Introductory Sociology 1

Introductory Sociology 1

Compiled from:

The Sociology Student Writer's Manual
Fifth Edition
by William A. Johnson, Jr., Richard P. Rettig,
Gregory M. Scott, and Stephen M. Garrison

Sociology: A Down-to-Earth Approach
Eighth Edition
by James M. Henslin

PEARSON
Custom
Publishing

Pearson Education Limited
Edinburgh Gate
Harlow
Essex CM20 2JE

And associated companies throughout the world

Visit us on the World Wide Web at:
www.pearsoned.co.uk

First published 2007
This Custom Book Edition © 2007 Published by Pearson Education Limited

Compiled from:

The Sociology Student Writer's Manual
by William A. Johnson, Jr., Richard P. Rettig,
Gregory M. Scott and Stephen M. Garrison
Fifth Edition
ISBN 0 13 192851 1
Copyright © 2006, 2004, 2002, 2000, 1998 by Pearson Education, Inc., Upper Saddle
River, New Jersey, 07458

Sociology: A Down-to-Earth Approach
Eighth Edition
by James M. Henslin
ISBN 0 205 47305 9
Copyright © 2007 by James M. Henslin

ISBN-10 1 84658 460 4
ISBN-13 978 1 84658 460 2

Printed and bound in Great Britain by Antony Rowe.

Contents

Preface

Dear Student,

Welcome to the customised text that has been prepared for you by us. The purpose of this text is to supplement the relevant chapters contained in the course textbook, Macionis & Plummer (2005) *Sociology: a global introduction*

This customised text contains helpful chapters on essay writing skills taken from Johnson et al (2006) *The sociology student writer's manual*. This will give you the opportunity to develop skills that you will use throughout your university career. The customised text also contains particularly good chapters from Henslin (2007) *Sociology: a down to earth approach* on the key topics of 'culture', 'socialisation', social structure and social interaction' and 'social networks'. These deal with major themes of the course:

- Why it is important to recognise that when we are born we enter a world that is already organised by social relationships.
- How we learn to both accept and react to a system of socially distributed and socially approved meanings.
- How these meanings affect not only how we act but also how we think and feel.
- How our sense of personal identity is learnt from and maintained by the social networks within which we live.

A particular strength of these chapters is that they make a point of showing the extraordinary nature of ordinary life. This is what we want to achieve in this course; to enable you to think about familiar events in a new way by making it possible for you to recognise the complex and fascinating systems of social relationships that maintain your familiar way of life.

Enjoy!

CHAPTER 1

WRITING AS COMMUNICATION

1.1   WRITING TO LEARN

Writing is a way of ordering your experience. Think about it: No matter what you are writing—a paper for your introductory sociology class, a short story, a limerick, or a grocery list—you are putting pieces of your world together in new ways and making yourself freshly conscious of these pieces. This is one of the reasons writing is so hard. From the infinite welter of data that your mind continually processes and locks in your memory, you are selecting only certain items significant to the task at hand, relating them to other items, and phrasing them in a new coherence. You are mapping a part of your universe that has hitherto been unknown territory. You are gaining a little more control over the processes by which you interact with the world around you.

This is why the act of writing, no matter where it leads, is never insignificant. It is always communication, a way of making a fresh connection with your world. Writing, therefore, is also one of the best ways to learn. This statement, at first, may sound odd. If you are an unpracticed writer, you may share a common notion that the only purpose writing can have is to express what you already know or think. Any learning that you as a writer might do has already been accomplished by the time your pen meets the paper. In this view, your task is to inform or even surprise the reader. But if you are a practiced writer, you know that, at any moment as you write, you are capable of surprising yourself. And it is surprise that you look for: the shock of seeing what happens in your own mind when you drop an old, established opinion into a batch of new facts or bump into a cherished belief from a different angle. Writing synthesizes new understanding for the writer. E. M. Forster's famous question "How do I know what I think until I see what I say?" is one that all of us could ask. We make meaning as we write, jolting ourselves by little, surprising discoveries into a larger and more interesting universe.

1.1.1   The Irony of Writing

Good writing often helps the reader become aware of the ironies and paradoxes of human existence. One such paradox is that good writing expresses that which is unique about the writer and, at the same time, that which is common, not to the writer alone, but to every human being. Many of our most famous political statements share this double attribute of mirroring the singular and the ordinary. For example, read the following excerpts from President Franklin Roosevelt's first inaugural address, spoken on March 4, 1933, in the middle of the Great Depression. Then answer this question: Is what Roosevelt said famous because its expression is extraordinary, or because it appeals to something that is basic to every human being?

> This is pre-eminently the time to speak the truth, the whole truth, frankly and boldly. Nor need we shrink from honestly facing conditions in our country today. This great nation will endure as it has endured, will revive and will prosper.
>
> So first of all let me assert my firm belief that the only thing we have to fear is fear itself—nameless, unreasoning, unjustified terror that paralyzes needed efforts to convert retreat into advance.
>
> In every dark hour of our national life a leadership of frankness and vigor has met with that understanding and support of the people themselves that is essential to victory. I am convinced that you will again give that support to leadership in these critical days.
>
> In such a spirit on my part and on yours we face our common difficulties. They concern, thank God, only material things. Values have shrunken to fantastic levels; taxes have risen; our ability to pay has fallen; government of all kinds is faced by serious curtailment of income; the means of exchange are frozen in the currents of trade; the withered leaves of industrial enterprise lie on every side; farmers find no markets for their produce; the savings of many years in thousands of families are gone.
>
> More important, a host of unemployed citizens face the grim problem of existence, and an equally great number toil with little return. Only a foolish optimist can deny the dark realities of the moment.
>
> Yet our distress comes from no failure of substance. We are stricken by no plague of locusts. Compared with the perils that our forefathers conquered because they believed and were not afraid, we have still much to be thankful for. Nature still offers her bounty and human efforts have multiplied it. Plenty is at our doorstep, but a generous use of it languishes in the very sight of the supply. . . .
>
> The measure of the restoration lies in the extent to which we apply social values more noble than mere monetary profit.
>
> Happiness lies not in the mere possession of money; it lies in the joy of achievement, in the thrill of creative effort.
>
> The joy and moral stimulation of work no longer must be forgotten in the mad chase of evanescent profits. These dark days will be worth all they cost us if they teach us that our true destiny is not to be ministered unto but to minister to ourselves and to our fellow-men. (quoted in Commager 1963:240)

The benefits of writing in learning and in controlling what we learn are why sociology instructors will require a great deal of writing in their classes. Learning the complex and diverse world of sociology takes more than a passive ingestion of facts. You have to understand and come to grips with social issues and with your own attitudes toward them. When you write in an introductory sociology or minorities in American society class, you are entering into the world of the sociologist in the same way he or she does—testing theory against fact, fact against belief, belief against reality.

Writing is the entryway into social and political life. Virtually everything that happens in education, politics, and so on, happens on paper first. Documents are wrestled into shape before their contents can affect institutions and/or the public. Great speeches are written before they are spoken. Meaningful social programs must be spelled out before they are implemented. The written word has helped free slaves, end wars, create new opportunities in the workplace, and shape the values of nations. Often, gaining recognition for our ourselves and our ideas depends less on what we say than on how we say it. Accurate and persuasive writing is absolutely vital to the sociologist.

1.1.2   Learning by Writing

Here is a way to test the notion that writing is a powerful learning tool: Rewrite the notes you have taken from a recent class lecture. It does not matter which class—it can be history, chemistry, or advertising. Choose a difficult class, if possible, one in which you are feeling somewhat unsure of the material and in which you have taken copious notes. As you rewrite, provide the transitional elements (connecting phrases, such as *in order to, because of, and, but, however*) that you were unable to supply in class because of time constraints. Furnish your own examples or illustrations of the ideas expressed in the lecture.

This experiment forces you to make your own thought processes coherent. See if the time it takes you to rewrite the notes is not more than compensated for by a gain in your understanding of the lecture material.

1.1.3   Challenging Yourself

There is no way around it—writing is a struggle. Do you think you are the only one to feel this way? Take heart! Writing is hard for everyone, great writers included. Bringing order into the world is never easy. Isaac Bashevis Singer, winner of the 1978 Nobel Prize in literature, once wrote: "I believe in miracles in every area of life except writing. Experience has shown me that there are no miracles in writing. The only thing that produces good writing is hard work" (quoted in Lunsford and Connors 1992:2). Hard work was evident in the words of John F. Kennedy's inaugural address. Each word is crafted to embed an image in the reader's mind. As you read the following excerpts from Kennedy's speech, what images come to mind? Historians tend to consider a president "great" when his words live longer than his deeds in the minds of the people. Do you think this will be true of Kennedy?

> We observe today not a victory of party but a celebration of freedom—symbolizing an end as well as a beginning—signifying renewal as well as change. For I

have sworn before you and Almighty God the same solemn oath our forebearers prescribed nearly a century and three-quarters ago.

The world is very different now. For man holds in his mortal hands the power to abolish all forms of human poverty and all forms of human life. And yet the same revolutionary beliefs for which our forebearers fought are still at issue around the globe—the belief that the rights of man come not from the generosity of the state but from the hand of God.

We dare not forget today that we are the heirs of that first revolution. Let the word go forth from this time and place, to friend and foe alike, that the torch has been passed to a new generation of Americans—born in this century, tempered by war, disciplined by a hard and bitter peace, proud of our ancient heritage—and unwilling to witness or permit the slow undoing of those human rights to which this nation has always been committed, and to which we are committed today at home and around the world. . . .

In the long history of the world, only a few generations have been granted the role of defending freedom in its hours of maximum danger. I do not shrink from this responsibility—I welcome it. I do not believe that any of us would exchange places with any other people or any other generation. The energy, the faith, the devotion that we bring to this endeavor will light our country and all who serve it—and the glow from that fire can truly light the world.

And so, my fellow Americans: ask not what your country can do for you—ask what you can do for your country.

My fellow citizens of the world: ask not what America will do for you, but what together we can do for the freedom of man. (quoted in Commager 1963:688–689)

One reason for the difficulty of writing is that it is not actually a single activity but a process consisting of several activities that can overlap each other, with two or more sometimes operating simultaneously as you labor to organize and phrase your thoughts (this will be discussed in greater detail later in this chapter). The writing process tends to be sloppy for everyone—an often frustrating search for the best way to articulate meaning.

Frustrating though that search may sometimes be, however, it need not be futile. Remember that the writing process makes use of skills that we all have. In other words, the ability to write is not some magical competence bestowed on the rare, fortunate individual. Although few of us may achieve the proficiency of Isaac Singer, we are all capable of phrasing thoughts clearly and in a well-organized fashion. But learning how to do so takes practice: The one sure way to improve your writing is to write.

Remember also that one of the toughest but most important jobs in writing is to maintain enthusiasm for your writing project. Commitment may sometimes be hard to come by given the difficulties inherent in the writing process—difficulties that can be made worse when the project assigned is unappealing at first glance. For example, how can you be enthusiastic about having to write a paper analyzing welfare reform, when you know little about the American welfare system and see no real use in doing the project?

One of the worst mistakes that unpracticed writers sometimes make is failing to assume responsibility for keeping themselves interested in their writing. No matter how hard it may seem at first to drum up interest in your topic, you have to do it—that is, if you want to write a paper you can be proud of, one that contributes useful material and a fresh point of view to the topic. One thing is guaranteed: If you are bored with your writing, your reader will be, too.

So what can you do to keep your interest and energy level high? Challenge yourself. Think of the paper not as an assignment for a grade, but as a piece of writing that has a point to make. Getting this point across persuasively is the real reason that you are writing, not the simple fact that a teacher has assigned a project.

If someone were to ask you why you are writing your paper, what would you answer? If your immediate, unthinking response is, "Because I've been given a writing assignment," or "Because I want a good grade," your paper may be in trouble. If, on the other hand, your first impulse is to explain the challenge of your main point—"I'm writing to show how welfare reform will benefit both welfare recipients and the American taxpayer"—then you are thinking usefully about your topic.

1.1.4   Maintaining Self-Confidence

Having a sense of confidence in your ability to write well about your topic is essential for good writing. This does not mean that you will always know what the end result of a particular writing activity will be. In fact, you have to cultivate your ability to tolerate a high degree of uncertainty while weighing evidence, testing hypotheses, and experimenting with organizational strategies and wording. Be ready for temporary confusion and for seeming dead-ends, and remember that every writer faces them. It is from your struggle to combine fact with fact, to buttress conjecture with evidence, that order arises.

Do not be intimidated by the amount and quality of work already done in your field of inquiry. The array of opinion and evidence that confronts you in the published literature can be confusing. But remember that no important topic is ever exhausted. There are always gaps—questions that have not yet been satisfactorily explored either in the published research on a subject or in the prevailing popular opinion. It is in these gaps that you establish your own authority, your own sense of control.

Remember that the various stages of the writing process reinforce one another. Establishing a solid motivation strengthens your sense of confidence about the project, which in turn influences how successfully you organize and write. If you start out well, using good work habits, and give yourself ample time for the various activities to gel, you should produce a paper that will reflect your best work, one that your audience will find both readable and useful.

1.2   THE WRITING PROCESS

As you engage in the writing process, you are doing many different things at once. While planning, you are no doubt defining the audience for your paper at the same time that you are thinking about the paper's purpose. As you draft the paper, you may organize your next sentence while revising the one you have just written. Different parts of the writing process overlap, and much of the difficulty of writing is that so many things happen at once. Through practice—in other words, through writing—it is possible to learn how to control those parts of the process that can be controlled and to encourage those mysterious, less controllable activities.

No two people go about writing in exactly the same way. It is important for you to recognize routines—modes of thought as well as individual exercises—that help you negotiate the process successfully. And it is also important to give yourself as much time as possible to complete the process. Procrastination is one of the writer's greatest enemies. It saps confidence, undermines energy, and destroys concentration. Working regularly and keeping as close as possible to a well-thought-out schedule often make the difference between a successful paper and an embarrassment.

Although the various parts of the writing process are interwoven, there is, naturally, a general order to the work you have to do. You have to start somewhere! What follows is a description of the various stages of the writing process—planning, using intervention strategies, outlining, drafting, revising, editing, and proofreading—along with suggestions as to how to get the most out of each.

1.2.1   Planning

Planning includes all activities that lead up to the writing of the first draft. These activities differ from person to person. For instance, some writers prefer to compile a formal outline before writing that draft. Others perform brief writing exercises to jump-start their imaginations. Some draw diagrams; others doodle. Later on we'll look at a few starting strategies, and you can determine which may be of help to you.

Right now, however, let us discuss some early choices that all writers must make during the planning stage. These choices concern topic, thesis, purpose, and audience—four elements that help make up the writing context, the terms under which we all write. Every time you write—even if you are writing a diary entry or a note to the delivery person—these four elements are present. You may not give conscious consideration to all of them in each piece of writing that you do, but it is extremely important to think carefully about them when writing a sociology paper. Some or all of these defining elements may be dictated by your assignment, yet you will always have a degree of control over them.

Selecting your topic.   No matter how restrictive an assignment may seem to be, there is no reason to feel trapped by it. Within any assigned subject you can find a range of topics to explore. What you are looking for is a topic that engages your own interest. Let your curiosity be your guide. For example, if you have been assigned the subject of welfare reform, then try to find some issues concerning welfare reform that interest you. (How does receiving something for nothing affect an individual's self-esteem? What would be the repercussions of limiting the amount of time anyone could receive welfare benefits?) Any good topic comes with a set of questions; you may well find that your interest picks up if you simply begin asking questions. One strong recommendation: Ask your questions on paper. Like most other mental activities, the process of exploring your way through a topic is transformed when you write down your thoughts as they come instead of letting them fly through your mind unrecorded. Remember the old adage from Louis Agassiz: "A pen is often the best of eyes" (quoted in Pearce 1958:106).

Although it is vital to be interested in your topic, you do not have to know much about it at the outset of your investigation. In fact, having too heartfelt a commitment to a topic can be an impediment to writing about it; emotions can get in the way of objectivity. Often it is better to choose a topic that has piqued your interest yet remained something of a mystery to you—a topic discussed in one of your classes, perhaps, or mentioned on television or in a conversation with friends.

Narrowing your topic.   The task of narrowing your topic offers you a tremendous opportunity to establish a measure of control over the writing project. It is up to you to hone your topic to just the right shape and size to suit both your own interests and the requirements of the assignment. Do a good job of it, and you will go a long way toward guaranteeing yourself sufficient motivation and confidence for the tasks ahead of you. Do it wrong, and somewhere along the way you may find yourself directionless and out of energy.

Generally, the first topics that come to your mind will be too large to handle in your research paper. For example, the topic of a national health policy has generated a tremendous number of news articles and reports recently published by experts in the field. Despite all the attention turned toward this topic, however, there is still plenty of room for you to investigate it on a level that has real meaning to you and that does not merely recapitulate the published research. What about an analysis of how one of the proposed U.S. health policies might affect insurance costs in a locally owned company?

The problem with most topics is not that they are too narrow or too completely explored; it is that they are too rich. There are so many useful ways to address a topic that choosing the best focus is often difficult. Take your time narrowing the topic. Think through the possibilities that occur to you, and—as always—jot down your thoughts.

The following is a list of topics assigned to undergraduate students in a course on social theory. Their task was to choose a topic and write an essay of 2,500 words. Next to each topic is an example of how a student narrowed it to make it a manageable paper topic.

General Topic	Paper Topic
Plato	Plato's philosophy of the role of women in politics
Freedom	A comparison of Rousseau's concept of freedom with Locke's

Community	Arguments for the necessity of community used by Amitai Etzioni
Max Weber	Weber's definition of bureaucracy

Without taking time to research them, see what kinds of viable narrowed topics you can make from the following general topics:

crime in America	political corruption
international terrorism	military spending
education	affirmative action hiring policies
freedom of speech	freedom of religion
gun control	abortion rights

Example

general topic:	the family
narrowed topics:	cultural demands that keep family members isolated the effect of substance abuse on family stability the impact of the single-parent family on work in America

Finding your thesis.   As you plan, be on the lookout for an idea that would serve as your thesis. A thesis is not a fact that can be immediately proven by recourse to recorded information, but a hypothesis worth discussing, an argument with more than one possible conclusion. Your thesis sentence will reveal to your reader not only the argument you have chosen, but also your orientation toward it—the conclusion that your paper will attempt to prove.

In looking for a thesis, you do many jobs at once:

1. You limit the amount and kind of material that you must cover, making it manageable.
2. You increase your own interest in the narrowing field of study.
3. You work to establish your paper's purpose—the reason that you are writing about your topic. (If the only reason you can see for writing is to earn a good grade, then you probably won't!)
4. You establish your notion of who your audience is and what sort of approach might best catch their interest.

In short, you gain control over your writing context. For this reason, it is a good idea to establish a thesis early on—a working thesis—that will very probably change as your thinking deepens but that will allow you to establish a measure of order in the planning stage.

Writing your thesis sentence.   The introduction of your paper will contain a sentence that expresses in a nutshell the task that you intend to accomplish. This thesis sentence communicates your main idea—the one you are going to support or defend or illustrate. The thesis sets up an expectation in the reader's mind that you must satisfy. But it is more than just the statement that informs your reader of your goal; in the planning stage, the thesis is a valuable tool to help you narrow your focus and confirm in your own mind your paper's purpose.

Developing your thesis.   A class on crime and society was assigned a twenty-page paper studying a problem currently being faced by the municipal authorities in their own city. The choice of the problem was left up to the students. One student, Richard Gonzales, decided to investigate the problem posed to the city by the large number of abandoned buildings in a downtown neighborhood that he drove through on his way to the university. Richard's first working thesis was: "Abandoned houses result in negative social effects to the city."

The problem with this thesis, as Richard found out, was that it was not an idea that could be argued, but a fact corroborated easily by the sources he began to consult. As he read reports from various sources, such as the Urban Land Institute and the City Planning Commission, and talked with representatives from the Community Planning Department, Richard began to get interested in the dilemma faced by his city in responding to the problem of abandoned buildings.

Richard's second working thesis was: "Removal of abandoned buildings is a major problem facing the city." This thesis narrowed the topic somewhat and gave Richard an opportunity to use material gleaned from his research, but there was still no real comment attached to it. It still states a bare fact, easily proved. At this point, Richard became interested in the still narrower topic of how building removal should best be handled. He found that the major issue was funding and that different civic groups favored different methods of funding the demolition. As Richard explored the arguments for and against funding plans, he began to feel that one of them might be best for the city.

Richard's third working thesis was: "Assessing a 'demolition fee' to each sale of a property offers a viable solution to the city's building removal problem." Note how this thesis narrowed the focus of his paper still further than the other two yet presents an arguable hypothesis. This thesis told Richard what he had to do in his paper, just as it tells his reader what to expect.

At some time during your preliminary thinking on a topic, you should consult the library to see how much published work has already been done. This search is beneficial in at least two ways:

1. It acquaints you with a body of writing that will become very important in the research phase.
2. It gives you a sense of how your topic is generally addressed by the community of scholars you are joining. Is the topic as important as you think it is? Has there already been so much research on the topic as to make your inquiry, in its present formulation, irrelevant? These questions can be answered by reviewing the literature.

As you go about determining your topic, remember that one goal of sociology writing in college is to enhance your own understanding of the social and/or social-psychological process, to build an accurate model of the way societies work. Let this goal help you: Aim your research into those subject areas that you know are important to your understanding of the discipline.

Defining your purpose.   There are many ways to classify the purposes of writing, but in general most writing is undertaken either to inform or to persuade an audience. The goal of informative or expository writing is, simply, to impart information about a particular subject, whereas the aim of persuasive writing is to convince your reader of your point of view on an issue. The distinction between expository and persuasive writing is not hard and fast. Most sociology writing has elements of both exposition and persuasion. However, most effective writing has a clearly chosen focus of either exposition or persuasion. When you begin writing, consciously select a primary aim of exposition or persuasion, and then set out to achieve that goal.

Suppose you have been required to write a paper explaining how parents' attitudes affect their children's choice of college. If you are writing an expository paper, your task could be to describe in a coherent and impartial way the attitudes of the parents and the choices of their children.

If, however, your paper attempts to convince your reader that parental attitudes often result in children making poor choices, you are now writing to persuade, and your strategy is radically different. You will now need to explain the negative effects of parental attitudes. Persuasive writing seeks to influence the opinions of its audience toward its subject. Writing assignments in sociology may break down the distinction between expository and persuasive writing in a number of ways. You may be called on to analyze sociopolitical situations, evaluate government programs, speculate on directions in social policy, identify or define problems within a range of fields, or suggest solutions and predict results. It is very important to spend planning time sharpening your sense of purpose.

Know what you want to say. By the time you begin working on your final draft, you must have a very sound notion of the point you wish to argue or the position you wish to support. If, during the writing of the final draft, someone were to ask you to state your thesis, you should be able to give a satisfactory answer with a minimum of delay and no prompting. On the other hand, if you have to hedge your answer because you cannot easily form a notion of your thesis in your own mind, you may not yet have arrived at a final draft.

For example, two writers have been asked what point they wish to make in their papers. One of these writers has a better grip on her writing task.

Writer 1: My paper is about tax reform for the middle class.

Writer 2: My paper argues that tax reform for the middle class would be unfair to the upper and lower classes, who would then have to share more responsibility for the cost of government.

The second writer has a clear view of her task; the first knows what her topic is—tax reform for the middle class—but may not yet know what it is about tax reform that she wishes to support. It may be that you will have to write a draft or two or engage in various prewriting activities to arrive at a secure understanding of your task.

Watch out for bias! There is no such thing as pure objectivity. You are not a machine. No matter how hard you may try to produce an objective paper, every

choice you make as you write is influenced to some extent by your personal beliefs and opinions. What you tell your readers is influenced—sometimes without
your knowing—by a multitude of factors: your environment, upbringing, and education; your attitude toward your audience; your political affiliation; your race
and gender; your career goals; and your ambitions for the paper you are writing.
The influence of these factors can be very subtle, and it is something you must
work to identify in your own writing as well as in the writing of others in order
not to mislead or be misled. Remember that one of the reasons you write is for
self-discovery. The writing you will do in sociology classes—as well as the writing you will do for the rest of your life—will give you a chance to discover and
confront honestly your own views on your subjects. Responsible writers keep an
eye on their own biases and are honest with their readers about them.

Defining your audience.   It may sometimes be difficult to remember that the
point of your writing is not simply to jump through the technical hoops imposed
by the assignment. The point is communication—the transmission of your knowledge and your conclusions—to the reader in a way that suits you. Your task is to
pass to your reader the spark of your own enthusiasm for the topic. Readers
who were indifferent to your topic should look at it in a new way after reading
your paper. This is the great challenge of writing: to enter into your reader's mind
and leave behind new knowledge and new questions.

It is tempting to think that most writing problems would be solved if the
writer could view his or her writing as if it had been produced by another person. The ego barrier between writer and audience is the single greatest impediment to accurate communication. To reduce the discrepancy between your
understanding and that of your audience, it is necessary to consider the audience's needs. By the time you begin drafting, most—if not all—of your ideas have
begun to attain coherent shape in your mind, so that virtually any words in which
you try to phrase those ideas will reflect your thought accurately—to you. Your
reader, however, does not already have in mind the conclusions that you have so
painstakingly achieved. If you leave out of your writing the material that is necessary to complete your reader's understanding of your argument, he or she may
not be able to supply that information himself.

The potential for misunderstanding is a given for any audience—whether it
is made up of general readers, experts in the field, or your professor, who is reading, in part, to see how well you have mastered the constraints that govern the
relationship between writer and reader. Make your presentation as complete as
possible, writing always as if to an audience whose previous knowledge of your
topic is limited to information easily available to the general public.

John F. Kennedy's Pastry Mistake

President Kennedy was one of America's greatest speechmakers. He had a gift for
understanding and speaking directly to the audience he was addressing. At one
point during the Cold War, the Soviet Union banned shipments of supplies across
East Germany to West Berlin, the part of the city governed by the Western, non-
communist countries. It was a tense moment in East–West relations.

> Going to Berlin on June 26, 1963, Kennedy spoke to the besieged people as if he were one of them. The people responded warmly, cheering his speech continuously. At the climactic moment, Kennedy boldly proclaimed, in words that became famous, "Ich bein ein Berliner." He was attempting to say, in German, "I am a citizen of Berlin," meaning, "I am one of you; I share your concerns in this moment of crisis." What he said instead was German for "I am a pastry." His mistake was in inserting the article *ein*—*ein Berliner* is a kind of pastry in Germany.

Communicating to your audience can sometimes be more difficult than it first appears.

1.2.2   Using Invention Strategies

In this chapter, we have discussed methods of selecting and narrowing the topic of a paper. As your focus on a specific topic sharpens, you naturally begin to think about the kinds of information that will go into the paper. In the case of papers not requiring formal research, that material comes largely from your own recollections. Indeed, one of the reasons why instructors assign unresearched papers is to convince you of the incredible richness of your memory, the vastness and variety of the "database" that you have accumulated and that, moment by moment, you continue to build.

So vast is your horde of information that it is sometimes difficult to find within it the material that would best suit your paper. In other words, finding out what you already know about a topic is not always easy. Invention—a term borrowed from classical rhetoric—refers to the task of discovering, or recovering from memory, information about your topic. As we write, all of us go through some sort of invention procedure that helps us explore our topic. Some writers seem to have little problem coming up with material; others need more help. Over the centuries writers have devised different exercises that can help locate useful material housed in memory. We shall look at a few of these briefly.

Freewriting.   Freewriting is an activity that forces you to get something down on paper. There is no waiting around for inspiration. Instead, you set yourself a time limit—three minutes or five minutes—and write for that length of time without stopping, not even to lift the pen from the paper or your hands from the typewriter or computer keyboard. Focus on the topic, and don't let the difficulty of finding relevant material stop you from writing. If necessary, you may begin by writing, over and over, some seemingly useless phrase, like, "I cannot think of anything to write about," or perhaps the name of your topic. Eventually, something else will occur to you. (It is surprising how long a three-minute freewriting can seem to take!) At the end of the freewriting, look over what you have produced for anything of use. Granted, much of the writing will be unusable, but there may be an insight or two that you did not know you possessed. In addition to its ability to recover usable material for your paper, freewriting yields a few other benefits. First, it takes little time to do, which means you may repeat the exercise as often as you like within a relatively short span of time. Second, it breaks down

AN EXAMPLE OF FREEWRITING

The professor in Shelby Johnson's second-year Family as a Social Institution class assigned a paper focusing on some aspect of American family life. Shelby, who felt her understanding of the family as an institution was modest, tried to get her mind started on the job of finding a topic that interested her with a three-minute freewriting exercise. Thinking about the family and child development, Shelby wrote steadily for three minutes without lifting her pen from the paper. Here is the result of her freewriting:

> Okay, now, what do I know about the family? I was raised in one. I have a father, mother, and sister. Both parents were present all my life. Both worked. Professionals. Sometimes I wished Mom was at home. That might be interesting: working parents, the effects on kids. Two-paycheck families. I like it. Where to start? I could interview my parents. I need to find some recent statistics on two-paycheck families.

some of the resistance that stands between you and the act of writing. There is no initial struggle to find something to say; you just write.

Brainstorming.   Brainstorming is simply the process of making a list of ideas about a topic. It can be done quickly and, initially, without any need to order items into a coherent pattern. The point is to write down everything that occurs to you as quickly and as briefly as possible, as individual words or short phrases. Once you have a good-sized list of items, you can then group the items according to relationships that you see among them. Brainstorming allows you both to uncover ideas stored in your memory and to make useful associations among those ideas.

A professor in a political sociology class asked her students to write a 700-word paper, in the form of a letter to be translated and published in a Warsaw newspaper, giving the Polish readers useful advice about living in a democracy. Carrie Nation, a student in the class, started thinking about the assignment by brainstorming. First, she simply wrote down anything that occurred to her:

Life in a Democracy

voting rights	welfare	freedom of the press
protest movements	everybody equal	minorities
racial prejudice	American Dream	injustice
the individual	no job security	lobbyists and PACs
justice takes time	psychological factors	aristocracy of wealth
size of bureaucracy	market economy	

Thinking through her list, Carrie decided to rearrange her list into two: one devoted to positive aspects of life in a democracy, the other to negative aspects. At this point she decided to discard some items that were redundant or did not seem to have much potential. As you can see, Carrie had some questions about where some of her items would fit.

Positive	**Negative**
voting rights	aristocracy of wealth
freedom of the press	justice takes time
everybody equal	racial prejudice
American Dream	welfare
psychological factors	lobbyists and PACs
protest movements	size of bureaucracy

At this point, Carrie decided that her strongest inclination was to explore the ways in which money and special interests affect a democratically elected government. Which of the remaining items in her two lists would be of help to Carrie?

Asking questions. It is always possible to ask most or all of the following questions about any topic: Who? What? When? Where? Why? How? These questions force you to approach it the way a journalist does, setting it within different perspectives that can then be compared to discover insights within the material.

For a class in the sociology of law, a professor asked her class to write a paper describing the impact of Supreme Court clerks on the decision-making process. Here are some questions that a student in the class might logically ask to begin thinking about a thesis.

- Who are the Supreme Court's clerks? (How old? What racial and gender mix are they? What are their politics?)
- What are their qualifications for the job?
- What exactly is their job?
- When during the court term are they most influential?
- Where do they come from? (Is there any discernible geographical pattern in the way they are chosen? Any pattern regarding religion? Do certain law schools contribute a significantly greater number of clerks than any others?)
- How are they chosen? (Are they appointed? elected?)
- When in their careers do they serve?
- Why are they chosen as they are?
- Who have been some influential court clerks? (Have any gone on to sit on the bench themselves?)

Can you think of other questions that would make for useful inquiry?

Being flexible.   As you engage in invention strategies, you are also doing other work. You are still narrowing your topic, for example, as well as making decisions that will affect your choice of tone or audience. You move forward on all fronts, with each decision you make affecting the others. This means you must be flexible enough in your understanding of the paper's development to allow for adjustments or alterations in your understanding of your goal. Never be so determined to prove a particular theory that you fail to notice when your own understanding of it changes. Stay objective.

1.2.3   Organizing Your Writing by Outlining

A paper that contains all the facts but provides them in an ineffective order will confuse rather than inform or persuade. Although there are various methods of grouping ideas, none is potentially more effective than outlining. Unfortunately, no organizing process is more often misunderstood.

Outlining for yourself.   There are really two jobs that outlining can do. First, it can serve as a means of forcing you, the writer, to gain a better understanding of your ideas by arranging them according to their interrelationships. As the following model indicates, there is one primary rule of outlining: Ideas of equal weight are placed on the same level within the outline. This rule requires you to determine the relative importance of your ideas. You must decide whether one idea is of the same type or order as another and which subtopic each idea best fits into. If you arrange your ideas with care in a coherent outline in the planning stage, your own grasp of your topic will be greatly enhanced. You will have linked your ideas together logically and given a skeleton to the body of the paper. This sort of subordinating and coordinating activity is difficult, however, and as a result, inexperienced writers sometimes fail to pay the necessary attention to the outline. They begin writing their first draft without an effective outline, hoping for the best. That hope usually disappears, especially in complex papers involving research. Garcia, a student in a second-year class in government management, researched the impact of a worker-retraining program in his state and came up with the following facts and theories. Number them in logical order.

___ A growing number of workers in the state do not possess the basic skills and education demanded by employers.

___ The number of dislocated workers in the state increased from 21,000 in 1982 to 32,000 in 1992.

___ A public policy to retrain uneducated workers would allow them to move into new and expanding sectors of the Oklahoma economy.

___ Investment in high technology would allow the state's employers to remain competitive in the production of goods and services in both domestic and foreign markets.

___ The economy is becoming more global and more competitive.

Outlining for your reader.   The second job of an outline is aimed not at the writer's understanding, but at the reader's. An outline accompanying your paper can serve the reader as its blueprint—a summary of the paper's points and their interrelationships. A busy person can consult your outline to quickly get a sense of your paper's goal and the argument you have used to promote it. This accompanying outline, then, is very important, since its clarity and coherence help to determine how much attention your audience will give to your ideas. As sociology students, you will be given a great deal of help with the arrangement of your material into an outline to accompany your paper. A look at the model presented in other chapters of this manual will show you how strictly these formal outlines are structured. But while you must pay close attention to the requirements of the accompanying outline, do not forget that an outline is a powerful tool in the early planning stages of your paper.

Formal outline pattern.   Following this pattern accurately during the planning stage of your paper helps to guarantee that your ideas are placed logically.

Thesis sentence (prefaces the organized outline)

I. First main idea
   A. First subordinate idea
      1. Reason, example, or illustration
      2. Reason, example, or illustration
         a. Detail supporting reason 2
         b. Detail supporting reason 2
         c. Detail supporting reason 2
   B. Second subordinate idea
II. Second main idea

Notice that each level of the paper must have more than one entry: For every A there must be at least a B (and, if required, a C, D, and so on); for every 1 there must be a 2. This arrangement forces you to compare ideas, looking carefully at each one to determine its place among the others. The insistence on assigning relative values to your ideas is what makes your outline an effective organizing tool.

The structure of any particular type of sociology paper is governed by a formal pattern. When rigid external controls are placed on their writing, some writers tend to feel stifled, their creativity impeded by this kind of paint-by-numbers approach to structure. It is vital to the success of your paper that you never allow yourself to be overwhelmed by the pattern rules of a particular type of paper. Remember that such controls are placed on papers not to limit your creativity but to make the paper easy to read and immediately useful to its intended audience. It is as necessary to write clearly and confidently in a social issue paper or a case study as it is in a term paper for English literature, a résumé, a short story, or a job application letter.

1.2.4   Writing Drafts

The rough draft.   After the planning comes the writing of the first draft. Using your thesis and outline as direction markers, you must now weave your amalgam of ideas, researched data, and persuasion strategies into logically ordered sentences and paragraphs. Though adequate prewriting may make the drafting easier than it might have been, it will still not be easy. Writers establish their own methods of encouraging themselves to forge ahead with the draft, but here are some tips to bear in mind:

1. Remember that this is a rough draft, not the final draft. At this stage, it is not necessary that every word you write be the best possible choice. Do not put that sort of pressure on yourself; you must not allow anything to slow you down now. Writing is not like sculpting, in which every chip is permanent— you can always go back to your draft later and add, delete, reword, or re-arrange. No matter how much effort you have put into planning, you cannot be sure how much of this first draft you will eventually keep. It may take several drafts to get one that you find satisfactory.

2. Give yourself sufficient time to write. Don't delay the first draft by telling yourself there is still more research to do. You cannot uncover all the material there is to know on a particular subject, so don't fool yourself into trying. Remember that writing is a process of discovery. You may have to begin writing before you can see exactly what sort of final research you need to do. Keep in mind that there are other tasks waiting for you after the first draft is finished, so allow for them as you determine your writing schedule. Giving yourself time is very important for another reason: The more time that passes after you write a draft, the better your ability to view it with greater objectivity. It is very difficult to evaluate your writing accurately soon after you complete it. You need to cool down, to recover from the effort of putting all those words together. The "colder" you get on your writing, the better able you are to read it as if it were written by someone else, which helps you acknowledge the changes needed to strengthen the paper.

3. Stay sharp. It is important to keep in mind the plan you created for yourself as you narrowed your topic, composed a thesis sentence, and outlined the material. But if, as you write, you feel a strong need to change the plan a bit, do not be afraid to do so. Be ready for surprises dealt you by your own growing understanding of your topic. Your goal is to render your best thinking on the subject as accurately as possible.

Authority.   To be convincing, your writing needs to be authoritative; that is, you have to sound as if you have confidence in your ability to convey your ideas in words. Sentences that sound stilted or that suffer from weak phrasing or the use of clichés are not going to win supporters for the aims that you express in your paper. Thus, sounding confident becomes a major concern. Consider the following points as you work to convey to your reader that necessary sense of authority.

Level of formality.   Tone is one of the primary methods by which you signal to the readers who you are and what your attitude is toward them and toward your topic. The major choice you make has to do with the level of language formality that you feel is most appropriate for your audience. The informal tone you would use in a letter to a friend might well be out of place in a paper called "Waste in Military Spending," written for your sociology professor. Remember that tone is only part of the overall decision that you make about how to present your information. To some extent, formality is a function of individual word choices and phrasing. Is it appropriate to use contractions like *isn't* or *they'll?* Would the strategic use of a sentence fragment for effect be out of place? The use of informal language, the personal *I,* and the second-person *you* is traditionally forbidden—for better or worse—in certain kinds of writing. Often, part of the challenge of writing a formal paper is, simply, how to give your prose bite while staying within the conventions.

Jargon.   One way to lose readers quickly is to overwhelm them with jargon—phrases that have a special, usually technical meaning within your discipline, but that are unfamiliar to the average reader. The occasional use of jargon may add an effective touch of atmosphere, but anything more than that will severely dampen a reader's enthusiasm for the paper. Often a reason for jargon is the writer's desire to impress the reader by sounding lofty or knowledgeable. Unfortunately, all jargon usually does is make for confusion. In fact, jargon is often an index of the writer's lack of connection to his audience.

Sociology writing is a haven for jargon. Perhaps writers of professional journals and certain issue papers believe their readers are all completely attuned to their terminology. It may be that these writers occasionally hope to obscure faulty information or potentially unpopular ideas in confusing language. Or the problem could simply be fuzzy thinking on the writer's part. Whatever the reason, sociology papers too often sound like prose made by machines to be read by machines.

Some students may feel that, in order to be accepted as sociologists, their papers should conform to the practices of their published peers. This is a mistake. Remember that it is always better to write a clear sentence than a cluttered or confusing one, and that burying your ideas in jargon defeats the effort that you went through to form them.

Clichés.   In the heat of composition, as you are looking for words to help you form your ideas, it is sometimes easy to plug in a cliché—a phrase that has attained universal recognition by overuse. (Note that clichés differ from jargon in that clichés are part of the general public's everyday language, while jargon is specific to the language of experts in a particular field.) Our vocabularies are brimming with clichés:

It's raining cats and dogs.

That issue is as dead as a doornail.

It's time for the governor to face the music.

Angry voters made a beeline for the ballot box.

The problem with clichés is that they are virtually meaningless. Once color-ful means of expression, they have lost their color through overuse, and they tend to bleed energy and color from the surrounding words. When revising, re-place clichés with words that more accurately convey the specific impression that you wish to create.

Descriptive language.   Language that appeals to the reader's senses will al-ways engage his or her interest more fully than language that is abstract. This is especially important for writing in disciplines that tend to deal in abstracts—such as sociology. The typical sociology paper—with its discussions of abstract principles, demographics, or deterministic outcomes—is often in danger of float-ing off on a cloud of abstractions, drifting farther away in each paragraph from the tangible life of the reader. Whenever appropriate, appeal to your reader's sense of sight, hearing, taste, touch, or smell. Consider the effectiveness of the following second sentence, as opposed to that of the first.

1. The housing project had deteriorated since the last inspection.
2. Since the last inspection, deterioration of the housing project had become ev-ident in stench rising from the plumbing, grime on the walls and floors, and the sound of rats scurrying in the hallways.

Bias-free and gender-neutral writing.   Language can be a very powerful method of either reinforcing or destroying cultural stereotypes. You should try to avoid gender bias and ethnic stereotyping in your writing. By treating the sexes in subtly different ways in your writing, you may unknowingly be commit-ting an act of discrimination. A common example is the use of the pronoun *he* to refer to a person whose gender has not been identified. But there are many other writing situations in which sexist and/or ethnic bias may appear. To avoid gen-der bias, the American Sociological Association (1997) recommends replacing words like *man, men,* or *mankind* with *person, people,* or *humankind.* When both sexes must be referred to in a sentence, use *he or she, her or him,* and *his or hers* instead of *he/she, him/her,* and *his/hers.* Consider the following examples of sex-ist and nonsexist language:

Sexist: A lawyer should always treat his client with respect.

Corrected: A lawyer should always treat his or her client with respect.

Or: Lawyers should always treat their clients with respect.

Sexist: Man is a political animal.

Corrected: People are political animals.

There are other methods of avoiding gender bias in your writing. Some writ-ers, faced with the aforementioned pronoun dilemma, alternate the use of male and female personal pronouns, identifying to the unknown referent as *he* in one section of their text, then as *she* in the next (a strategy often used in this manu-al). You can also change the subject to plural—there is no gender bias in *they.*

Sexist language denies to a large number of your readers the basic right to fair and equal treatment. Be aware of this subtle form of discrimination. Remember that language is more than the mere vehicle of your thoughts; your words shape perceptions for your reader. How well you say something will profoundly affect your reader's response to it.

1.2.5   Revising

After all the work you have gone through writing it, you may feel "married" to the first draft of your paper. However, revising is one of the most important steps in assuring your paper's success. Although unpracticed writers often think of revision as little more than making sure all the i's are dotted and t's are crossed, it is much more than that. Revising is reseeing the paper, looking at it from other perspectives, trying always to align your view with the view that will be held by your audience. Research in the process of composition indicates that we are actually revising all the time, in every phase of the writing process as we reread phrases, rethink the placement of a item in an outline, or test a new topic sentence for a paragraph. Subjecting your entire hard-fought draft to cold, objective scrutiny is one of the most difficult activities to master in the writing process, but it is absolutely necessary. You must make sure that you have said everything that needs to be said clearly and in logical order. One confusing passage, and the reader's attention is deflected from where you want it to be. Suddenly she has to become a detective, trying to figure out why you wrote what you did and what you meant by it. You don't want to throw such obstacles in the path of meaning.

Here are some tips to help you with revision:

1. Give yourself adequate time to revise. As mentioned, you need time to become "cold" on your paper in order to analyze it objectively. After you have written your draft, spend some time away from it. Try to come back to it as if it had been written by someone other than yourself.

2. Read the paper carefully. This is tougher than it sounds. One good strategy is to read it aloud or to have a friend read it aloud while you listen. (Note: Having friends critique your writing may be helpful, but friends do not usually make the best critics. They are rarely trained in revision techniques and are usually so close to you that they are unwilling—often unconsciously so—to risk disappointing you by giving your paper a really thorough examination.)

3. Prepare a list of specific items to check. It is important to revise in an orderly fashion—in stages—looking first at large concerns, such as the overall structure, and then rereading for problems with smaller elements, such as paragraph organization or sentence structure.

4. Check for unity—the clear and logical relation of all parts of the essay to its thesis. Make sure that every paragraph relates well to the whole paper and that it is in the right place.

5. Check for coherence. Make sure there are no gaps among the different parts of the argument and that you have adequate transition everywhere it is needed. Transitional elements are markers indicating places where the paper's focus or attitude changes. Transitional elements can be one-word long—*however, although, unfortunately, luckily*—or as long as a sentence or a paragraph:

"In order to fully appreciate the importance of democracy as a shaping presence in post–Cold War Polish politics, it is necessary to examine briefly the Poles' last historical attempt to implement democratic government." Transitional elements rarely introduce new material. Instead, they are direction pointers, either indicating a shift to new subject matter or signaling how the writer wishes certain material to be interpreted by the reader. Because you—the writer—already know where and why your paper changes direction and how you want particular passages to be received, it can be very difficult for you to determine where transition is needed.

6. Avoid unnecessary repetition.

Avoiding repetition.   There are two types of repetition that can annoy a reader: repetition of content and repetition of wording. Repetition of content leads to redundancy. Ideally, you want to cover a topic once, memorably, and then move on to your next topic. Organizing a paper is a difficult task, however, one that usually occurs through a process of enlightenment as to purposes and strategies. It is possible for an early draft to circle back to a subject you have already covered, and to begin to treat the same material over again. This sort of repetition can happen even if you have made use of prewriting strategies. What is worse, it can be difficult for you as a writer to acknowledge the repetition—to admit to yourself that the material you have worked so hard to shape on page 2 returns on page 5 in much the same shape. As you write and revise, bear this in mind: Any unnecessary repetition of content that you allow into your final draft is a potential annoyance to your reader, who is working to make sense of the argument she or he is reading and does not want to be distracted by a passage that repeats material already encountered. Train yourself, through practice, to read through your draft, looking for material that you have repeated unnecessarily.

Repetition of wording results in boring material. Make sure that you do not overuse any phrases or individual words. This sort of repetition can make your prose sound choppy and uninspired. It is important that your language sound fresh and energetic. Before you turn in your final draft, make sure to read through your paper carefully, looking for such repetition. Here are some examples of repetition of wording:

> The subcommittee's report on education reform will surprise a number of people. A number of people will want copies of the report.

> The chairman said at a press conference that he is happy with the report. He will circulate it to the local news agencies in the morning. He will also make sure that the city council has copies.

> I became upset when I heard how the committee had voted. I called the chairman and expressed my reservations about the committee's decision. I told him I felt that he had let the teachers and students of the state down. I also issued a press statement.

The last passage illustrates a condition known by composition teachers as the "I-syndrome." Can you hear how such duplicated phrasing can make a paper sound disconnected and unimaginative?

Note that not all repetition is bad. You may wish to repeat a phrase for rhetorical effect or special emphasis: "I came. I saw. I conquered." Just make sure that any repetition in your paper is intentional—placed there to produce a specific effect.

1.2.6 Editing

Editing is sometimes confused with the more involved process of revising. But editing happens later, after you have wrestled through your first draft—and maybe your second and third—and arrived at the final draft. Even though your draft now contains all the information you want to impart and the information is arranged to your satisfaction, there are still many factors to check, such as sentence structure, spelling, and punctuation.

It is at this point that an unpracticed writer might let down his guard. After all, most of the work on the paper is finished; the big jobs of discovering material and organizing and drafting it have been completed. But watch out! Editing is as important as any other step in the writing process. Any error that you allow in the final draft will count against you in the reader's mind. It may not seem fair, but a minor error—a misspelling or the confusing placement of a comma—will make a much greater impression on your reader than it perhaps should. Remember that everything about your paper is your responsibility, including getting even the supposedly little jobs right. Careless editing undermines the effectiveness of your paper. It would be a shame if all the hard work you put into prewriting, drafting, and revising were to be damaged because you carelessly allowed a comma splice!

Most of the preceding tips for revising hold for editing as well. It is best to edit in stages, looking for only one or two kinds of errors each time you reread the paper. Focus especially on errors that you remember committing in the past. For instance, if you know you have a tendency to misplace commas, go through your paper looking at each comma carefully. If you have a weakness for writing unintentional sentence fragments, read each sentence aloud to make sure that it is, indeed, a complete sentence. Have you accidentally shifted verb tenses anywhere, moving from past to present tense for no reason? Do all the subjects in your sentences agree in number with their verbs? Now is the time to find out.

Watch out for miscues—problems with a sentence that the writer can easily overlook. Remember that your search for errors is hampered in two ways:

1. As the writer, you hope not to find any errors with your writing. This desire can lead you to miss sighting them when they occur.
2. Because you know your material so well, it is easy, as you read, to unconsciously supply missing material—a word, correct punctuation—as if it were present.

How difficult is it to see that something is missing in the following sentence?

Unfortunately, legislators often have too little regard their constituents.

We can even guess that the missing word is probably *for,* which should be inserted after *regard.* However, it is quite possible that the writer of the sentence will supply the missing *for* automatically as he reads it, as if he has seen it on the page. This is a miscue, and miscues can be hard for the writer to spot because he is so close to his own material.

Editing is the stage in which you finally answer those minor questions that you put off earlier when you were wrestling with wording and organization. Any ambiguities regarding the use of abbreviations, italics, numerals, capital letters, titles (for example, when do you capitalize the title *president?*), hyphens, dashes (usually created on a typewriter or computer by striking the hyphen key twice), apostrophes, and quotation marks have to be cleared up. You must check to see that you have used the required formats for footnotes, endnotes, margins, and page numbers.

Guessing is not allowed. Sometimes unpracticed writers who realize that they don't quite understand a particular rule of grammar, punctuation, or format often do nothing to fill that knowledge gap. Instead they rely on guesswork and their own logic—which is not always up to the task of dealing with so contrary a language as English—to get them through problems that they could solve if only they referred to a writing manual. Remember that it does not matter to the reader why or how an error shows up in your writing; it only matters that you as the writer have dropped your guard. You must not allow a careless error to diminish your hard work.

One tactic for catching mistakes in sentence structure is to read the sentences aloud, starting with the last one in the paper, moving to the next to last, and then the previous sentence, thus going backward through the paper (reading each sentence in the normal, left-to-right manner, of course) until you reach the first sentence of the introduction. This backward progression strips each sentence of its rhetorical context and helps you to focus on its internal structure.

1.2.7   Proofreading

Before you hand in your final version of the paper, it is vital that you check it over one more time to make sure there are no errors of any sort. This job is called *proofreading* or *proofing.* In essence, you are looking for many of the same things you checked for during editing, but now you are doing it on the last draft, which has been typed and is about to be submitted to your audience. Proofreading is as important as editing; you may have missed an error in the previous stages, or an error may have been introduced when the draft was recopied or typed for the last time. Like every other stage of the writing process, proofreading is your responsibility.

At this stage, it is essential that you check for typing mistakes—letters transposed or left out of words, or missing words, phrases, or punctuation. If you have had the paper professionally typed, you still must check it carefully. Do not rely solely on the typist's proofreading abilities. If you typed your paper on a computer or a word processor, it is possible that you unintentionally inserted a command that alters your document drastically—slicing out a word or a line or a sentence at the touch of a key. Make sure such accidental deletions have not occurred.

Above all else, remember that your paper represents you. It is a product of your best thoughts, your most energetic and imaginative response to a writing challenge. If you have maintained your enthusiasm for the project and worked through the different stages of the writing process honestly and carefully, you should produce a paper you can be proud of and one that will serve its readers well.

1.3 LEVELS OF ACADEMIC WRITING

Researchers who study the written work of college students find that several patterns of effort and expertise emerge. Morgan (1981:5–6) refers to these patterns as "levels of academic writing," and believes that they appear in nearly every college class, graduate and undergraduate alike. Although writing quality increases with grade level, many students—no matter what their grade level—have trouble using words effectively.

1.3.1 Level One: The Fact-Gathering Level

Students at this level have little more to offer in their writing than opinions that they have heard others state or that they found in a newspaper or periodical. If asked, "What is Social Security?" a level-one student might answer, "Social Security is welfare for the elderly or disabled," or "Social Security is a liberal program." Students who are stranded at level one or below are unable to advance much further than presenting a fact or two to support their statements. This is the lowest level of scholarship. The level-one student, when assigned a report, will simply go to the library and assemble facts and opinions incoherently and return with a paper. At best, this is a very simple presentation of "What is?" However, mastery of level one is a necessary learning experience.

1.3.2 Level Two: The Informational Level

At this level, students learn to clarify facts and understand them more completely through the process of comparison. When asked the question, "What is Social Security?" the student writing at level two might draw on what she has learned of political science and economics to suggest different ideological perspectives, each with its own facts. A level-two answer shows greater depth of knowledge than a level-one answer; the student has advanced beyond a recitation of facts, taking the initial steps toward analysis.

1.3.3 Level Three: The Analytical Level

At this level, the student becomes familiar with and somewhat proficient in completing various types of sociological analysis. Using the same example, "What is Social Security?" some students might present their facts in numerical terms, using formulas, mathematical curves, statistical tests, or tables to express relationships among variables. Other students might reduce their data to common prose, utilizing different theories to analyze and explain the same phenomena.

1.3.4 Level Four: The Creative Level

This is the highest and most difficult level of academic writing. The student is able to use facts, theories, and analytical ability to reach levels of creativity. At the creative level, the student is essentially alone, trying to discover something new, perhaps an insight that colleagues can't appreciate initially.

To the question, "What is Social Security?" the creative sociologist, utilizing the sociological imagination described in the Introduction, might employ both historical analysis and creative forecasting to discover new information. The creative level is where knowledge is advanced, its frontiers pushed inevitably outward.

It is the purpose of this book to help you advance, from whatever level at which you presently find yourself, to the full professional expression of level four—creative and insightful writing in sociology.

CHAPTER

2

WRITING COMPETENTLY

2.1 GUIDELINES FOR THE COMPETENT WRITER

Good writing places your thoughts in your reader's mind in exactly the way you want them to be there. It tells your reader just what you want him to know without revealing anything you do not wish to say. That may sound odd, but the fact is that writers have to be careful not to let unwanted messages slip into their writing. For example, look at the following passage, taken from a paper analyzing the impact of a worker-retraining program. Hidden within the prose is a message that jeopardizes the paper's success. Can you detect the message?

> Recent articles written on the subject of dislocated workers have had little to say about the particular problems dealt with in this paper. Since few of these articles focus on the problem at the local level.

Chances are, when you reached the end of the second "sentence," you sensed something missing, a gap in logic or coherence, and your eye ran back through both sentences to find the place where things went wrong. The second sentence is actually not a sentence at all. It does have certain features of a sentence—a subject, for example (*few*), and a verb (*focus*), but its first word (*Since*) subordinates the entire clause that follows, taking away its ability to stand on its own as a complete idea. The second "sentence," which is properly called a subordinate clause, merely fills in some information about the first sentence, explaining why recent articles about dislocated workers fail to deal with problems discussed in the present paper.

This sort of error is commonly called a sentence fragment, and it conveys to the reader a message that no writer wants to send: that the writer either is careless or—worse—has not mastered the language she is using. Language errors, such as fragments, misplaced commas, or shifts in verb tense send up little red

39

flags in the reader's mind. The result is that the reader loses a little of his concentration on the issue being discussed. He becomes distracted and begins to wonder about the language competency of the writer. The writing loses effectiveness. Remember that whatever goal you set for your paper—whether you want it to persuade, describe, analyze, or speculate—you must also set another goal: to display language competence. Without it, your paper will not completely achieve its other aims. Language errors spread doubt like a virus; they jeopardize all the hard work you have done on your paper.

Credibility in the job market depends on language competence. Anyone who doubts this should remember the beating that Dan Quayle took in the press when he was vice president of the United States for misspelling the word potato at a Trenton, New Jersey, spelling bee. His error caused a storm of humiliating publicity for the hapless Quayle, and contributed to an impression of his general incompetence.

Although they may seem minor, these sorts of language errors—which are often called surface errors—can be extremely damaging in certain kinds of writing. Surface errors come in a variety of types, including misspellings, punctuation problems, grammar errors, and the inconsistent use of abbreviations, capitalization, and numerals. They are an affront to your reader's notion of correctness—and therein lies one of the biggest problems with surface errors. Different audiences tolerate different levels of correctness. You already know that you can get away with surface errors in, say, a letter to a friend, who will not judge you harshly for them, while those same errors in a job application letter might eliminate you from consideration for the job. Correctness depends to an extent on context.

Another problem is that the rules governing correctness shift over time. What would have been an error to your grandmother's generation—the splitting of an infinitive, for example, or the ending of a sentence with a preposition—is taken in stride today by most readers. So how do you write correctly when the rules shift from person to person and over time? Following are some tips.

2.1.1   Consider Your Audience

One of the great risks of writing is that even the simplest of choices you make regarding wording or punctuation can sometimes prejudice your audience against you in ways that may seem unfair. For example, look again at the old grammar "rule" forbidding the splitting of infinitives. After decades of counseling students to never split an infinitive (something this sentence has just done), composition experts now concede that a split infinitive is not a grammar crime. But suppose you have written a position paper trying to convince your city council of the need to hire security personnel for the library, and half of the council members—the people you wish to convince—remember their eighth-grade grammar teacher's outdated warning about splitting infinitives. How will they respond when you tell them, in your introduction, that "librarians are ordered to always accompany visitors to the rare book room because of the threat of vandalism"? How much of their attention have you suddenly lost because of their automatic recollection of a nonrule? It is possible, in other words, to write correctly and still offend your readers' notions of language competence.

Make sure that you tailor the surface features of your writing to the level of competency that your readers require. When in doubt, take a conservative approach. The same goes for the level of formality you should assume. Your audience might be just as distracted by contractions as by a split infinitive.

2.1.2   Aim for Consistency

When dealing with a language question for which there are different answers—such as whether to place a comma after the second item in a series of three ("The mayor's speech addressed taxes, housing for the poor, and the job situation.")—always use the same strategy. If, for example, you avoid splitting one infinitive, avoid splitting all infinitives in your paper.

2.1.3   Have Confidence in What You Already Know about Writing

It is easy for unpracticed writers to allow their occasional mistakes to discourage them about their writing ability. But most of what we know about writing is right. For example, we are all capable of writing sentences that are grammatically sound—even if we cannot identify the grammar rules by which we achieve coherence. Most writers who worry about their chronic errors have fewer than they think. Becoming distressed about errors makes writing more difficult. In fact, you already know more about grammar than you think you do. As various composition theorists have pointed out, the word *grammar* has several definitions. One meaning is "the formal patterns in which words must be arranged in order to convey meaning." We learn these patterns very early in life and use them spontaneously without thinking about them. Our understanding of grammatical patterns is extremely sophisticated, despite the fact that few of us can actually cite the rules that the patterns follow.

Hartwell (1985:111) tested grammar learning by asking native English-speakers of different ages and levels of education, including high school teachers, to arrange these words in natural order:

French the young girls four

Everyone he asked could produce the natural order for this phrase: "the four young French girls." Yet none of Hartwell's respondents said they knew the rule that governs the order of the words.

2.1.4   Eliminate Chronic Errors

The question then arises: If just thinking about our errors has a negative effect on our writing, how do we learn to write with greater accuracy? One important way is simply to write as often as possible. Give yourself practice in putting your thoughts into written shape, and get lots of practice in revising and proofing your work. And as you write and revise, be honest—and patient—with yourself. Chronic errors are like bad habits; getting rid of them takes time. You probably know of one or two problem areas in your writing that you could have eliminated but have not done so. Instead, you have "fudged" your writing at the critical points, relying on half-remembered formulas from past English classes or trying to come up with logical solutions to your writing problems. (Warning: Rules governing the English language are not always logical.) You may have simply decided that comma rules are unlearnable or that you will never understand the difference between the verbs *lay* and *lie*. And so you guess—and get the rule wrong a good part of the time. What a shame, when just a little extra work would give you mastery over those few gaps in your understanding and boost your confidence as well.

Instead of continuing with this sort of guesswork, instead of living with the gaps, why not face the problem areas now and learn the rules that have heretofore escaped you? What follows is a discussion of those surface features of a paper in which errors most commonly occur. You will probably be familiar with most—if not all—of the rules discussed, but there may be a few you have not yet mastered. Now is the time to do so.

2.2   SOME RULES OF PUNCTUATION AND GRAMMAR

2.2.1   Apostrophes

An apostrophe is used to show possession; when you wish to say that something belongs to someone or to another thing, you add either an apostrophe and an *s* or an apostrophe alone to the word that represents the owner.

When the owner is singular (a single person or thing), the apostrophe precedes an added *s:*

> According to Mr. Pederson's secretary, the board meeting has been canceled.
>
> The school's management team reduced crime problems last year.
>
> Somebody's briefcase was left in the classroom.

The same rule applies if the word showing possession is a plural that does not end in *s:*

> The women's club provided screening services for at-risk youth and their families.
>
> Professor Logan has proven himself a tireless worker for children's rights.

When the word expressing ownership is a plural ending in *s,* the apostrophe follows the *s:*

> The new procedure was discussed at the youth workers' conference.

There are two ways to form the possessive for two or more nouns:

1. To show joint possession (both nouns owning the same thing or things), the last noun in the series is possessive:

   Billy and Richard's first draft was completed yesterday.

2. To indicate that each noun owns an item or items individually, each noun must show possession:

   Professor Wynn's and Professor Camacho's speeches took different approaches to the same problem.

The apostrophe is important, an obvious statement when you consider the difference in meaning between the following two sentences:

Be sure to pick up the psychiatrist's things on your way to the airport.

Be sure to pick up the psychiatrists' things on your way to the airport.

In the first of these sentences, you have only one psychiatrist to worry about, while in the second, you have at least two!

2.2.2 Capitalization

When to capitalize. Following is a brief summary of some hard-to-remember capitalization rules.

Rule 1: You may, if you choose, capitalize the first letter of the first word in a complete sentence that follows a colon (but remember to be consistent throughout your paper).

Our instructions are explicit: Do not allow anyone into the conference without an identification badge.

Rule 2: Capitalize proper nouns (nouns naming specific people, places, or things) and proper adjectives (adjectives made from proper nouns). A common noun following the proper adjective is usually not capitalized, nor is a common adjective preceding the proper adjective (such as *a, an,* or *the*):

Proper Nouns	**Proper Adjectives**
England	English sociologists
Iraq	the Iraqi educator
Shakespeare	a Shakespearean tragedy

Proper nouns include the following:

- *Names of famous monuments and buildings:* the Washington Monument, the Empire State Building, the Library of Congress
- *Historical events, eras, and certain terms concerning calendar dates:* the Civil War, the Dark Ages, Monday, December, Columbus Day

- *Parts of the country:* North, Southwest, Eastern Seaboard, the West Coast, New England (Note that when words like *north, south, east, west,* and *northwest* are used to designate direction rather than geographical region, they are not capitalized: "We drove east to Boston and then made a tour of the East Coast.")
- *Words referring to race, religion, and nationality:* Islam, Muslim, Caucasian, White (or white), Asian, African American, Black (or black), Slavic, Arab, Jewish, Hebrew, Buddhism, Buddhists, Southern Baptists, the Bible, the Koran, American
- *Names of languages:* English, Chinese, Latin, Sanskrit
- *Titles of corporations, institutions, businesses, universities, and organizations:* Dow Chemical, General Motors, the National Endowment for the Humanities, University of Tennessee, Colby College, Kiwanis Club, American Association of Retired Persons, the Oklahoma State Senate (Note: Some words once considered proper nouns or adjectives have, over time, become common: french fries, pasteurized milk, arabic numerals, italics, panama hat.)

Rule 3: Titles of individuals should be capitalized when they precede a proper name; otherwise, titles are usually not capitalized.

The committee honored Chairperson Furmanski.

The committee honored the chairperson from the sociology department.

We phoned Doctor MacKay, who arrived shortly afterward.

We phoned the doctor, who arrived shortly afterward.

A story on Queen Elizabeth's health appeared in yesterday's paper.

A story on the queen's health appeared in yesterday's paper.

Pope John Paul's visit to Colorado was a public relations success.

The pope's visit to Colorado was a public relations success.

When not to capitalize.   In general, do not capitalize nouns when your reference is nonspecific. For example, you would not capitalize the phrase *the senator,* but you would capitalize *Senator Smith.* The second reference is as much a title as it is a term of identification, while the first reference is a mere identifier. Likewise, there is a difference in degree of specificity between the phrase *the state treasury* and the *Texas State Treasury.*

Note that the meaning of a term may change somewhat depending on capitalization. What, for example, might be the difference between a Democrat and a democrat? (When capitalized, the word refers to a member of a specific political party; when not capitalized, the word refers to someone who believes in a democratic form of government.)

Capitalization depends to some extent on the context of your writing. For example, if you are writing a policy analysis for a specific corporation, you may capitalize words and phrases—Board of Directors, Chairperson of the Board, the Institute—that would not be capitalized in a paper written referring to boards of directors, chairpersons, and institutes in general. Likewise, in some contexts it is not unusual to see titles of certain powerful officials capitalized even when not accompanying a proper noun:

The President's visit to the Oklahoma City bombing site was considered timely.

In this case the reference is to a specific president, President Clinton.

2.2.3   Colons

There are uses for the colon that we all know. For example, a colon can separate the parts of a statement of time (4:25 A.M.), separate chapter and verse in a biblical quotation (John 3:16), and close the salutation of a business letter (Dear Senator Keaton:). But there are other uses for the colon that writers sometimes don't quite learn that can add an extra degree of flexibility to sentence structure.

The colon can introduce into a sentence certain kinds of material, such as a list, a quotation, or a restatement or description of material mentioned earlier in the paper.

> *List:* The committee's research proposal promised to do three things: (1) establish the extent of the problem; (2) examine several possible solutions; and (3) estimate the cost of each solution.

> *Quotation:* In his speech, the mayor challenged us with these words: "How will your council's work make a difference in the life of our city?"

> *Restatement or description:* Ahead of us, according to the senator's chief of staff, lay the biggest job of all: convincing our constituents of the plan's benefits.

2.2.4   Commas

The comma is perhaps the most troublesome of all punctuation marks, no doubt because its use is governed by so many variables, such as sentence length, rhetorical emphasis, and changing notions of style. Following are the most common problems.

Comma splices.   Joining two complete sentences by only a comma makes a comma splice. Examine the following examples of comma splices:

> An impeachment is merely an indictment of a government official, actual removal usually requires a vote by a legislative body.

> An unemployed worker who has been effectively retrained is no longer an economic problem for the community, he has become an asset.

> It might be possible for the city to assess fees on the sale of real estate, however, such a move would be criticized by the community of real estate developers.

In each of these passages, two complete sentences (also called independent clauses) have been "spliced" together by a comma. When a comma splice is taken out of context, it becomes easy to see what is wrong: The break between the two sentences is inadequate. Simply reading the draft through to try to "hear" the comma splices may not work, however, since the rhetorical features of your prose—its "movement"—may make it hard to detect this kind of sentence error.

There is one foolproof way to check your paper for comma splices. Locate the commas in your draft and then read carefully the structures on both sides of each comma to determine whether you have spliced together two complete sentences. If you find a complete sentence on both sides of a comma, and if the sentence following the comma does not begin with a coordinating conjunction (*and, but, for, nor, or, so, yet*), then you have found a comma splice.

There are five commonly used ways to correct comma splices:

1. Place a period between the two independent clauses

   Splice: A physician receives many benefits from his or her affiliation with clients, there are liabilities as well.

   Correction: A physician receives many benefits from his or her affiliation with clients. There are liabilities as well.

2. Place a comma and a coordinating conjunction (*and, but, for, or, nor, so, yet*) between the sentences:

   Splice: The chairperson's speech described the major differences of opinion over the departmental situation, it also suggested a possible course of action.

   Correction: The chairperson's speech described the major differences of opinion over the departmental situation, and it also suggested a possible course of action.

3. Place a semicolon between the independent clauses:

   Splice: Some people believe that the federal government should play a large role in establishing a housing policy for the homeless, many others disagree.

   Correction: Some people believe that the federal government should play a large role in establishing a housing policy for the homeless; many others disagree.

4. Rewrite the two clauses of the comma splice as one independent clause:

   Splice: Television programs play some part in the development of delinquent attitudes, however they were not found to be the deciding factor in determining the behavior of juvenile delinquents.

   Correction: Television programs were found to play a minor but not a decisive role in determining the delinquent behavior of juveniles.

5. Change one of the two independent clauses into a dependent clause by beginning it with a subordinating word. A subordinating word introducing a clause prevents the clause from being able to stand on its own as a complete sentence. Words that can be used as subordinators include *although, after, as, because, before, if, though, unless, when, which,* and *where.*

   Splice: The student meeting was held last Tuesday, there was a poor turnout.

   Correction: When the student meeting was held last Tuesday, there was a poor turnout.

Comma missing in a compound sentence.   A compound sentence is comprised of two or more independent clauses—two complete sentences. When these two clauses are joined by a coordinating conjunction, the conjunction should be preceded by a comma. (In the previous section, the second solution for fixing a comma splice calls for the writer to transform the splice into this sort of compound sentence.) The error is that writers sometimes fail to place the comma before the conjunction. Remember, the comma is there to signal the reader that another independent clause follows the coordinating conjunction. In other words, the comma is like a road sign, telling a driver what sort of road she is about to encounter. If the comma is missing, the reader does not expect to find the second half of a compound sentence and may be distracted from the text. As the following examples indicate, the missing comma is especially a problem in longer sentences or in sentences in which other coordinating conjunctions appear:

> *Missing comma:* The senator promised to visit the hospital and investigate the problem and then he called the press conference to a close.
>
> *With the comma added:* The senator promised to visit the hospital and investigate the problem, and then he called the press conference to a close.
>
> *Missing comma:* The water board can neither make policy nor enforce it nor can its members serve on auxiliary water committees.
>
> *With the comma added:* The water board can neither make policy nor enforce it, nor can its members serve on auxiliary water committees.

Notice how the comma sorts out the two main parts of the compound sentence, eliminating confusion. However, an exception to the rule must be noted. In shorter sentences, the comma may not be necessary to make the meaning clear:

> The mayor phoned and we thanked him for his support.

Placing a comma between the independent clauses after the conjunction is never wrong, however. If you are the least bit unsure of your audience's notions about what makes for "proper" grammar, it is a good idea to take the conservative approach and use the comma:

> The mayor phoned, and we thanked him for his support.

Missing comma or commas with a nonrestrictive element.   A nonrestrictive element is part of a sentence—a word, phrase, or clause—that adds information about another element in the sentence without restricting or limiting the meaning of that element. In other words, a nonrestrictive element simply says something about some other part of the sentence without changing radically our understanding of it. Although the information it carries may be useful, we do not have to have the nonrestrictive element for the sentence to make sense. To signal the nonessential nature of the element, we set it off from the rest of the sentence with commas.

Failure to indicate the nonrestrictive nature of an element by using commas can cause confusion. For example, see how the presence or absence of commas affects our understanding of the following sentence:

> The judge was talking with the police officer, who won the outstanding service award last year.
>
> The judge was talking with the police officer who won the outstanding service award last year.

Can you see that the comma changes the meaning of the sentence? In the first version of the sentence, the comma makes the information that follows it incidental: The judge was talking with the police officer, who happens to have won the service award last year. In the second version of the sentence, the information following the term *police officer* is important to the sense of the sentence; it tells us, specifically, which police officer—presumably there are more than one— the judge was addressing. The lack of a comma has transformed the material following the term *police officer* into a restrictive element—meaning one necessary to our understanding of the sentence. Be sure that in your paper you make a clear distinction between nonrestrictive and restrictive elements by setting off the nonrestrictive elements with commas.

Missing comma in a series.   A series is any two or more items of a similar nature that appear consecutively in a sentence. The items may be individual words, phrases, or clauses. One of the rules that we all learned a long time ago is that the items in a series of three or more items are separated by commas. In the following examples the series items are in italics:

> The *senator, the mayor,* and *the police chief* all attended the ceremony.

> Because of the new zoning regulations, *all trailer parks must be moved out of the neighborhood, all small businesses must apply for recertification and tax status,* and *the two local churches must repave their parking lots.*

The final comma, the one before the *and,* is sometimes left out, especially in newspaper writing. This practice, however, can make for confusion, especially in longer, complicated sentences like the second example. Here is the way the sentence would read without the final comma:

> Because of the new zoning regulations, all trailer parks must be moved out of the neighborhood, all small businesses must apply for recertification and tax status and the two local churches must repave their parking lots.

Notice how the second *and,* which is not set off from the sequence in front of it, seems at first to be an extension of the second clause in the series instead of the beginning of the third. This is the sort of ambiguous structure that can cause a reader to backtrack and lose concentration.

To avoid the possibility of causing this sort of confusion, it is a good idea always to include that final comma. And remember that if you do decide to include it, be consistent; make sure it appears in every series in your paper.

2.2.5   Misplaced Modifiers

A modifier is a word or group of words used to describe—to "modify" our understanding of—another word in the sentence. A misplaced modifier is one that appears either at the beginning or ending of a sentence and seems to describe some word other than the one the writer obviously intended. The modifier is disconnected from its intended meaning. Because the writer knows what she wishes to say, it is often hard for her to spot a misplaced modifier. But other readers find them, and the result can be disastrous for the sentence.

Incorrect: Flying low over Washington, the White House was seen.

Correct: Flying low over Washington, we saw the White House.

Incorrect: Worried about the cost of the program, sections of the bill were trimmed in committee.

Correct: Worried about the cost of the program, the committee trimmed sections of the bill.

Correct: The committee trimmed sections of the bill because they were worried about the cost of the program.

Incorrect: To lobby for prison reform, a lot of effort went into the TV ads.

Correct: The lobby group put a lot of effort into the TV ads advocating prison reform.

Incorrect: Stunned, the television network broadcast the defeated senator's concession speech.

Correct: The television network broadcast the stunned senator's concession speech.

You will note that in the first two incorrect sentences, the confusion is largely due to the use of passive-voice verbs: the White House was seen, sections of the bill were trimmed. Often, though not always, the cause of a misplaced modifier is the fact that the actor in the sentence—*we* in the first example, *the committee* in the second—is either distanced from the modifier or obliterated by the passive-voice verb. It is a good idea to avoid passive voice unless you have a specific reason for using it.

One way to check for misplaced modifiers is to examine all modifiers at the beginnings or endings of your sentences. Look especially for *to be* phrases (to lobby) or for words ending in *–ing* or *–ed* at the start of the modifier. Then check to see whether the word being modified is in plain sight and close enough to the phrase to be properly connected.

2.2.6   *Parallelism*

Series of two or more words, phrases, or clauses within a sentence should be structured in the same grammatical way. Parallel structures can add power and balance to your writing by creating a strong rhetorical rhythm. Here is a famous example of parallelism from the U.S. Constitution. (The capitalization, preserved from the original document, follows eighteenth-century custom. Parallel structures have been italicized.)

Preamble to the Constitution

We the People of the United States, in Order to *form a more perfect Union, establish Justice, insure Domestic Tranquillity, provide for the Common Defense, promote the general Welfare,* and *secure the Blessings of Liberty to ourselves and our Posterity,* do ordain and establish this Constitution for the United States of America.

Note that there are actually two series in this sentence, the first composed of several phrases that each complete the infinitive phrase beginning with the word *to* (*to form,* [to] *Establish,* [to] *insure*), the second consisting of two verbs (*do ordain* and *establish*). These parallel series appeal to our love of balance and pattern, and give an authoritative tone to the sentence. We feel the writer has thought long and carefully about the subject, and has taken firm control of it.

We find a special satisfaction in balanced structures and so are more likely to remember ideas phrased in parallelisms than in less highly ordered language. For this reason—as well as for the sense of authority and control that they suggest—parallel structures are common in well-written speeches. Consider the following examples:

> We hold these truths to be self-evident, that all men are created equal, that they are endowed by their Creator with certain unalienable Rights, that among these are Life, Liberty, and the pursuit of Happiness.
>
> —Declaration of Independence

> But, in a larger sense, we can not dedicate—we can not consecrate—we can not hallow—this ground. The brave men, living and dead, who struggled here, have consecrated it, far above our poor power to add or detract. The world will little note, nor long remember what we say here, but it can never forget what they did here.
>
> —Abraham Lincoln, Gettysburg Address

> Let us never negotiate out of fear. But never let us fear to negotiate. . . . Ask not what your country can do for you; ask what you can do for your country.
>
> —John F. Kennedy, Inaugural Address

If the parallelism of a passage is not carefully maintained, the writing can seem sloppy and out of balance. To check for parallelism, scan your writing for any series of two or more items in a sentence. These items should be parallel in structure. In other words, if one item depends on an *–ing* construction, as in the second example following, so should its partners. Any lists in your paper should consist of items that are parallel in structure. Note the following examples of incorrect and correct constructions:

> *Incorrect:* The mayor promises not only to reform the police department, but also the giving of raises to all city employees.

> *Correct:* The mayor promises not only to reform the police department, but also to give raises to all city employees. [Connective structures such as *not only . . . but also* introduce elements that should be parallel.]

> *Incorrect:* The cost of doing nothing is greater than the cost to renovate the apartment block.

Correct: The cost of doing nothing is greater than the cost of renovating the apartment block.

Incorrect: Here are the items on the committee's agenda: (1) to discuss the new property tax; (2) to revise the wording of the city charter; and (3) a vote on the city manager's request for an assistant.

Correct: Here are the items on the committee's agenda: (1) to discuss the new property tax; (2) to revise the wording of the city charter; and (3) to vote on the city manager's request for an assistant.

2.2.7 Fused (Run-On) Sentences

A fused sentence is one in which two or more independent clauses (passages that can stand as complete sentences) have been joined together without the aid of any suitable connecting word, phrase, or punctuation; the sentences run together. As you can see, there are several ways to correct a fused sentence:

Incorrect: The council members were exhausted they had debated for two hours.

Correct: The council members were exhausted. They had debated for two hours. [The linked independent clauses have been separated into two sentences.]

Correct: The council members were exhausted; they had debated for two hours. [A semicolon marks the break between the two clauses.]

Correct: The council members were exhausted, having debated for two hours. [The second independent clause has been rephrased as a dependent clause.]

Incorrect: Our policy analysis impressed the committee it also convinced them to reconsider their action.

Correct: Our policy analysis impressed the committee by convincing them to reconsider their action. [The second clause has been rephrased as part of the first clause.]

Correct: Our policy analysis impressed the committee, and it also convinced them to reconsider their action. [The two clauses have been separated by a comma and a coordinating word.]

Although a fused sentence is easily noticeable to the reader, it can be maddeningly difficult for the writer to catch in proofreading. Unpracticed writers tend to read through the fused spots, sometimes supplying the break that is usually heard when sentences are spoken. To check for fused sentences, read the independent clauses in your paper carefully, making sure that there are adequate breaks among all of them.

2.2.8 Pronoun Errors

The difference between *its* and *it's*. Do not make the mistake of trying to form the possessive of it in the same way that you form the possessive of most nouns. The pronoun *it* shows possession by simply adding an *s:*

The prosecuting attorney argued the case on its merits.

The word *it's* is a contraction, meaning "it is":

It's the most expensive program ever launched by the prison.

What makes the *its/it's* rule so confusing is that most nouns form the singular possessive by adding an apostrophe and an *s:* The jury's verdict startled the crowd. When proofreading, any time you come to the word *it's,* substitute the phrase *it is* while you read. If the phrase makes sense, you have used the correct form. Consider the following examples:

If you have used the word *it's:*

The newspaper article was misleading in it's analysis of the election.

Then read *it's* as *it is:*

The newspaper article was misleading in it is analysis of the election.

If the phrase makes no sense, substitute *its* for *it's:*

The newspaper article was misleading in its analysis of the election.

Vague pronoun reference.   Pronouns are words that stand in place of nouns or other pronouns that have already been mentioned in your writing. The most common pronouns include *he, she, it, they, them, those, which,* and *who.* You must make sure that each pronoun reference is clear; in other words, that there is no confusion about the reference. Examine the following clear pronoun references:

The mayor said that he would support our bill if the city council would also back it.

The piece of legislation that drew the most criticism was the bill concerning housing for the poor.

The word that is replaced by the pronoun is called its *antecedent.* To check the accuracy of your pronoun references, ask yourself this question: To what does the pronoun refer? Then answer the question carefully, making sure that there is not more than one possible antecedent. Consider the following sentence:

Several special interest groups decided to defeat the new health care bill. This became the turning point of the government's reform campaign.

To what does the word *this* refer? The immediate answer seems to be the word *bill* at the end of the previous sentence. It is more likely the writer was referring to the attempt of the special interest groups to defeat the bill, but there is no word in the first sentence that refers specifically to this action. The reference is unclear. One way to clarify the reference is to change the beginning of the second sentence:

Several special interest groups decided to defeat the new health care bill. Their attack on the bill became the turning point of the government's reform campaign.

Here is another example:

When John F. Kennedy appointed his brother Robert to the position of U.S. Attorney General, he had little idea how widespread the corruption in the Teamsters Union was.

To whom does the word *he* refer? It is unclear whether the writer is referring to John or to Robert Kennedy. One way to clarify the reference is simply to repeat the antecedent instead of using a pronoun:

When President John F. Kennedy appointed his brother Robert to the position of U.S. Attorney General, Robert had little idea how widespread the corruption in the Teamsters Union was.

Pronoun agreement.   Remember that a pronoun must agree in gender and in number with its antecedent. This rule is generally easy for us to remember. Study the following examples of pronoun agreement:

Mayor Smith said that he appreciated our club's support in the election.

One reporter asked the senator what she would do if the President offered her a cabinet post.

Having listened to our case, the judge decided to rule on it within the week.

Engineers working on the housing project said they were pleased with the renovation so far.

The following words, however, can become troublesome antecedents. They may look like plural pronouns but are actually singular:

everybody	nobody	everyone
no one	somebody	each
someone	either	anyone

A pronoun referring to one of these words in a sentence must be singular, too. Pronoun agreement errors appear in the following examples:

Incorrect: Each of the women in the support group brought their children.

Correct: Each of the women in the support group brought her children.

Incorrect: Has everybody received their ballot?

Correct: Has everybody received his or her ballot? [The two gender-specific pronouns are used to avoid sexist language.]

Correct: Have all the delegates received their ballots? [The singular antecedent has been changed to a plural one.]

Shift in person.   It is important to avoid shifting among first person (*I, we*), second person (*you*), and third person (*she, he, it, one, they*) unnecessarily. Such shifts can cause confusion:

Incorrect: Most people [third person] who seek a job find that if you [second person] tell the truth during your interviews, you will gain the interviewers' respect.

Correct: Most people who seek a job find that if they tell the truth during their interviews, they will win the interviewers' respect.

2.2.9   Quotation Marks

It can be difficult to remember when to use quotation marks and where they go in relation to other marks of punctuation. When faced with a gap in their knowledge of the rules, unpracticed writers often try to rely on logic rather than referring to a rule book. But the rules governing quotation marks do not always seem to us to rely on logic. The only way to make sure of your use of quotation marks is to memorize the rules. There are not many.

When to use quotation marks.   Use quotation marks to enclose direct quotations, if they are four typed lines or less:

In his farewell address to the American people, George Washington warned, "The great rule of conduct for us, in regard to foreign nations, is, in extending our commercial relations, to have with them as little political connection as possible." (U.S. Senate 1991)

Longer quotes are indented left and right and single-spaced—without quotation marks:

Lincoln explained his motive for continuing the Civil War clearly in his response to Horace Greeley's open letter:

I would save the Union. I would save it the shortest way under the Constitution. The sooner the National authority can be restored, the nearer the Union will be the Union as it was. If there be those who would not save the Union unless they could at the same time save Slavery, I do not agree with them. If there be those who would not save the Union unless they could at the same time destroy Slavery, I do not agree with them. (Lincoln 1862)

Use single quotation marks to set off quotations within quotations:

"I intend," said the professor, "to use in my lecture a line from Frost's poem, 'The Road Not Taken.'"

Note that when the interior quote occurs at the end of the sentence, both single and double quotation marks are placed outside the period. Use quotation marks to set off the following kinds of titles:

- The title of a short poem: "The Second Coming," by William Butler Yeats [But note that the title of a long poem published as a book does not appear in quotation marks; instead, it is italicized as a book would be: *The Dark Sister,* by Winfield Townley Scott]
- The title of a short story
- The title of an article or essay
- The title of a song
- An episode of a television or radio show

Use quotation marks to set off words or phrases used in special ways:

To convey irony: The so-called "liberal" administration has done nothing but cater to big business.

To set off a technical term: To have "charisma," Weber would argue, is to possess special powers. Many believe that John F. Kennedy had great charisma. [Note that once the term is defined, it is not placed in quotation marks again.]

Placement of quotation marks in relation to other punctuation.   Always place commas and periods inside closing quotation marks:

"My fellow Americans," said the President, "there are tough times ahead of us."

Place colons and semicolons outside closing quotation marks:

In his speech on voting, the sociologist warned against "an encroaching indolence"; he was referring to the middle class.

There are several victims of the government's campaign to "Turn Back the Clock": the homeless, the elderly, and the mentally impaired.

Place question marks, exclamation points, and dashes inside or outside closing quotation marks, depending on context. If the punctuation is part of the quotation, it goes inside the quotation mark:

"When will the tenure committee make up its mind?" asked the dean.

The demonstrators shouted, "Free the hostages!" and "No more slavery!"

If the punctuation is not part of the quotation, it goes outside the quotation mark:

Which president said, "We have nothing to fear but fear itself"?

Note that although the quote was a complete sentence, you do not place a period after it. There can only be one mark of "terminal" punctuation (punctuation that ends a sentence).

2.2.10   Semicolons

The semicolon is a little-used punctuation mark that is worth incorporating into your writing strategy because of its many potential applications. A semicolon can be used to correct a comma splice:

Incorrect: The union representatives left the meeting in good spirits, their demands were met.

Correct: The union representatives left the meeting in good spirits; their demands were met.

Incorrect: Several guests at the fund-raiser had lost their invitations, however, we were able to seat them, anyway.

Correct: Several guests at the fund-raiser had lost their invitations; however, we were able to seat them, anyway.

It is important to remember that conjunctive adverbs like *however, therefore,* and *thus* are not coordinating words (such as *and, but, or, for, so,* and *yet*) and cannot be used with a comma to link independent clauses. If the second independent clause begins with *however,* it must be preceded by either a period or a semicolon. As you can see from the second example, connecting the two independent clauses with a semicolon instead of a period preserves the suggestion that there is a strong relationship between the clauses.

Semicolons can separate items in a series. Usually commas separate items in a series:

We ate breakfast, lunch, and dinner in the hotel.

But when the series items themselves contain commas, the items may be separated from one another with semicolons.

The newspaper account of the rally stressed the march, which drew the biggest crowd; the mayor's speech, which drew tremendous applause; and the party afterwards in the park.

Avoid misusing semicolons. Do not use a semicolon to separate an independent clause from a dependent clause:

Incorrect: Students from the college volunteered to answer phones during the pledge drive; which was set up to generate money for the new arts center.

Correct: Students from the college volunteered to answer phones during the pledge drive, which was set up to generate money for the new arts center.

Although you can use a semicolon to separate two independent clauses, you should use a comma to separate an independent clause from a dependent clause. Do not overuse semicolons. Useful though semicolons are, if too many of them appear in your writing, they can distract your reader's attention. Avoid monotony by using semicolons sparingly.

2.2.11   Sentence Fragments

A fragment is a part of a sentence that is punctuated and capitalized as if it were an entire sentence. It is an especially disruptive kind of error, because it obscures the kinds of connections that the words of a sentence must make in order to complete the reader's understanding. Students sometimes write fragments because they are concerned that a particular sentence is growing too long and needs to be shortened. Remember that cutting the length of a sentence merely by adding a period somewhere along the way often creates a fragment. When checking your writing for fragments, it is essential that you read each sentence carefully to determine (1) whether there is a complete subject and a verb; and (2) whether there is a subordinating word preceding the subject and verb, making the construction a subordinate clause rather than a complete sentence.

Some fragments lack a verb:

Incorrect: The chairperson of our committee, having received a letter from the mayor. [It may look as if there is a verb in this passage, but the word *having,* which can be used as a verb, is used here as a gerund introducing a participial phrase. Watch out for words that look like verbs but are used in another way.]

Correct: The chairperson of our committee received a letter from the mayor.

Some fragments lack a subject:

Incorrect: Our study shows that there is broad support for improvement in the health care system. And in the unemployment system.

Correct: Our study shows that there is broad support for improvement in the health care system and in the unemployment system.

Some fragments are subordinate clauses:

Incorrect: After the latest edition of the newspaper came out. [This clause has the two major components of a complete sentence: a subject (*edition*) and a verb (*came*). Indeed, if the first word (*After*) were deleted, the clause would be a complete sentence. But that first word is a subordinating word, which acts to prevent the following clause from standing on its own as a complete sentence. Watch out for this kind of construction. It is called a subordinate clause, and it is not a sentence.]

Correct: After the latest edition of the newspaper came out, the mayor's press secretary was overwhelmed with phone calls. [A subordinate clause is connected in meaning to the independent clause either before or after it. A common method of revising a subordinate clause that has been punctuated as a complete sentence is to connect it to the complete sentence to which its meaning is most closely connected.]

Incorrect: Several members of Congress asked for copies of the Vice President's position paper. Which called for reform of the Environmental Protection Agency. [The clause beginning after the first period is a subordinate clause written as if it were a complete sentence.]

Correct: Several members of Congress asked for copies of the Vice President's position paper, which called for reform of the Environmental Protection Agency.

2.3   SPELLING

All of us have special spelling problems, words whose correct spelling we have not yet committed to memory. Most writers are not as bad at spelling as they believe themselves to be. Usually it is just a handful of words that the individual finds troubling. The most important thing to do when confronting your spelling problems is to be as sensitive as possible to those words with which you know you have trouble and keep a dictionary handy. No writer should be without a dictionary. There is no excuse for failing to look up a questionable spelling.

When using a computer to type your paper, take advantage of the "spell check" feature available with most word-processing software. It allows you to check those words listed in the program's dictionary. But do not rely entirely on your computer's spell checker. It will miss a variety of words that are properly spelled but are improperly used variants within a particular context. Notice that the mistakes in the following sentences would go unnoticed by a computer's spell checker:

> Wilbur wood rather dye than admit that he had been their. When he cited the bare behind the would pile, he thought,"Isle just lye hear until he goes buy."

Following are two lists of words that often give writers trouble. Read through the lists, looking for those words that tend to give you trouble.

2.3.1   Commonly Confused Words

The words in each pair listed below are often confused with each other. If you do not know the difference in a particular pair, consult your dictionary:

accept/except	complement/compliment
advice/advise	conscience/conscious
affect/effect	corps/corpse
aisle/isle	council/counsel
allusion/illusion	dairy/diary
an/and	descent/dissent
angel/angle	desert/dessert
ascent/assent	device/devise
bare/bear	die/dye
brake/break	dominant/dominate
breath/breathe	elicit/illicit
buy/by	eminent/immanent/imminent
capital/capitol	envelop/envelope
choose/chose	every day/everyday
cite/sight/site	fair/fare

formally/formerly

rain/reign/rein

forth/fourth

raise/raze

hear/here

reality/realty

heard/herd

respectfully/respectively

hole/whole

reverend/reverent

human/humane

right/rite/write

its/it's

road/rode

know/no

scene/seen

later/latter

sense/since

lay/lie

stationary/stationery

lead/led

straight/strait

lessen/lesson

taught/taut

loose/lose

than/then

may be/maybe

their/there/they're

miner/minor

threw/through

moral/morale

too/to/two

of/off

track/tract

passed/past

waist/waste

patience/patients

waive/wave

peace/piece

weak/week

personal/personnel

weather/whether

plain/plane

were/where

precede/proceed

which/witch

presence/presents

whose/who's

principal/principle

your/you're

quiet/quite

2.3.2   Commonly Misspelled Words

acceptable

arguing/argument

accessible

authentic

accommodate

before

accompany

begin/beginning

accustomed

believe

acquire

bulletin

against

business

a lot

cannot

annihilate

category

apparent

committee

condemn	irritate
courteous	knowledge
definitely	license
dependent	likelihood
desperate	maintenance
develop	manageable
different	meanness
disappear	mischievous
disappoint	missile
easily	necessary
efficient	nevertheless
environment	no one
equipped	noticing/noticeable
exceed	nuisance
exercise	occasion/occasionally
existence	occurred/occurrences
experience	omit/omission
fascinate	opinion
finally	opponent
foresee	parallel
forty	parole
fulfill	peaceable
gauge	performance
guaranteed	pertain
guard	practical
harass	preparation
hero/heroes	probably
humorous	process
hurried/hurriedly	professor
hypocrite	prominent
ideally	pronunciation
immediately	psychology
immense	publicly
incredible	pursue/pursuing
innocuous	questionnaire
intercede	realize
interrupt	received/receipt
irrelevant	recession
irresistible	recommend

referring

religious

remembrance

reminisce

repetition

representative

rhythm

ridiculous

roommate

satellite

scarcity

scenery

science

secede/secession

secretary

senseless

separate

sergeant

shining

significant

sincerely

skiing

stubbornness

studying

succeed/success/successfully

susceptible

suspicious

technical

temporary

tendency

therefore

tragedy

truly

tyranny

unanimous

unconscious

undoubtedly

until

vacuum

valuable

various

vegetable

visible

without

women

writing

CITING SOURCES

One of your most important jobs as a research writer is to document your use of source material carefully and clearly. Failure to do so will cause your reader confusion, damage the effectiveness of your paper, and perhaps make you vulnerable to a charge of plagiarism. Proper documentation is more than just good form; it is a powerful indicator of your own commitment to scholarship and the sense of authority that you bring to your writing. Good documentation demonstrates your expertise as a researcher and increases the reader's trust in you and your work; it gives credibility to what you are writing.

Unfortunately, as anybody who has ever written a research paper knows, getting the documentation right can be a frustrating, confusing job, especially for the novice writer. Positioning each element of a single reference citation accurately can require what seems an inordinate amount of time spent thumbing through the style manual. Even before you begin to work on specific citations, there are important questions of style and format to answer.

4.1   PRELIMINARY CONSIDERATIONS

Direct quotes must always be credited, as must certain kinds of paraphrased material. Information that is basic—important dates, and facts or opinions universally acknowledged—need not be cited. Information that is not widely known, whether fact or opinion, should be documented.

What if you are unsure whether or not a certain fact is widely known? You are, after all, very probably a newcomer to the field in which you are conducting your research. If in doubt, supply the documentation. It is better to overdocument than to fail to do justice to a source.

Although the question of which documentation style to use may be decided for you in some classes by your instructor, others may allow you to choose.

There are several styles available, each designed to meet the needs of writers in particular fields. The citation and reference systems approved by the Modern Language Association (MLA) and the American Psychological Association (APA) are often used in the humanities and social sciences.

The American Sociological Association (ASA) has its own system that is widely used by sociology students and professionals. The ASA has adopted a modification of the style elaborated in the *Chicago Manual of Style* (CMS), perhaps the most universally approved of all documentation authorities. One of the advantages of using the ASA style, which is outlined in a pamphlet entitled *ASA Style Guide* (1997), is that it is designed to guide the professional sociologist in preparing a manuscript for submission to a journal. The ASA style is required for all papers submitted to the *American Sociological Review,* the official journal of the ASA and the most influential sociology journal in publication. It is also required for all the leading journals in sociology and many of the less prestigious ones.

4.2   CITING SOURCES IN ASA FORMAT

A parenthetical reference or citation is a note placed within the text, near where the source material occurs. In order not to distract the reader from the argument, the citation is as brief as possible, containing just enough information to refer the reader to the full reference listing that appears in the bibliography or reference section following the text. Usually the minimum information necessary is the author's last name—meaning the name by which the source is alphabetized in the references at the end of the paper—and the year of the publication of the source. As indicated by the following models, this information can be given in a number of ways. Models for listing bibliographical entries that correspond to parenthetical citations are given in the next section of this chapter.

4.2.1   Text Citations

Citations within the text should include the author's last name and the year of publication. Page numbers should be included only when quoting directly from a source or referring to specific passages. Subsequent citations of the same source should be identified the same way as the first. The following examples identify the *ASA Style Guide*'s (1997) citation system for a variety of possibilities.

When the author's name is in the text, it should be followed by the publication year in parentheses:

Freedman (2004) postulates that when individuals . . .

When the author's name is not in the text, the last name and publication date should be enclosed in parentheses:

. . . encourage more aggressive play (Perrez 1999).

As noted previously, the page number should be included when the material referred to is quoted directly, or when you wish to refer the reader to a specific page of the source text. However, some instructors prefer page numbers for all citations in order to check for plagiarism. Ask your instructor what system you should follow. When the page number is included, it should follow the publication year and be preceded by a colon, with no space between the colon and the page number:

Thomas (1999:741) builds on this scenario . . .

When the publication has two authors, cite both last names:

. . . establish a sense of self (Holmes and Watson 1872:114–116).

When a publication has three authors, cite all three last names in the first citation, with *et al.* (in roman type) used for subsequent citations in the text. Thus a first citation would read:

. . . found the requirements very restrictive (Mollar, Querley, and McLarry 1926).

Thereafter, the following form is sufficient:

. . . proved to be quite difficult (Mollar et al. 1926).

For more than three authors, list the first author's last name and use *et al.* (in roman type) for the remaining authors in all citations.

When citing two authors with the same last name, use a first initial to differentiate between them.

. . . the new budget cuts (K. Grady 1994).
. . . stimulate economic growth (B. Grady 1993).

When citing two works by the same author, in the same note, place a comma between the publication dates of the works.

George (1996, 2004) argues for . . .

If the two works were published in the same year, differentiate between them by adding lowercase letters to the publication dates. Be sure to add the letters to the references in the bibliography, too.

. . . the city government (Estrada 2002a, 2002b).

Direct quotes of fewer than four lines should be placed in the text, with quotation marks at the beginning and end. The citation should include the page number in one of the following formats:

The majority of these ads promote the notion that "If you are slim, you will also be beautiful and sexually desirable" (Rockett and McMinn 1999:278).

Smith and Hill (1997) found that "women are far more likely to obsess about weight" (p. 127).

Direct quotes of four lines or more should be indented, single spaced, and presented in a smaller font or type when possible. They should be blocked—no tab set for the first line—with no quotation marks, as follows:

According to Brown (2005):

> There are few girls and women of any age or culture raised in white America, who do not have some manifestation of the concerns discussed here, i.e., distortion of body image, a sense of being "out-of-control" in relationship to food, addiction to dieting, binging, or self-starvation. (P. 61)

Note that in the block quote the author, date, and/or page number follows the period at the end, and that the *P* for *page* is capitalized when the page number appears alone without the author and date, as in this example.

Sometimes information is obtained from a source that is cited in a secondary source. Although it is always best to locate and cite the original source, sometimes this is not possible. When citing a source that is itself cited in a secondary source, refer in your parenthetical citation to the original source, and not to the later source in which the original is quoted. For example, if you wish to cite a passage from a 1999 article by John Smith that you found cited in a 2003 article by Arleen Michaels, your citation should look like this:

. . . the promise of a subsequent generation (Smith 1999).

See "Article Cited in a Secondary Source" on page 92 for information on how to list this citation in your references.

The *ASA Style Guide* only briefly discusses reference formats for works published anonymously. Section 17.34 of the *Chicago Manual of Style* (2003) indicates that if the authorship of an anonymous work is known, the name is given in brackets:

([Morey, Cynthia] 1977)

According to section 17.32 of the *Chicago Manual of Style,* if the name of the author of an anonymous work cannot be ascertained, the reference begins with the title of the work. The first of the following models refers to a magazine article, the second to a book. Note that in the case of the book title, the initial article "The" is moved to the end of the title.

("The Case for Prosecuting Deadbeat Dads" 1996:36–38)
(*Worst Way to Learn: The Government's War on Education, The* 2003)

Section 17.41 of the *Chicago Manual of Style* recommends including the name of an editor, compiler, or translator, without an abbreviation such as "ed.," "comp.," or "trans.," when there is no author's name given.

Cite chapters, tables, appendixes, and the like as follows:

... (Johnson 1995, chap. 6).
... (Blake 2005, table 4:34).
... (Shelby 1976, appendix C:177).

When citing a work reprinted from an earlier publication, give the earliest date of publication in brackets, followed immediately by the date of the version you have used:

... Baldwin ([1897] 2002) interpreted this ...

When citing more than one source, separate the citations by a semicolon and order them in a manner of your choice. You may arrange them in alphabetical order, date order, or order of importance to your argument, but whatever order you choose, use it consistently throughout your paper:

... are related (Harmatz 1999:48; Marble et al. 1996:909; Powers and Erickson 2001:48; Rackley et al. 1988:10; Thompson and Thompson 2000:1067).

Give the date for dissertation and unpublished papers. When the date is not available, use "n.d." (no date) in place of the date. Use the word "forthcoming" when materials cited are unpublished but scheduled for publication.

Studies by Barkley (forthcoming) and Jorden (n.d.) lend support ...

When citing National Archives or other archival sources, abbreviate the citations. The *Chicago Manual of Style* (section 17.324) suggests that the parenthetical citation should include the record group (RG) as well, leaving other information for the citation in the reference section:

(NA, RG 43)

Classic texts.   When citing classic texts, such as the Bible, standard translations of ancient Greek texts, or numbers of the Federalist Papers, you may use the systems by which they are subdivided. Since any edition of a classic text employs the standard subdivisions, this reference method has the advantage of allowing your reader to find the source passage in any published edition of the text. It is not necessary to include a citation for a classic text in the reference section.

You may cite a biblical passage by referring to the particular book, chapter, and verse, all in roman type, with the translation given after the verse number:

"But the path of the just is as the shining light, that shineth more and more unto the perfect day" (Proverbs 4:18 King James Version).

The Federalist Papers are numbered:

Madison addresses the problem of factions in a republic (Federalist 10).

Newspapers.   According to the *Chicago Manual of Style* (2003, section 17.191), references to material in daily newspapers should be handled within the syntax of your sentence:

> In an August 10, 1999, editorial, the *New York Times* painted the new regime in glowing colors.
>
> An article entitled "Abuse in Metropolis," written by Harry Black and published in the *Daily News* on December 24, 2001, took exception to the mayor's remarks.

According to the *Chicago Manual of Style,* references to newspaper items are not usually included in the reference list or bibliography. If you wish to include newspaper references, however, there is a model of a bibliographical entry in the next section of this chapter.

Public documents.   When citing a public/government document or one with institutional authorship, you should supply the minimum identification:

> . . . (U.S. Bureau of the Census 1993:223).

Since the *ASA Style Guide* gives formats for only two types of government publications, the following models are based not only on practices from the ASA guide but also on formats found in the *Chicago Manual of Style* (sections 17.290–355). Corresponding bibliography entries appear in the next section.
Parenthetical text references to both the *Senate Journal* and the *House Journal* start with the journal title in place of the author, the session year, and, if applicable, the page:

> (*Senate Journal* 1997:24)

Congressional debates are printed in the daily issues of the *Congressional Record,* which are bound biweekly and then collected and bound at the end of the session. Whenever possible, you should consult the bound yearly collection instead of the biweekly compilations. Your parenthetical reference should begin with the title *Congressional Record* (or *Cong. Rec.*) in place of the author's name and include the year of the congressional session, the volume and part of the *Congressional Record,* and finally the page:

> (*Cong. Rec.* 1930, 72, pt. 8:9012)

References to congressional reports and documents, which are numbered sequentially in one- or two-year periods, include the name of the body generating the material, the year, and the page:

> (U.S. Congress 1997:12)

Note that any reference that begins with *U.S. Senate* or *U.S. House* may omit the *U.S.* if it is clear from the context that you are referring to the United States.

Whichever form you use, be sure to use it consistently, in both the notes and the bibliography.

Bills and resolutions.   According to the *Chicago Manual of Style* (section 17.309), bills and resolutions, which are published in pamphlets called slip bills, on microfiche, and in the *Congressional Record,* are not always given a parenthetical text reference and a corresponding bibliography entry. Instead, the pertinent reference information appears in the syntax of the sentence. If, however, you wish to cite such information in a text reference, the form depends on the source from which you took your information. If citing to a slip bill, use one of these forms:

(U.S. Senate 1996)

(*Visa Formalization Act of 1996*)

You may cite either the body that authored the bill or the title of the work itself. Whichever method you choose, remember to begin your bibliography entry with the same material. Here is a model for citing to the *Congressional Record:*

(U.S. Senate 1996:S7658)

The number following the date and preceded by an *S* (for Senate; *H* for House) is the page in the *Congressional Record.*

As with bills and resolutions, laws (also called statutes) are not necessarily given a parenthetical text reference and a bibliography entry. Instead, the identifying material is included in the text. If you wish to make a formal reference for a statute, you must structure it according to the place where you found the law published. Initially published separately in pamphlets, as slip laws, statutes are eventually collected and incorporated, first into a set of volumes called *U.S. Statutes at Large* and later into the *U.S. Code,* a multivolume set that is revised every six years. You should use the latest edition. When citing to a slip law, you should either use *U.S. Public Law* (in roman type) and the number of the piece of legislation, or the title of the law:

(U.S. Public Law 678:16–17)

(*Library of Congress Book Preservation Act of 1997*:16–17)

When citing to the *Statutes at Large,* use this form:

(*Statutes at Large* 2005:466)

The following form is for citing to the *U.S. Code:*

(*Library of Congress Book Preservation Act of 1997, U.S. Code,* Vol. 38, sec. 1562)

United States Constitution. According to the *Chicago Manual of Style* (section 17.321), references to the United States Constitution include the number of the article or amendment, the section number, and the clause, if necessary:

(U.S. Constitution, art. 3, sec. 3)

It is not necessary to include the Constitution in the bibliography.

A reference to a report, bulletin, circular, or any other type of material issued by the Executive Department starts with the name of the agency issuing the document, although you may use the name of the author, if known:

(Department of Labor 2004:334)

United States Supreme Court. As with laws, Supreme Court decisions are rarely given their own parenthetical text reference and bibliography entry but are instead identified in the text. If you wish to use a formal reference, however, you may place within the parentheses the title of the case, in italics, followed by the source (for cases after 1875 this is the *United States Supreme Court Reports,* abbreviated U.S.), which is preceded by the volume number and followed by the page number. You should end the first reference to the case that appears in your paper with the date of the case, in brackets. You need not include the date in subsequent references:

(*State of Nevada v. Goldie Warren* 324 U.S. 123 [1969])

Before 1875, Supreme Court decisions were published under the names of official court reporters. The reference below is to William Cranch, *Reports of Cases Argued and Adjudged in the Supreme Court of the United States, 1801–1815,* 9 vols. (Washington, D.C., 1804–1817). The number preceding the clerk's name is the volume number; the last number is the page:

(1 Cranch 137)

For most of these parenthetical references, it is possible to move some or all of the material outside the parentheses simply by incorporating it in the text:

In 1969, in *State of Nevada v. Goldie Warren* (324 U.S. 123), the judge ruled that an observer of a traffic accident has an obligation to offer assistance to survivors.

Lower courts. Decisions of lower federal courts are published in the *Federal Reporter.* The note should give the volume of the *Federal Reporter* (F.); the series, if it is other than the first (2d, in the model below); the page; and, in brackets, an abbreviated reference to the specific court (the example below is to the Second Circuit Court) and the year:

(*United States v. Sizemore,* 183 F. 2d 201 [2d Cir. 1950])

Government commissions. According to the *Chicago Manual of Style* (section 17.320), references to bulletins, circulars, reports, and study papers that are issued by various government commissions should include the name of the commission, the date of the document, and the page:

(Securities and Exchange Commission 1985:57)

Because government documents are often credited to a corporate author with a lengthy name, you may devise an acronym or a shortened form of the name and indicate in your first reference to the source that this name will be used in later citations:

(*Bulletin of Labor Statistics* 1997, 1954; *hereafter BLS*)

The practice of using a shortened name in subsequent references to any corporate author, whether a public or private organization, is sanctioned in most journals and approved in the *Chicago Manual of Style* (section 17.47). Thus, if you refer often to the *U.N. Monthly Bulletin of Statistics,* you may, after giving the publication's full name in the first reference, use a shortened form of the title—perhaps an acronym such as *UNMBS*—in all later citations.

Local government.   According to the *Chicago Manual of Style* (section 17.323), references to state and local government documents are similar to those for the corresponding national government sources:

(Oklahoma Legislature 1995:24)

The *Chicago Manual of Style* restricts bibliographical information concerning state laws or municipal ordinances to running text or notes. (See section 17.312 for examples of note citations.)

Interviews.   According to the *Chicago Manual of Style* (sections 17.205, 17.208), in the author-date system, citations to interviews should be handled by references within the text—in the syntax of a sentence—rather than in parentheses:

In a March 1997 interview with O. J. Simpson, Barbara Walters asked questions that seemed to upset and disorient the former superstar.

For published or broadcast interviews, no parenthetical reference is necessary, but there should be a complete citation under the interviewer's name in the bibliography.

An unpublished interview conducted by the writer of the paper should also be cited in the syntax of the sentence:

In an interview with the author on April 23, 2003, Dr. Kennedy expressed her disappointment with the new court ruling.

If you are citing material from an interview that you conducted, identify yourself as "the author" and give the date of the interview. Cite the interview by placing the date in parentheses following the name of the person whom you interviewed:

> Marsha Cummings (2000), Director of the Children's Hospital in Oklahoma City, was interviewed by the author on November 14, 2000.

4.2.2   References

Parenthetical citations in the text point the reader to the fuller source descriptions at the end of the paper known as the references or bibliography. This reference list, which always directly follows the text under the heading REFERENCES, is arranged alphabetically according to the first element in each citation. As stated in Chapter 3, some instructors prefer papers to be structured in article format, with everything presented as tightly compressed and succinct as possible. If your instructor favors this system, your reference section should immediately follow (after a double space) the last line of your discussion section. Other instructors prefer the references to be listed on a separate page. Ask your instructor which system you should follow.

As with most alphabetically arranged bibliographies, there is a kind of reverse-indentation system: After the first line of a citation, all subsequent lines are indented five spaces. The entire references section is double-spaced.

The ASA uses standard, or "headline style," capitalization for titles in the reference list. In this style, all first and last words in a title, and all other words except articles (*a, an, the*), coordinating words (*and, but, or, for, nor*), and prepositions (*among, by, for, of, to, toward,* and so on) are capitalized.

Remember that every source cited in the text, with those exceptions noted in the examples below, must have a corresponding entry in the references section. Do not include references to any work not cited in the text of your paper.

Most of the following formats are based on those given in the *ASA Style Guide* (1997). Formats for bibliographical situations not covered by the ASA guide are taken from the *Chicago Manual of Style* (2003).

Books

ONE AUTHOR.   First comes the author's name, inverted, then the date of publication, followed by the title of the book, the place of publication, and the name of the publishing house. Use first names for all authors or initials if no first name is provided. Add a space after each initial, as in the example below. For place of publication, always identify the state unless the city is New York. Use postal abbreviations to denote states (OK, MA, and so on).

Periods divide most of the elements in the citation, although a colon separates the place of publication from the name of the publisher. Custom dictates that the main title and subtitle be separated by a colon, even though a colon may not appear in the title as printed on the title page of the book.

> Northrup, A. K. 2002. *Living High off the Hog: Recent Pork Barrel Legislation in the Senate.* Cleveland, OH: Johnstown.

TWO AUTHORS.   Only the name of the first author is reversed, since it is the one by which the citation is alphabetized. Note that there is no comma between the first name of the first author and the *and* following:

Spence, Michelle and Kristen Ruell. 1996. *Hiring and the Law.* Boston, MA: Tildale.

THREE OR MORE AUTHORS.   The use of *et al.* is not acceptable in the references section; list the names of all authors of a source. While the ASA style places commas between all names in the text citation—(Moore, Rice, and Traylor 2002)—it deletes the comma separating the next-to-last and last names in the bibliographical reference. Note also that the ASA does not advocate abbreviating the word University in the name of a press, as indicated in the model below.

Moore, J. B., Allen Rice and Natasha Traylor. 2002. *Down on the Farm: Culture and Folkways.* Norman, OK: University of Oklahoma Press.

ANONYMOUS SOURCE.   Section 17.34 of the *Chicago Manual of Style* states that if you can ascertain the name of the author when that name is not given in the work itself, place the author's name in brackets:

[Morey, Cynthia]. 1977. *How We Mate: American Dating Customs, 1950–2000.* New York: Putney.

Do not use *anonymous* to designate an author whose name you cannot determine; instead, according to section 17.32 of the *Chicago Manual of Style,* begin your reference entry with the title of the book, followed by the date. You may move initial articles (*a, an, the*) to the end of the title:

Worst Way to Learn: The Government's War on Education, The. 1997. San Luis Obispo, CA: Blakeside.

EDITOR, COMPILER, OR TRANSLATOR AS AUTHOR.   When no author is listed on the title page, begin the citation with the name of the editor, compiler, or translator:

Trakas, Dylan, comp. 1998. *Making the Road-Ways Safe: Essays on Highway Preservation and Funding.* El Paso, TX: Del Norte Press.

EDITOR, COMPILER, OR TRANSLATOR WITH AUTHOR

Pound, Ezra. 1953. *Literary Essays.* Edited by T. S. Eliot. New York: New Directions.

Stomper, Jean. 2000. *Grapes and Rain.* Translated by John Picard. New York: Baldock.

UNTRANSLATED BOOK.   If your source is in a foreign language, it is not necessary, according to section 17.64 of the *Chicago Manual of Style,* to translate the title into English. Use the capitalization format of the original language.

Picon-Salas, Mariano. 1950. *De la Conquesta a la Independencia.* Mexico, DF: Fondo de Cultura Económica.

If you wish to provide a translation of the title, do so in brackets or parentheses following the title. Set the translation in roman type, and capitalize only the first word of the title and subtitle, proper nouns, and proper adjectives:

Wharton, Edith. 1916. *Voyages au front* (Visits to the Front). Paris, France: Plon.

TWO OR MORE WORKS BY THE SAME AUTHOR.   If you wish you may replace the author's name in all citations after the first by a three-em dash (six strokes of the hyphen):

Russell, Henry. 1978. *Famous Last Words: Notable Supreme Court Cases of the Last Five Years.* New Orleans, LA: Liberty Publications.

———. 1988. *Great Court Battles.* Denver, CO: Axel and Myers.

CHAPTER IN A MULTIAUTHOR COLLECTION

Gray, Alexa North. 1998. "Foreign Policy and the Foreign Press." Pp. 188–204 in *Current Media Issues,* edited by Barbara Bonnard and Luke F. Guinness. New York: Boulanger.

The parenthetical text reference may include the page reference:

(Gray 1998:195–197)

You must repeat the name if the author and the editor are the same person:

Farmer, Susan A. 1995. "Tax Shelters in the New Dispensation: How to Save Your Income." Pp. 58–73 in *Making Ends Meet: Strategies for the Nineties,* edited by Susan A. Farmer. Nashville, TN: Burkette and Hyde.

AUTHOR OF A FOREWORD OR INTRODUCTION.   According to section 17.46 of the *Chicago Manual of Style,* there is no need to cite the author of a foreword or introduction in your bibliography, unless the foreword or introduction is of major significance. In that case, list the bibliography entry under the name of the author of the work itself. Place the name of the author of the foreword or introduction after the title of the work:

Givan, Basil. 2000. *Marital Stress among the Professoriat: A Case Study,* with foreword by Carla Farris. New York: Galapagos.

The parenthetical text reference cites the name of the author of the foreword or introduction, not the author of the book:

(Farris 2000)

SUBSEQUENT EDITIONS.   If you are using an edition of a book other than the first, you must cite the number of the edition or the status, such as *Rev. ed.* for *Revised edition,* if there is no edition number:

Hales, Sarah. 2002. *The Coming Water Wars.* 3d ed. Pittsburgh, PA: Blue Skies.

MULTIVOLUME WORK.   If you are citing a multivolume work in its entirety, use the following format:

Graybosch, Charles. 1988–1989. *The Rise of the Unions.* 3 vols. New York: Starkfield.

If you are citing only one of the volumes in a multivolume work, use the following format:

Graybosch, Charles. 1988. *The Beginnings.* Vol. 1 of *The Rise of the Unions.* New York: Starkfield.

REPRINTS

Adams, Sterling R. [1964] 2001. *How to Win an Election: Promotional Campaign Strategies.* New York: Starkfield.

CLASSIC TEXTS.   According to the *Chicago Manual of Style* (sections 17.247, 17.250), references to classic texts such as sacred books and Greek verse and drama are usually confined to the text and not given citations in the bibliography.

Periodicals

JOURNAL ARTICLES.   Journals are periodicals, usually published either monthly or quarterly, that specialize in serious scholarly articles in a particular field.

Journal with Continuous Pagination.   Most journals are paginated so that each issue of a volume continues the numbering of the previous issue. The reason for such pagination is that most journals are bound in libraries as complete volumes of several issues; continuous pagination makes it easier to consult these large compilations:

Hunzecker, Joan. 2002. "Teaching the Toadies: Cronyism in Municipal Politics." *Review of Local Politics* 4:250–262.

Johnson, J. D., N. E. Noel and J. Sutter-Hernandez. 2000. "Alcohol and Male Acceptance of Sexual Aggression: The Role of Perceptual Ambiguity." *Journal of Applied Social Psychology* 30:1186–1200.

Note that the name of the journal, which is italicized, is followed without punctuation by the volume number, which is itself followed by a colon and the page numbers. There should be no space between the colon and the page numbers, which are inclusive. Do not use *p.* or *pp.* to introduce the page numbers.

Journal in Which Each Issue Is Paginated Separately.   The issue number appears in parentheses immediately following the volume number.

Skylock, Browning. 1991. "'Fifty-Four Forty or Fight!': Sloganeering in Early America." *American History Digest* 28(3):25–34.

Entwisle, Doris, Karl Alexander and Linda Olson. 2000. "Urban Youth, Jobs, and High School." *American Sociological Review* 65(2):279–297.

Article Published in More Than One Journal Issue

Crossitch, Vernelle. 1997. "Evaluating Evidence: Calibrating Ephemeral Phenomena," parts 1–4. *Epiphanic Review* 15:22–29; 16:46–58; 17:48–60.

Articles Published in Foreign-Language Journals

Sczaflarski, Richard. 2001. "The Trumpeter in the Tower: Solidarity and Legend"
(in Polish). *World Political Review* 32:79–95.

Article Cited in a Secondary Source.   When referencing a source that has itself
been cited in a secondary source, first list the complete citation of the source you
cited, followed by the words *cited in,* and a listing of the source from which you
obtained your citation.

Johnson, William A. and Richard P. Rettig. 1999. "Drug Assessment of Juveniles
in Detention." *Social Forces* 28(3):56–69, cited in John Duncan and Mary Ann
Hopkins. 2004. "Youth and Drug Involvement: Families at Risk." *British Journal of Addiction* 95:45.

Gonzalez, Tim, Lucy Hammond, Fred Luntz and Virginia Land. 2002. "Free Love
and Nickel Beer: On Throwaway Relationships." *The Journal of Sociology and
Religion* 12(2):14–29, cited in Emanuel Hiddocke, Cheryl Manson and Ruth
Mendez. 2005. *The Death of the American Family.* Upper Saddle River, NJ:
Prentice Hall, p. 107.

MAGAZINE ARTICLES.   Magazines, which are usually published weekly, bimonthly, or monthly, appeal to the popular audience and generally have a wider circulation than journals. *Newsweek* and *Scientific American* are examples of magazines.

Monthly Magazine

Stapleton, Bonnie and Ellis Peters. 1981. "How It Was: On the Trail with Og Mandino." *Lifetime Magazine,* April, pp. 23–24, 57–59.

Weekly or Bimonthly Magazine

Bruck, Connie. 1997. "The World of Business: A Mogul's Farewell." *The New York-
er,* October 18, pp. 12–15.

NEWSPAPER ARTICLES

Everett, Susan. 2002. "Beyond the Alamo: How Texans View the Past." *The Car-
rollton Tribune,* February 16, D1, D4.

Sources stored in archives.   According to the *ASA Style Guide,* if you refer to
a number of archival sources, you should group them in a separate part of the
references section and name it *Archival Sources.* A sample entry follows:

Clayton Fox Correspondence, Box 12. July–December 1903. File: Literary Figures
2. Letter to Edith Wharton, dated September 11.

According to the *Chicago Manual of Style* (section 17.324), materials housed in the National Archives or in one of its branches are cited according to their record group (RG) number. The citation may also include title, subsection, and file number:

> National Archives. RG 43. Records of the National Committee on Poverty and Aging. File 78A-M22.

Public documents.   Since the *ASA Style Guide* gives formats for only two types of government publications, the following bibliographical models are based not only on practices from the ASA guide but also on formats found in the *Chicago Manual of Style* (sections 17.290–355).

CONGRESSIONAL JOURNALS.   References to either the *Senate Journal* or the *House Journal* begin with the journal's title and include the years of the session, the number of the Congress and session, and the month and day of the entry:

> *U.S. Senate Journal.* 1997. 105th Cong., 1st sess., 10 December.

The ordinal numbers *second* and *third* may be represented as *d* (*52d, 103d*) or as *nd* and *rd,* respectively.

CONGRESSIONAL DEBATES

> *Congressional Record.* 1930. 71st Cong., 2d sess. Vol. 72, pt. 8.

CONGRESSIONAL REPORTS AND DOCUMENTS

> U.S. Congress. 1997. House Subcommittee on the Study of Governmental/Public Rapport. *Report on Government Efficiency as Perceived by the Public.* 105th Cong., 2d sess., pp. 11–26.

BILLS AND RESOLUTIONS

Slip Bill.   The abbreviation *S. R.* in the first model below stands for *Senate Resolutions,* and the number following is the bill or resolution number. For references to House bills, the abbreviation is *H. R.* Notice that the second model refers the reader to the more complete first entry. The choice of formats depends upon the one you used in the parenthetical text reference.

> U.S. Senate. 1996. *Visa Formalization Act of 1996.* 105th Cong., 1st sess. S. R. 1437.
>
> *Visa Formalization Act of 1996.* See U.S. Senate. 1996.

CONGRESSIONAL RECORD

> Senate. 1997. *Visa Formalization Act of 1997.* 105th Cong., 1st sess., S. R. 1437. *Congressional Record* 135, no. 137, daily ed. (10 December): S7341.

LAWS

Slip Law

U.S. Public Law 678. 105th Cong., 1st sess., 4 December 1997. *Library of Congress Book Preservation Act of 1997.*

Library of Congress Book Preservation Act of 1997. U.S. Public Law 678. 105th Cong., 1st sess., 4 December 1997.

Statutes at Large

Statutes at Large. 1998. Vol. 82, p. 466. *Library of Congress Book Preservation Act of 1997.*

Library of Congress Book Preservation Act of 1997. Statutes at Large 82:466.

United States Code

Library of Congress Book Preservation Act of 1997. U.S. Code, Vol. 38, sec. 1562.

UNITED STATES CONSTITUTION.   According to the *Chicago Manual of Style,* the Constitution is not listed in the bibliography.

EXECUTIVE DEPARTMENT DOCUMENT

Department of Labor. 1998. *Report on Urban Growth Potential Projections.* Washington, D.C.: GPO.

The abbreviation for the publisher in the above model, GPO, stands for the Government Printing Office, which prints and distributes most government publications. According to the *Chicago Manual of Style* (section 17.295), you may use any of the following formats to refer to the GPO:

Washington, D.C.: U.S. Government Printing Office, 2004.

Washington, D.C.: Government Printing Office, 2004.

Washington, D.C.: GPO, 2004.

Washington, 2004.

Washington 2004.

Remember to be consistent in using the form you choose.

LEGAL REFERENCES

Supreme Court.   Federal court decisions are only rarely listed in bibliographies. If you do wish to include such an entry, here is a suitable format:

State of Nevada v. Goldie Warren. 1969. 324 U.S. 123.

For a case prior to 1875, use the following format:

Marbury v. Madison. 1803. 1 Cranch 137.

Lower Courts

United States v. Sizemore. 1950. 183 F. 2d 201 (2d Cir.).

PUBLICATIONS OF GOVERNMENT COMMISSIONS

U.S. Securities and Exchange Commission. 1984. *Annual Report of the Securities and Exchange Commission for the Fiscal Year.* Washington, D.C.: GPO.

PUBLICATIONS OF STATE AND LOCAL GOVERNMENTS.   Remember that references for state and local government publications are modeled on those for corresponding national government documents:

Oklahoma Legislature. 1991. *Joint Committee on Public Recreation. Final Report to the Legislature,* 1995, Regular Session, on Youth Activities. Oklahoma City.

Interviews.   According to section 17.205 of the *Chicago Manual of Style,* interviews need not be included in the bibliography, but if you or your instructor wants to list such entries, here are possible formats:

PUBLISHED INTERVIEW

Untitled Interview in a Book

Jorgenson, Mary. 1998. Interview by Alan McAskill. Pp. 62–86 in *Hospice Pioneers,* edited by Alan McAskill. Richmond, VA: Dynasty Press.

Titled Interview in a Periodical

Simon, John. 1997. "Picking the Patrons Apart: An Interview with John Simon," by Selena Fox. *Media Week,* March 14, pp. 40–54.

INTERVIEW ON TELEVISION

Snopes, Edward. 2002. Interview by Klint Gordon. *Oklahoma Politicians.* WKY Television, June 4.

UNPUBLISHED INTERVIEW

Kennedy, Melissa. 1997. Interview by author. Tape recording. Portland, ME, April 23.

Unpublished sources

PERSONAL COMMUNICATIONS.   According to section 17.208 of the *Chicago Manual of Style,* references to personal communications may be handled completely in the text of the paper:

In a letter to the author, dated July 16, 1997, Mr. Bentley admitted the organizational plan was flawed.

If, however, you wish to include a reference to an unpublished communication in the bibliography, you may do so using one of the following models:

Bentley, Jacob. 1997. Letter to author, July 16.

Duberstein, Cindy. 2003. Telephone conversation with the author, June 5.

Timrod, Helen. 1997. E-mail to author, April 25.

THESES AND DISSERTATIONS

Hochenauer, Klint. 1999. "Populism and the Free Soil Movement." Ph.D. dissertation, Department of Sociology, Lamont University, Cleveland.

PAPER PRESENTED AT A MEETING

Zelazny, Kim and Ed Gilmore. 2005. "Art for Art's Sake: Funding the NEA in the Twenty-First Century." Presented at the annual meeting of the Conference of Metropolitan Arts Boards, June 15, San Francisco.

UNPUBLISHED MANUSCRIPTS

Borges, Rita V. 1993. "Mexican-American Border Conflicts, 1915–1970." Department of History, University of Texas at El Paso, El Paso. Unpublished manuscript.

WORKING AND DISCUSSION PAPERS

Blaine, Emory and Ralph Cohn. 2004. "Analysis of Social Structure in Closed Urban Environments." Discussion Paper No. 312, Institute for Sociological Research, Deadwood College, Deadwood, SD.

Electronic sources

ON-LINE SOURCES.   The need for a reliable online citation system continues to grow, but attempts to establish one are hampered by a number of factors. For one thing, there is no foolproof method of clearly reporting even such basic information as the site's author(s), title, or date of establishment. Occasionally authors identify themselves clearly; sometimes they place a link to their home page at the bottom of the site. But it is not always easy to determine exactly who authored a particular site. Likewise, it can be difficult to determine whether a site has its own title or instead exists as a subsection of a larger document with its own title. Perhaps the biggest problem facing online researchers is the instability of Internet sites. Although some sites may remain in place for weeks or months, many either move to another site—not always leaving a clear path for you to find it—or disappear.

The ASA Style Guide (1997:37–38) lists only a few models for electronic sources. Therefore,until such time as an authoritative ASA citation system for the Internet is available, we suggest the following simple formats, based in part on the models found in the *ASA Style Guide*.

On-Line Journal Article.   The *retrieval date* in the models below is the most recent date on which you accessed the source for your research project.

Bucknell, Vespasia. 2003. "Servitude as a Way of Life: Religious Denominations in Middle America." *Skeptic's Journal* 4:22–37. Retrieved February 21, 2005 (http://www.religiosk.org/protesta.buck.html).

On-Line Newpaper Article

Squires, Amanda. 2000. "Hard Times for Social Workers, Says Mayor." *El Paso Sun Times,* July 14, p. 2. Retrieved November 12, 2000 (http://www.elpasosun. com/2000-12/12.html).

The question of whether to break a lengthy site address at the end of a line is not discussed in the *ASA Style Guide,* but one of the guide's models does make such a line break. Other sources suggest breaking a site address only after a slash (/). Do not place a hyphen following the slash. Remember, the one thing that is absolutely required in order to find a site on the Internet is the site address, so make sure that you copy it accurately.

E-Mail Document.   Due to the ephemeral nature of e-mail sources, most researchers recommend not including citations to e-mail in the bibliography. Instead, you may handle e-mail documentation within the text of the paper.

In an e-mail dated March 22, 1997, Bennett assured the author that the negotiations would continue.

If, however, you would like to include an e-mail citation in your references section, here is a possible format:

Bennett, Suzanne. sbb@mtsu.socka.edu. 15 March 1997. RE: Progress on education reform petition [E-mail to Courtney Cline (coline@usc.cola.edu)].

The name of the author of the e-mail message is placed first, followed by the author's e-mail address and the date of the message. Next comes a brief statement of the subject of the message, followed by the recipient's name and e-mail address, in brackets.

CD-ROM.   The publisher of a CD-ROM can usually be identified in the same way as a book's publisher. The following model is for a source with an unascertainable author. Note that it is still necessary to include the latest date on which you accessed the database.

Dissertation Abstracts Ondisc. 1861–1994. CD-ROM: UMI/Dissertation Abstracts Ondisc. Retrieved December 15, 1996.

A sample reference page is shown on page 98.

References

Entwisle, Doris, Karl Alexander and Linda Olson. 2000. "Urban Youth, Jobs, and High School." *American Sociological Review* 65(2):279–297.

Johnson, J. D., N. E. Noel and J. Sutter-Hernandez. 2000. "Alcohol and Male Acceptance of Sexual Aggression: The Role of Perceptual Ambiguity." *Journal of Applied Social Psychology* 30(6):1186–1200.

Johnson, William A. and Richard P. Rettig. 1999. "Drug Assessment of Juveniles in Detention." Social Forces 28(3):56–69, cited in John Duncan and Mary Ann Hopkins. 2004. "Youth and Drug Involvement: Families at Risk." *British Journal of Addiction* 95:45.

Moore, J. B., Allen Rice and Natasha Traylor. 1998. *Down on the Farm: Culture and Folkways.* Norman, OK: University of Oklahoma Press.

Sczaflarski, Richard. 2001. "The Trumpeter in the Tower: Solidarity and Legend" (in Polish). *World Political Review* 32:79–95.

Squires, Amanda. 2000. "Hard Times for Social Workers, Says Mayor." *El Paso Sun Times,* July 14, p. 2. Retrieved November 12, 2000 (http://www.elpasosun.com/2000-12/12.html).

Stapleton, Bonnie and Ellis Peters. 1981. "How It Was: On the Trail with Og Mandino." *Lifetime Magazine,* April, pp. 23–24, 57–59.

Stomper, Jean. 2000. *Grapes and Rain.* Translated by John Picard. New York: Baldock.

Culture

R. C. Gorman, *Night Stories*, 1994

I had never felt heat like this before. This was *northern* Africa, and I wondered what it must be like closer to the equator. Sweat poured off me as the temperature climbed past 110 degrees Fahrenheit.

As we were herded into the building—which had no air conditioning—hundreds of people lunged toward the counter at the rear of the structure. With body crushed against body, we waited as the uniformed officials behind the windows leisurely examined each passport. At times like this, I wondered what I was doing in Africa.

When I first arrived in Morocco, I found the sights that greeted me exotic—not far removed from my memories of *Casablanca, Raiders of the Lost Ark,* and other movies that over the years had become part of my collective memory. The men, women, and even the children really did wear those white robes that reached down to their feet. What was especially striking was that the women were almost totally covered. Despite the heat, they wore not only full-length gowns but also head coverings that reached down over their foreheads and veils that covered their faces from the nose down. All you could make out were their eyes—and every eye the same shade of brown.

And how short everyone was! The Arab women looked to be, on average, 5 feet, and the men only about three or four inches taller. As the only blue-eyed, blonde, 6-foot-plus person around, and the only one who was wearing jeans and a pullover shirt, in a world of white-robed short people I stood out like a creature from another planet. Everyone stared. No matter where I went, they stared. Wherever I looked, I found brown eyes watching me intently. Even staring back at those many dark brown eyes had no effect. It was so different from home, where, if you caught someone staring at you, that person would immediately look embarrassed and glance away.

And lines? The concept apparently didn't even exist. Buying a ticket for a bus or train meant pushing and shoving toward the ticket man (always a man—no women were visible in any public position), who took the money from whichever outstretched hand he decided on.

And germs? That notion didn't seem to exist here either. Flies swarmed over the food in the restaurants and the unwrapped loaves of bread in the stores. Shopkeepers would considerately shoo off the flies before handing me a loaf. They also offered home delivery. I still remember watching a bread vendor deliver a loaf to a woman who stood on a second-floor balcony. She first threw her money to the bread vendor, and he then threw the unwrapped bread up to her. Only, his throw was off. The bread bounced off the wrought-iron balcony railing and landed in the street, which was filled with people, wandering dogs, and the ever-present, defecating burros. The vendor simply picked up the unwrapped loaf and threw it again. This certainly wasn't his day, for he missed again. But he made it on his third

(continued)

Everyone stared. No matter where I went, they stared.

attempt. The woman smiled as she turned back into her apartment, apparently to prepare the noon meal for her family.

Now, standing in the oppressive heat on the Moroccan-Algerian border, the crowd once again became unruly. Another fight had broken out. And once again, the little man in uniform appeared, shouting and knocking people aside as he forced his way to a little wooden box nailed to the floor. Climbing onto this makeshift platform, he shouted at the crowd, his arms flailing about him. The people fell silent. But just as soon as the man left, the shouting and shoving began again.

The situation had become unbearable. His body pressed against mine, the man behind me decided that this was a good time to take a nap. Determining that I made a good support, he placed his arm against my back and leaned his head against his arm. Sweat streamed down my back at the point where his arm and head touched me.

Finally, I realized that I had to abandon U.S. customs. So I pushed my way forward, forcing my frame into every square inch of vacant space that I could create. At the counter, I shouted in English. The official looked up at the sound of this strange tongue, and I thrust my long arms over the heads of three people, shoving my passport into his hand.

What Is Culture?

culture the language, beliefs, values, norms, behaviors, and even material objects that are passed from one generation to the next

material culture the material objects that distinguish a group of people, such as their art, buildings, weapons, utensils, machines, hairstyles, clothing, and jewelry

nonmaterial culture (also called *symbolic culture*) a group's ways of thinking (including its beliefs, values, and other assumptions about the world) and doing (its common patterns of behavior, including language and other forms of interaction)

What is culture? The concept is sometimes easier to grasp by description than by definition. For example, suppose you meet a young woman who has just arrived in the United States from India. That her culture is different from yours is immediately evident. You first see it in her clothing, jewelry, makeup, and hairstyle. Next you hear it in her speech. It then becomes apparent by her gestures. Later, you might hear her express unfamiliar beliefs about relationships or about what is valuable in life. All these characteristics are indicative of **culture**—the language, beliefs, values, norms, behaviors, and even material objects that are passed from one generation to the next.

In northern Africa, I was surrounded by a culture quite alien to my own. It was evident in everything I saw and heard. The **material culture**—such things as jewelry, art, buildings, weapons, machines, and even eating utensils, hairstyles, and clothing—provided a sharp contrast to what I was used to seeing. There is nothing inherently "natural" about material culture. That is, it is no more natural (or unnatural) to wear gowns on the street than it is to wear jeans.

I also found myself immersed in a contrasting **nonmaterial culture,** that is, a group's ways of thinking (its beliefs, values, and other assumptions about the world) and doing (its common patterns of behavior, including language, gestures, and other forms of interaction). North African assumptions about pushing others aside to buy a ticket and staring in public are examples of nonmaterial culture. So are U.S. assumptions about not doing either of these things. Like material culture, neither custom is "right." People simply become comfortable with the customs they learn during childhood, and—as in the case of my visit to northern Africa—uncomfortable when their basic assumptions about life are challenged.

Culture and Taken-for-Granted Orientations to Life

To develop a sociological imagination, it is essential to understand how culture affects people's lives. If we meet someone from a different culture, the encounter may make us aware of culture's pervasive influence on that person. Attaining the same level of awareness regarding our own culture, however, is quite another matter. *Our* speech, *our* gestures, *our* beliefs, and *our* customs are usually taken for granted. We assume that they are "normal" or "natural," and we almost always follow them without question. As anthropologist Ralph Linton (1936) said, "The last thing a fish would ever notice would be water." So also with people: Except in unusual circumstances, our own culture remains imperceptible to us.

Yet culture's significance is profound; it touches almost every aspect of who and what we are. We came into this life without a language; without values and morality; with no ideas about religion, war, money, love, use of space, and so on. We possessed none of these fundamental orientations that we take for granted and that are so essential in determining the type of people we become. Yet by this point in our lives, we all have acquired them. Sociologists call this *culture within us*. These learned and shared ways of believing and of doing (another definition of culture) penetrate our beings at an early age and quickly become part of our taken-for-granted assumptions about what normal behavior is. *Culture becomes the lens through which we perceive and evaluate what is going on around us.* Seldom do we question these assumptions, for, like water to a fish, the lens through which we view life remains largely beyond our perception.

The rare instances in which these assumptions are challenged, however, can be upsetting. Although as a sociologist I should be able to look at my own cultures "from the outside," my trip to Africa quickly revealed how fully I had internalized my culture. My upbringing in Western society had given me strong assumptions about aspects of social life that had become deeply rooted in my being—staring, hygiene, and the use of space. But in this part of Africa these assumptions were useless in helping me navigate everyday life. No longer could I count on people to stare only surreptitiously, to take precautions against invisible microbes, or to stand in line in an orderly fashion, one behind the other.

As you can tell from the opening vignette, I found these assumptions upsetting, for they violated my basic expectations of "the way people *ought* to be"—although I did not realize how firmly I held these expectations until they were so abruptly challenged. When my nonmaterial culture failed me—when it no longer enabled me to make sense out of the world—I experienced a disorientation known as **culture shock**. In the case of buying tickets, the fact that I was several inches taller than most Moroccans and thus able to outreach others helped me to adjust partially to their different ways of doing things. But I never did get used to the idea that pushing ahead of others was "right," and I always felt guilty when I used my size to receive preferential treatment.

An important consequence of culture within us is **ethnocentrism**, a tendency to use our own group's ways of doing things as the yardstick for judging others. All of us learn that the ways of our own group are good, right, proper, and even superior to other ways of life. As sociologist William Sumner (1906), who developed this concept, said, "One's own group is the center of everything, and all others are scaled and rated with reference to it." Ethnocentrism has both positive and negative consequences. On the positive side, it creates in-group loyalties. On the negative side, ethnocentrism can lead to discrimination against people whose ways differ from ours.

The many ways in which culture affects our lives fascinate sociologists. In this chapter, we'll examine how profoundly culture affects everything we are. This will serve as a basis from which you can start to analyze your own assumptions of reality. I should give you a warning at this point: This can result in a changed perspective on social life and your role in it. If so, life will never look the same.

IN SUM To avoid losing track of the ideas under discussion, let's pause for a moment to summarize, and in some instances clarify, the principles we have covered.

culture shock the disorientation that people experience when they come in contact with a fundamentally different culture and can no longer depend on their taken-for-granted assumptions about life

ethnocentrism the use of one's own culture as a yardstick for judging the ways of other individuals or societies, generally leading to a negative evaluation of their values, norms, and behaviors

1. There is nothing "natural" about material culture. Arabs wear gowns on the street and feel that it is natural to do so. Americans do the same with jeans.
2. There is nothing "natural" about nonmaterial culture. It is just as arbitrary to stand in line as it is to push and shove.
3. Culture penetrates deep into our thinking, becoming a taken-for-granted lens through which we see the world and obtain our perception of reality.
4. Culture provides implicit instructions that tell us what we ought to do and how we ought to think. It provides a fundamental basis for our decision making.
5. Culture also provides a "moral imperative"; that is, the culture that we internalize becomes the "right" way of doing things. (I, for example, believed deeply that it was wrong to push and shove to get ahead of others.)
6. Coming into contact with a radically different culture challenges our basic assumptions of life. (I experienced culture shock when I discovered that my deeply ingrained cultural ideas about hygiene and the use of space no longer applied.)
7. Although the particulars of culture differ from one group of people to another, culture itself is universal. That is, all people have culture, for a society cannot exist without developing shared, learned ways of dealing with the challenges of life.
8. All people are ethnocentric, which has both positive and negative consequences.

Practicing Cultural Relativism

To counter our tendency to use our own culture as the standard by which we judge other cultures, we can practice **cultural relativism**; that is, we can try to understand a culture on its own terms. This means looking at how the elements of a culture fit together, without judging those elements as superior or inferior to our own way of life.

Because we tend to use our own culture as a standard for judging others, cultural relativism presents a challenge to ordinary thinking. For example, most U.S. citizens appear to have strong feelings against raising bulls for the purpose of stabbing them to death in front of crowds that shout "Olé!" According to cultural relativism, however, bullfighting must be viewed from the perspective of the culture in which it takes place—*its* history, *its* folklore, *its* ideas of bravery, and *its* ideas of sex roles.

You may still regard bullfighting as wrong, of course, if your culture, which is deeply ingrained in you, has no history of bullfighting. We all possess culturally specific ideas about cruelty to animals, ideas that have evolved slowly and match other elements of our culture. In the United States, for example, practices that once were common in some areas—cock fighting, dog fighting, bear–dog fighting, and so on—have been gradually eliminated.

None of us can be entirely successful at practicing cultural relativism. Look at the Cultural Diversity box on the next page. My best guess is that you will evaluate these "strange" foods through the lens of your own culture. Cultural relativism, however, is an attempt to refocus that lens so we can appreciate other ways of life rather than simply asserting, "Our way is right."

As you view the photos on page 40, try to appreciate the cultural differences in standards of beauty.

Although cultural relativism helps us to avoid cultural smugness, this view has come under attack. In a provocative book, *Sick Societies* (1992), anthropologist Robert Edgerton suggests that we develop a scale for evaluating cultures on their "quality of life," much as we do for U.S. cities. He also asks why we should consider cultures that practice female circumcision, gang rape, or wife beating,

Many Americans perceive bullfighting, which is illegal in the United States, as a cruel activity that should be abolished everywhere. To Spaniards and those who have inherited Spanish culture, however, bullfighting is a beautiful, artistic sport in which matador and bull blend into a unifying image of power, courage, and glory. *Cultural relativism* requires that we suspend our own perspectives in order to grasp the perspectives of others, something that is much easier described than attained.

You Are What You Eat? An Exploration in Cultural Relativity

HERE IS A CHANCE TO TEST your ethnocentrism and ability to practice cultural relativity. You probably know that the French like to eat snails and that in some Asian cultures, chubby dogs and cats are considered a delicacy ("Ah, lightly browned with a little doggy sauce!"). But did you know about this?

Marston Bates (1967), a zoologist, reports:

I remember once, in the llanos of Colombia, sharing a dish of toasted ants at a remote farmhouse. . . . My host and I fell into conversation about the general question of what people eat or do not eat, and I remarked that in my country people eat the legs of frogs.

The very thought of this filled my ant-eating friends with horror; it was as though I had mentioned some repulsive sex habit.

And then there is the experience of the production coordinator of this text, Dusty Friedman, who told me:

When traveling in Sudan, I ate some interesting things that I wouldn't likely eat now that I'm back in our society. Raw baby camel's liver with chopped herbs was a delicacy. So was camel's milk cheese patties that had been cured in dry camel's dung.

You might be able to see yourself eating frog legs, toasted ants, perhaps raw camel liver or even dogs and cats, but this custom may provide a better test of your ethnocentrism and cultural relativity ("Monkey Rescued . . ."

Wild animals? Pets? Beasts of burden? For pleasure riding? For racing? All of these. But food? Not for many Americans—who became upset when the French, who are fond of horse-burgers and horse steaks—bought these wild horses for food.

2004). Maxine Kingston (1975), an English professor whose parents grew up in China, wrote:

"Do you know what people in [the Nantou region of] China eat when they have the money?" my mother began. "They buy into a monkey feast. The eaters sit around a thick wood table with a hole in the middle. Boys bring in the monkey at the end of a pole. Its neck is in a collar at the end of the pole, and it is screaming. Its hands are tied behind it. They clamp the monkey into the table; the whole table fits like another collar around its neck. Using a surgeon's saw, the cooks cut a clean line in a circle at the top of its head. To loosen the bone, they tap with a tiny hammer and wedge here and there with a silver pick. Then an old woman reaches out her hand to the monkey's face and up to its scalp, where she tufts some hairs and lifts off the lid of the skull. The eaters spoon out the brains."

for your Consideration

1. What is your opinion about eating toasted ants? About eating fried frog legs? About eating puppies and kittens? About eating raw monkey brains?

2. If you were reared in U.S. society, more than likely you think that eating frog legs is okay, eating ants is disgusting, and eating dogs, cats, and monkey brains is downright repugnant. How would you apply the concepts of ethnocentrism and cultural relativism to your perceptions of these customs?

or cultures that sell little girls into prostitution as morally equivalent to those that do not. Cultural values that result in exploitation, he says, are inferior to those that enhance people's lives.

Edgerton's sharp questions and incisive examples bring us to a topic that comes up repeatedly in this text: the disagreements that arise among scholars as they confront contrasting views of reality. It is such questioning of assumptions that keeps sociology interesting.

Components of Symbolic Culture

Sociologists sometimes refer to nonmaterial culture as **symbolic culture,** because its central component is the symbols that people use. A **symbol** is something to which people attach meaning and that they then use to communicate with

cultural relativism not judging a culture but trying to understand it on its own terms

symbolic culture another term for nonmaterial culture

symbol something to which people attach meanings and then use to communicate with others

Standards of beauty vary so greatly from one culture to another that what one group finds attractive, another may not. Yet, in its *ethnocentrism*, each group thinks that its standards are the best—that the appearance reflects what beauty "really" is.

As indicated by these photos, around the world men and women aspire to their group's norms of physical attractiveness. To make themselves appealing to others, they try to make their appearance reflect those standards.

Tibet

Cameroon

Thailand

New Guinea

Japan

India (Gypsy)

Peru

United States

one another. Symbols include gestures, language, values, norms, sanctions, folkways, and mores. Let's look at each of these components of symbolic culture.

Gestures

Gestures, using one's body to communicate with others, are shorthand ways to convey messages without using words. Although people in every culture of the world use gestures, a gesture's meaning may change completely from one culture to another. North Americans, for example, communicate a succinct message by raising the middle finger in a short, upward stabbing motion. I wish to stress "North Americans," for that gesture does not convey the same message in most parts of the world.

I once was surprised to find that this particular gesture was not universal, having internalized it to such an extent that I thought everyone knew what it meant. When I was

gestures the ways in which people use their bodies to communicate with one another

comparing gestures with friends in Mexico, however, this gesture drew a blank look from them. After I explained its intended meaning, they laughed and showed me their rudest gesture—placing the hand under the armpit and moving the upper arm up and down. To me, they simply looked as if they were imitating monkeys, but to them the gesture meant "Your mother is a whore"— the worst possible insult in that culture.

With the current political, military, and cultural dominance of the United States, "giving the finger" is becoming well known in other cultures. Following 9/11, the United States began to photograph and fingerprint foreign travelers. Feeling insulted, Brazil retaliated by doing the same to U.S. visitors. Angry at this, a U.S. pilot raised his middle finger while being photographed. Having become aware of the meaning of this gesture, Brazilian police arrested him. To gain his release, the pilot had to pay a fine of $13,000 ("Brazil Arrests" . . . 2004).

Gestures not only facilitate communication but also, because they differ around the world, they can lead to misunderstanding, embarrassment, or worse. One time in Mexico, for example, I raised my hand to a certain height to indicate how tall a child was. My hosts began to laugh. It turned out that Mexicans use three hand gestures to indicate height: one for people, a second for animals, and yet another for plants. They were amused because I had ignorantly used the plant gesture to indicate the child's height. (See Figure 2.1.)

To get along in another culture, then, it is important to learn the gestures of that culture. If you don't, not only will you fail to achieve the simplicity of communication that gestures allow but also you may overlook or misunderstand much of what is happening, run the risk of appearing foolish, and possibly offend people. In some cultures, for example, you would provoke deep offense if you were to offer food or a gift with your left hand, because the left hand is reserved for dirty tasks, such as wiping after going to the toilet. Left-handed Americans visiting Arabs, please note!

Suppose for a moment that you are visiting southern Italy. After eating one of the best meals in your life, you are so pleased that when you catch the waiter's eye, you smile broadly and use the standard U.S. "A-OK" gesture of putting your thumb and forefinger together and making a large "O." The waiter looks horrified, and you are struck speechless when the manager asks you to leave. What have you done? Nothing on purpose, of course, but in that culture this gesture refers to a part of the human body that is not mentioned in polite company (Ekman et al. 1984).

Is it really true that there are no universal gestures? There is some disagreement on this point. Some anthropologists claim that no gesture is universal. They point out that even nodding the head up and down to indicate "yes" is not universal, because in some parts of the world, such as areas of Turkey, nodding the head up and down means "no" (Ekman et al. 1984). However, ethologists, researchers who study biological bases of behavior, claim

Figure 2.1 Gestures to Indicate Height, Southern Mexico

that expressions of anger, pouting, fear, and sadness are built into our biology and are universal (Eibl-Eibesfeldt 1970:404). They point out that even infants who are born blind and deaf, who have had no chance to *learn* these gestures, express themselves in the same way.

Although this matter is not yet settled, we can note that gestures tend to vary remarkably around the world. It is also significant that certain gestures can elicit emotions; some gestures are so closely associated with emotional messages that the gestures themselves summon up emotions. For example, my introduction to Mexican gestures took place at a dinner table. It was evident that my husband-and-wife hosts were trying to hide their embarrassment at using their culture's obscene gesture at their dinner table. And I felt the same way—not about *their* gesture, of course, which meant nothing to me—but about the one I was teaching them.

Although most gestures are learned, and therefore vary from culture to culture, some gestures that represent fundamental emotions such as sadness, anger, and fear appear to be inborn. This crying child whom I photographed in India differs little from a crying child in China—or the United States or anywhere else on the globe. In a few years, however, this child will demonstrate a variety of gestures highly specific to his Hindu culture.

Language

Gestures and words go hand in hand, as is evident when you watch people talking. We use gestures to supplement our words, to provide emphasis and a deeper understanding of what we are communicating. Written language lacks the subtle cues that gestures provide, and with online communications so common, we miss these cues. To help supply them, people use *emoticons*. These "written gestures" that help to convey the feelings that go with our words are the topic of the Down-to-Earth Sociology box on the next page.

The primary way in which people communicate with one another is through **language**—symbols that can be combined in an infinite number of ways for the purpose of communicating abstract thought. Each word is actually a symbol, a sound to which we have attached a particular meaning. Because we share these meanings, we can use language to communicate with one another. Language itself is universal in the sense that all human groups have language, but there is nothing universal about the meanings given to particular sounds. Thus, like gestures, in different cultures the same sound may mean something entirely different—or may have no meaning at all.

The significance of language for human life is difficult to overstate. As will become apparent from the following discussion, *language allows culture to exist.*

Language Allows Human Experience to Be Cumulative   By means of language, we pass ideas, knowledge, and even attitudes on to the next generation, allowing it to build on experiences that it may never undergo. This building process enables humans to modify their behavior in light of what previous generations have learned. Hence the central sociological significance of language: *Language allows culture to develop by freeing people to move beyond their immediate experiences.*

Without language, human culture would be little more advanced than that of the lower primates. If we communicate by grunts and gestures, we would be limited to a small time span—to events now taking place, those that have just taken place, or those that will take place immediately—a sort of "slightly extended present." You can grunt and gesture, for example, that you want a drink of water, but in the absence of language how could you share ideas concerning past or future events? There would be little or no way to communicate to others what event you had in mind, much less the greater complexities that humans communicate—ideas and feelings about events.

Language Provides a Social or Shared Past   Without language, our memories would be extremely limited, for we associate experiences with words and then use words to recall the experience. Such memories as would exist in the absence of language would be highly individualized, for only rarely and incompletely could we communicate them to others, much less discuss them and agree on something. By attaching words to an event,

language a system of symbols that can be combined in an infinite number of ways and can represent not only objects but also abstract thought

Down-to-Earth Sociology

Emoticons: "Written Gestures" for Expressing Yourself Online

TALKING ONLINE HAS BECOME A FAVORITE activity of millions of people. Teenagers rehash the day's events with friends; grandparents keep in touch with grandchildren; businesspeople seal their deals with the click of a "send" button. All of them love the speed of online communications. They send an e-mail or post a note in a chat room, and in an instant people across the country or in distant lands can read or respond to it.

There is something nagging about online talk, though. It leaves a dissatisfying taste because it is so one-dimensional. People miss the nuances of emotion and overlays of meaning that we transmit during face-to-face conversations. Lacking are the gestures and tones of voice that give color and life to our communications, the subtleties by which we monitor and communicate submessages.

To help fill this gap, computer users have developed symbols to convey their humor, disappointment, sarcasm, and other moods and attitudes. Although these symbols are not as varied or spontaneous as the nonverbal cues of face-to-face interaction, they are useful. Here are some of them. If you tilt your head to the left as you view them, the symbols will be clearer.

:-)	Smile
:-))	Laugh
:-(	Frowning, or Sad
:-((	Very sad
:,(	Crying
>:-(	Angry, annoyed
:-X	My lips are sealed (or a Kiss)

;-)	Wink, wink—know what I mean?
:-')	Tongue in cheek
:-P	Sticking out your tongue
:-$	Put your money where your mouth is
(:-D	Has a big mouth
:-O	WOW! (Shocked)
#-)	Oh what a night!

Some correspondents prefer more aesthetically pleasing emoticons. They use the profile version: :^) :^)) :^(

Some correspondents also use abbreviations to indicate their emotions:

IAB	I Am Bored
ILY	I Love You
JK	Just Kidding
LOL	Laughing Out Loud
OTF	On The Floor (laughing)
ROTF	Rolling On The Floor
ROFLWTIME	Rolling On Floor Laughing With Tears In My Eyes

Another form of emoticons are the many smilies. Each of the symbols below is meant to indicate a particular emotion—from happiness and greed to shock and embarrassment.

With advancing technology, such shorthand might become unnecessary. Now that we can include video in our e-mail, recipients can see our image and hear our voice. Eventually, messages that include verbal and facial cues may replace much written e-mail. As long as written e-mail exists, however, some system of symbols to substitute for gestures will remain.

---

however, and then using those words to recall it, we are able to discuss the event. As we talk about past events, we develop shared understandings about what those events mean. In short, through talk, people develop a shared past.

Language Provides a Social or Shared Future   Language also extends our time horizons forward. Because language enables us to agree on times, dates, and places, it allows us to plan activities with one another. Think about it for a moment. Without language, how could you ever plan future events? How could you possibly communicate goals, times, and plans? Whatever planning could exist would be limited to rudimentary communications, perhaps to an agreement to meet at a certain place when the sun is in a certain position. But think of the difficulty, perhaps the impossibility, of conveying just a slight change in this simple arrangement, such as "I can't make it tomorrow, but my neighbor can, if that's all right with you."

Language Allows Shared Perspectives   Our ability to speak, then, provides us a social (or shared) past and future. This is vital for humanity. It is a watershed that distinguishes us from animals. But speech does much more than this. When we talk with one

Language is the basis of human culture around the world. The past decade has seen a major development in communication—the ease and speed with which we can "speak" to people across the globe. This development is destined to have vital effects on culture.

another, we are exchanging ideas about events; that is, we are sharing perspectives. Our words are the embodiment of our experiences, distilled into a readily exchangeable form, mutually understandable to people who have learned that language. *Talking about events allows us to arrive at the shared understandings that form the basis of social life.* To not share a language while living alongside one another, however, invites miscommunication and suspicion. This risk, which comes with a diverse society, is discussed in the Cultural Diversity box on the next page.

Language Allows Complex, Shared, Goal-Directed Behavior   Common understandings enable us to establish a *purpose* for getting together. Let's suppose you want to go on a picnic. You use speech not only to plan the picnic but also to decide on reasons for the picnic—which may be anything from "because it's a nice day and it shouldn't be wasted studying" to "because it's my birthday." Language permits you to blend individual activities into an integrated sequence. In other words, through discussion you decide where you will go; who will drive; who will bring the hamburgers, the potato chips, the soda; where you will meet; and so on. Only because of language can you participate in such a common yet complex event as a picnic—or build roads and bridges, or attend college classes.

IN SUM   The sociological significance of language is that it takes us beyond the world of apes and allows culture to develop. Language frees us from the present, actually giving us a social past and a social future. That is, language gives us the capacity to share understandings about the past and to develop shared perceptions about the future. Language also allows us to establish underlying purposes for our activities. As in the example of planning a picnic, each individual is able to perform a small part of a larger activity, aware that others are carrying out related parts. In this way, language enables a series of separate activities to become united into a larger whole.

In short, *language is the basis of culture.* Like most aspects of culture, its linguistic base is usually invisible to us.

Language and Perception: The Sapir-Whorf Hypothesis   In the 1930s, two anthropologists, Edward Sapir and Benjamin Whorf, became intrigued when they noted that the Hopi Indians of the southwestern United States had no words to distinguish among the past, the present, and the future. English, in contrast—as well as French, Spanish,

Miami—Language in a Changing City

SINCE CASTRO SEIZED POWER IN Cuba in 1959, the city of Miami has been transformed from a quiet southern city to a Latin American mecca. Nothing reflects Miami's essential character today as much as its long-simmering feud over language: English versus Spanish. Half of the city's 360,000 residents have trouble speaking English. Only *one-fourth* of Miami residents speak English at home.

As this chapter stresses, language is a primary means by which people learn—and communicate—their social worlds. Consequently, language differences in Miami reflect not only cultural diversity but also the separate social worlds of the city's inhabitants.

Although its ethnic stew makes Miami culturally one of the richest cities in the United States, the language gap sometimes creates misunderstanding and anger. The aggravation felt by Anglos—which often seems tinged with hostility—is seen in the bumper stickers that used to read, "Will the Last American Out Please Bring the Flag?"

Latinos, now a majority in Miami, are similarly frustrated. Many think that Anglos should be able to speak at least some Spanish. Nicaraguan immigrant Pedro Falcon, for example, is studying English and wonders why more people don't try to learn his language. "Miami is the capital of Latin America," he says. "The population speaks Spanish."

Language and cultural flare-ups sometimes make headlines in the city. Latinos were outraged when an employee at the Coral Gables Board of Realtors lost her job for speaking Spanish at the office. And protesters swarmed a Publix supermarket after a cashier was fired for chatting with a friend in Spanish.

What's happening in Miami, says University of Chicago sociologist Douglas Massey, is what happened in cities such as Chicago a hundred years ago. Then, as now, the rate of immigration exceeded the speed with which new residents learned English, creating a pile-up effect in the proportion of non-English speakers. "Becoming comfortable with English is a slow process," he points out, "whereas immigration is fast."

Massey expects Miami's percentage of non-English speakers to grow. But he says that this "doesn't mean that Miami is going to end up being a Spanish-speaking city." Instead, Massey believes that bilingualism will prevail. "Miami is the first truly bilingual city," he says. "The people who get ahead are not monolingual English speakers or monolingual Spanish speakers. They're people who speak both languages."

Source: Based on Sharp 1992; Usdansky 1992.

Swahili, and other languages—distinguishes carefully among these three time frames. From this observation, Sapir and Whorf concluded that the commonsense idea that words are merely labels that people attach to things is wrong. *Language, they concluded, has embedded within it ways of looking at the world.* Language, they said, not only expresses our thoughts but also shapes the way we think. Language not only communicates what we perceive but also helps determine what we perceive. When we learn a language, we learn not only words but also ways of thinking and perceiving (Sapir 1949; Whorf 1956).

The **Sapir-Whorf hypothesis** reverses common sense: It indicates that rather than objects and events forcing themselves onto our consciousness, it is our language that determines our consciousness, and hence our perception of objects and events. Sociologist Eviatar Zerubavel (1991) gives a good example. Hebrew, his native language, does not have separate words for jam and jelly. Both go by the same term, and only when Zerubavel learned English could he "see" this difference, which is "obvious" to native English speakers. Similarly, if you learn to classify students as Jocks, Goths, Stoners, Skaters, and Preps, you will perceive students in an entirely different way from someone who does not know these classifications.

Although Sapir and Whorf's observation that the Hopi do not have tenses was wrong (Edgerton 1992:27), they stumbled onto a major truth about social life. Learning a language means not only learning words but also acquiring the perceptions embedded in that language (Zhang and Schmitt 1998). In other words, language both reflects and shapes cultural experiences. The racial-ethnic terms that our culture provides, for example, influence how we see both ourselves and others, a point that is discussed in the Cultural Diversity box on the next page.

Sapir-Whorf hypothesis Edward Sapir's and Benjamin Whorf's hypothesis that language creates ways of thinking and perceiving

Cultural Diversity *in the* United States

Race and Language: Searching for Self-Labels

THE GROUPS THAT DOMINATE society often determine the names that are used to refer to racial-ethnic groups. If those names become associated with oppression, they take on negative meanings. For example, the terms *Negro* and *colored people* came to be associated with submissiveness and low status. To overcome these meanings, those referred to by these terms began to identify themselves as *black* or *African American*. They infused these new terms with respect—a basic source of self-esteem that they felt the old terms denied them.

In a twist, African Americans—and to a lesser extent Latinos, Asian Americans, and Native Americans—have changed the rejected term *colored people* to *people of color*. Those who embrace this modified term are imbuing it with meanings that offer an identity of respect. The term also has political meanings. It indicates bonds that cross racial-ethnic lines, a growing sense of mutual ties and identity rooted in historical oppression.

There is *always* disagreement about racial-ethnic terms, and this one is no exception. Although most rejected the term *colored people*, some found in it a sense of respect and claimed it for themselves. The acronym NAACP, for example, stands for the National Association for the Advancement of Colored People. The new term, *people of color*, arouses similar feelings. Some individuals whom this term would include claim that it is inappropriate. They point out that this new label still makes color the primary identifier of people. They stress that humans transcend race-ethnicity, that what we have in common as human beings goes much deeper than what you see on the surface. They stress that we should avoid terms that focus on differences in the pigmentation of our skin.

The language of self-reference in a society that is so conscious of skin color is an ongoing issue. As long as our society continues to emphasize such superficial differences, the search for adequate terms is not likely to ever be "finished." In this quest for terms that strike the right chord, the term *people of color* may become a historical footnote. If it does, it will be replaced by another term that indicates a changing self-identification in a changing historical context.

Values, Norms, and Sanctions

To learn a culture is to learn people's **values**, their ideas of what is desirable in life. When we uncover people's values, we learn a great deal about them, for values are the standards by which people define what is good and bad, beautiful and ugly. Values underlie our preferences, guide our choices, and indicate what we hold worthwhile in life.

Every group develops expectations concerning the right way to reflect its values. Sociologists use the term **norms** to describe those expectations (or rules of behavior) that develop out of a group's values. The term **sanctions** refers to the reactions people receive for following or breaking norms. A **positive sanction** expresses approval for following a norm, while a **negative sanction** reflects disapproval for breaking a norm. Positive sanctions can be material, such as a prize, a trophy, or money, but in everyday life they usually consist of hugs, smiles, a pat on the back, or even handshakes and "high fives." Negative sanctions can also be material—being fined in court is one example—but they, too, are more likely to be symbolic: harsh words, or gestures such as frowns, stares, clenched jaws, or raised fists. Getting a raise at work is a positive sanction, indicating that you have followed the norms clustering around work values. Getting fired, however, is a negative sanction, indicating that you have violated these norms. The North American finger gesture discussed earlier is, of course, a negative sanction.

Because people can find norms stifling, some cultures relieve the pressure through *moral holidays,* specified times when people are allowed to break norms. Moral holidays such as Mardi Gras often center on getting drunk and being rowdy. Some activities for which people would otherwise be arrested are permitted—and expected—including public drunkenness and some nudity. The norms are never completely dropped, however—just loosened a bit. Go too far, and the police step in.

Some societies have *moral holiday places,* locations where norms are expected to be broken. Red light districts of our cities are examples. There prostitutes are allowed to work

values the standards by which people define what is desirable or undesirable, good or bad, beautiful or ugly

norms expectations, or rules of behavior, that reflect and enforce values

sanctions expressions of approval or disapproval given to people for upholding or violating norms

positive sanction a reward or positive reaction for following norms, ranging from a smile to a prize

negative sanction an expression of disapproval for breaking a norm, ranging from a mild, informal reaction such as a frown to a formal reaction such as a prison sentence or an execution

Many societies relax their norms during specified occasions. At these times, known as *moral holidays,* behavior that is ordinarily not permitted is allowed. From a functional standpoint, *moral holidays,* such as the Mardi Gras held at New Orleans, and spring break in Florida and Mexico, serve as safety valves, allowing a release of deviance. When the *moral holiday* is over, the usual enforcement of rules follows.

the streets, bothered only when political pressure builds. If these same prostitutes attempt to solicit customers in adjacent areas, however, they are promptly arrested. Lake of the Ozarks in Missouri, a fairly straight-laced area, has "Party Cove." There, hundreds of boaters—from those operating cabin cruisers to jet skis—moor their vessels together in a highly publicized cove, where many get drunk and nude, and dance on the boats. In one of the more humorous incidents, boaters complained that a nude woman was riding a jet ski outside of the cove. The water patrol investigated but refused to arrest her because the woman was within the law—she had sprayed shaving cream on certain parts of her body. The Missouri Water Patrol has even given a green light to Party Cove, announcing in the local newspaper that officers will not enter this cove, supposedly because "there is so much traffic that they might not be able to get out in time to handle an emergency elsewhere."

Folkways and Mores

Norms that are not strictly enforced are called **folkways.** We expect people to comply with folkways, but we are likely to shrug our shoulders and not make a big deal about it if they don't. If someone insists on passing you on the right side of the sidewalk, for example, you are unlikely to take corrective action although if the sidewalk is crowded and you must move out of the way, you might give the person a dirty look.

Other norms, however, are taken much more seriously. We think of them as essential to our core values, and we insist on conformity. These are called **mores** (MORE-rays). A person who steals, rapes, or kills has violated some of society's most important mores. As sociologist Ian Robertson (1987:62) put it,

A man who walks down a street wearing nothing on the upper half of his body is violating a folkway; a man who walks down the street wearing nothing on the lower half of his body is violating one of our most important mores, the requirement that people cover their genitals and buttocks in public.

It should also be noted that one group's folkways may be another group's mores. Although a man walking down the street with the upper half of his body uncovered is deviating from a folkway, a woman doing the same thing is violating the mores. In

folkways norms that are not strictly enforced

mores norms that are strictly enforced because they are thought essential to core values or the well-being of the group

The violation of *mores* is a serious matter. In this case, it is serious enough that the police at this rugby match in Dublin, Ireland, have swung into action to protect the public from seeing a "disgraceful" sight, at least one so designated by this group.

addition, the folkways and mores of a subculture (discussed in the next section) may be the opposite of mainstream culture. For example, to walk down the sidewalk in a nudist camp with the entire body uncovered would conform to that subculture's folkways.

A **taboo** refers to a norm so strongly ingrained that even the thought of its violation is greeted with revulsion. Eating human flesh and having sex with one's parents are examples of such behaviors. When someone breaks a taboo, the individual is usually judged unfit to live in the same society as others. The sanctions are severe, and may include prison, banishment, or death.

Many Cultural Worlds

Subcultures

What common condition do you think this doctor is describing? Here is what he said:

> [It accompanies] diaphragmatic pleurisy, pneumonia, uremia, or alcoholism . . . Abdominal causes include disorders of the stomach, and esophagus, bowel diseases, pancreatitis, pregnancy, bladder irritation, hepatic metastases, or hepatitis. Thoracic and mediastinal lesions or surgery may be responsible. Posterior fossa tumors or infarcts may stimulate centers in the medulla oblongata. (Chambliss 2003:443)

My best guess is that you don't have the slightest idea what this doctor was talking about. For most of us, he might as well be speaking Greek. Physicians who are lecturing students in medical school, however, talk like this. This doctor is describing hiccups!

Physicians form a **subculture,** *a world within the larger world of the dominant culture.* Subcultures consist of people whose experiences have led them to have distinctive ways of looking at life or some aspect of it. Even if we cannot understand the preceding quote, it makes us aware that the physician's view of life is not quite the same as ours.

taboo a norm so strong that it often brings revulsion if violated

subculture the values and related behaviors of a group that distinguish its members from the larger culture; a world within a world

U.S. society contains tens of thousands of subcultures. Some are as broad as the way of life we associate with teenagers, others as narrow as those we associate with body builders—or with doctors. Some U.S. ethnic groups also form subcultures: Their values, norms, and foods set them apart. So might their religion, language, and clothing. Occupational groups also form subcultures, as anyone who has hung out with artists (McCall 1980), construction workers (Haas 1972), or undertakers (Thompson 2005) can attest. Even sociologists form a subculture. As you are learning, they use a unique language for carving up the world.

For a visual depiction of subcultures, see the photo montage on the next two pages.

Countercultures

Consider this quote from another subculture:

> If everyone applying for welfare had to supply a doctor's certificate of sterilization, if everyone who had committed a felony were sterilized, if anyone who had mental illness to any degree were sterilized—then our economy could easily take care of these people for the rest of their lives, giving them a decent living standard—but getting them out of the way. That way there would be no children abused, no surplus population, and, after a while, no pollution. . . .
>
> Now let's talk about stupidity. The level of intellect in this country is going down, generation after generation. The average IQ is always 100 because that is the accepted average. However, the kid with a 100 IQ today would have tested out at 70 when I was a lad. You get the concept . . . the marching morons. . . .
>
> When the . . . present world system collapses, it'll be good people like you who will be shooting people in the streets to feed their families. (Zellner 1995:58, 65)

Welcome to the world of the Survivalists, where the message is much clearer than that of physicians—and much more disturbing.

The values and norms of most subcultures blend in with mainstream society. In some cases, however, such as these survivalists, some of the group's values and norms place it at odds with the dominant culture. Sociologists use the term **counterculture** to refer to such groups. Another example would be Satanists. To better see this distinction, consider motorcycle enthusiasts and motorcycle gangs. Motorcycle enthusiasts—who emphasize personal freedom and speed *and* affirm cultural values of success—are members of a subculture. In contrast, the Hell's Angels not only stress freedom and speed, but also value dirtiness and contempt toward women and work. This makes them a counterculture (Watson 1988).

Countercultures do not have to be negative, however. Back in the 1800s, the Mormons were a counterculture that challenged the dominant culture's core value of monogamy.

An assault on core values is always met with resistance. To affirm their own values, members of the mainstream culture may ridicule, isolate, or even attack members of the counterculture. The Mormons, for example, were driven out of several states before they finally settled in Utah, which was then a wilderness. Even there the federal government would not let them practice *polygyny* (one man having more than one wife), and Utah's statehood was made conditional on its acceptance of monogamy (Anderson 1942/1966).

Values in U.S. Society

An Overview of U.S. Values

As you know, the United States is a **pluralistic society,** made up of many different groups. The United States has numerous religious and racial–ethnic groups, as well as countless interest groups that focus on such divergent activities as collecting Barbie dolls and

counterculture a group whose values, beliefs, and related behaviors place its members in opposition to the broader culture

pluralistic society a society made up of many different groups

Looking at Subcultures

Subcultures can form around any interest or activity. Each subculture has its own values and norms that its members share, giving them a common identity. Each also has special terms that pinpoint the group's corner of life and that its members use to communicate with one another. Some of us belong to several subcultures simultaneously.

As you can see from these photos, most subcultures are compatible with the values of the dominant or mainstream culture. They represent specialized interests around which its members have chosen to build tiny worlds. Some subcultures, however, conflict with the mainstream culture. Sociologists give the name contraculture to subcultures whose values (such as those of outlaw motorcyclists) or activities and goals (such as those of terrorists) are opposed to the mainstream culture. Contracultures, however, are exceptional, and few of us belong to them.

Membership in this subculture is not easily awarded. Not only must **high-steel iron-workers** prove that they are able to work at great heights but also that they fit into the group socially. Newcomers are tested by members of the group, and they must demonstrate that they can take joking without offense.

This Native American also represents a subculture within this subculture, for many Mohawk Native Americans specialize in this occupation.

t anyone who has visited a casino recognizes that
is something different about the people who work
Servers have developed their own norms—their
able practices for maximizing tips.

Why would someone decorate themselves like
this? Among the many reasons, one is to show
their solidarity with the **football subculture**.

"Showing" dogs is a highly specialized
subculture. To be a member in good
standing, intricate rules must be followed.

▲ The **motorcyclist clubs** and groups that students and workers participate in on
weekends are subcultures. Those that outlaw motorcyclists participate in are
countercultures. Can you see why sociologists make this distinction?

◀ **Truckers** participate in a huge subculture, one that combines its
own values and language. Can you identify other subcultures that
truckers are also likely to participate in?

The **cabbies'** subculture, centering
on their occupational activities and
nterests, is also broken into smaller
subcultures that reflect their experiences of race-ethnicity.

Participants in the **rodeo** subculture "advertise" their membership by wearing special clothing. The clothing symbolizes
a set of values that unites its members. Among those
values is the awarding of hyper-masculine status through
the conquest of animals.

Each subculture provides its members
with values and distinctive ways of view-
ing the world. What values and perceptions do you think are common among
body builders?

Introductory Sociology 1

hunting deer. This state of affairs makes the job of specifying U.S. values difficult. Nonetheless, sociologists have tried to identify the underlying core values that are shared by the many groups that make up U.S. society. Sociologist Robin Williams (1965) identified the following:

1. *Achievement and success.* Americans place a high value on personal achievement, especially outdoing others. This value includes getting ahead at work and school, and attaining wealth, power, and prestige.

2. *Individualism.* Americans have traditionally prized success that comes from individual efforts and initiative. They cherish the ideal that an individual can rise from the bottom of society to its very top. If someone fails to "get ahead," Americans generally find fault with that individual, rather than with the social system for placing roadblocks in his or her path.

3. *Activity and work.* Americans expect people to work hard and to be busy doing some activity even when not at work. This value is becoming less important.

4. *Efficiency and practicality.* Americans award high marks for getting things done efficiently. Even in everyday life, Americans consider it important to do things fast, and they seek ways to increase efficiency.

5. *Science and technology.* Americans have a passion for applied science, for using science to control nature—to tame rivers and harness winds—and to develop new technology, from iPods to Segways.

6. *Progress.* Americans expect rapid technological change. They believe that they should constantly build "more and better" gadgets that will help them move toward some vague goal called "progress."

7. *Material comfort.* Americans expect a high level of material comfort. This comfort includes not only good nutrition, medical care, and housing, but also late-model cars and recreational playthings—from Hummers to X-boxes.

8. *Humanitarianism.* Americans emphasize helpfulness, personal kindness, aid in mass disasters, and organized philanthropy.

9. *Freedom.* This core value pervades U.S. life. It underscored the American Revolution, and Americans pride themselves on their personal freedom. The Mass Media in Social Life box on the next page highlights an interesting study on how this core value applies to Native Americans.

10. *Democracy.* By this term, Americans refer to majority rule, to the right of everyone to express an opinion, and to representative government.

11. *Equality.* It is impossible to understand Americans without being aware of the central role that the value of equality plays in their lives. Equality of opportunity (part of the ideal culture discussed later), has significantly influenced U.S. history and continues to mark relations among the groups that make up U.S. society.

12. *Racism and group superiority.* Although it contradicts freedom, democracy, and equality, Americans value some groups more than others and have done so throughout their history. The slaughter of Native Americans and the enslaving of Africans are the most notorious examples.

In an earlier publication, I updated Williams' analysis by adding these three values.

13. *Education.* Americans are expected to go as far in school as their abilities and finances allow. Over the years, the definition of an "adequate" education has changed, and today a college education is considered an appropriate goal for most Americans. Those who have an opportunity for higher education and do not take it are sometimes viewed as doing something "wrong"—not merely as making a bad choice, but as somehow being involved in an immoral act.

14. *Religiosity.* There is a feeling that "every true American ought to be religious." This does not mean that everyone is expected to join a church, synagogue, or mosque, but that everyone ought to acknowledge a belief in a Supreme Being and follow some set of matching precepts. This value is so pervasive that Americans stamp "In God We Trust" on their money and declare in their national pledge of allegiance that they are "one nation under God."

mass **Media in social life**

Why Do Native Americans Like Westerns?

U.S. audiences (and even German, French, and Japanese ones) devour Western movies. In the United States, it is easy to see why Anglos might like Westerns. It is they who are portrayed as heroes who tame the savage wilderness and defend themselves from the attacks of cruel, barbaric Indians who are intent on their destruction. But why would Indians like Westerns?

Sociologist JoEllen Shively, a Chippewa who grew up on Indian reservations in Montana and North Dakota, observed that Westerns are so popular that Native Americans bring bags of paperbacks into taverns to trade with one another. They even call each other "cowboy."

Intrigued, Shively decided to investigate the matter by showing a Western to adult Native Americans and Anglos in a reservation town. She matched the groups in education, age, income, and percentage of unemployment. To select the movie, Shively (1991, 1992) previewed more than seventy Westerns. She chose a John Wayne movie, *The Searchers,* because it not only focuses on conflict between Indians and cowboys but also shows the cowboys defeating the Indians. After the movie the viewers filled out question-

naires, and Shively interviewed them.

She found something surprising: *All* Native Americans and Anglos identified with the cowboys; *none* identified with the Indians. Anglos and Native Americans, however, identified with the cowboys in different ways. Each projected a different fantasy onto the story. While Anglos saw the movie as an accurate portrayal of the Old West and a justification of their own status in society, Native Americans saw it as embodying a free, natural way of life. In fact, Native Americans said that they were the "real cowboys." They said, "Westerns relate to the way I wish I could live"; "He's not tied down to an eight-to-five job, day after day"; "He's his own man."

Shively adds,

What appears to make Westerns meaningful to Indians is the fantasy of being free and independent like the cowboy. . . . Indians . . . find a fantasy in the cowboy story in which the important parts of their ways of life triumph and are morally good, validating their own cultural group in the context of a dramatically satisfying story.

To express their real identity—a combination of marginality on the one hand, with a set of values which are about the land, autonomy, and being

Although John Wayne often portrayed an Anglo who kills Indians, Wayne is popular among Indian men. These men tend to identify with the cowboys, who reflect their values of bravery, autonomy, and toughness.

free—they (use) a cultural vehicle written for Anglos about Anglos, but it is one in which Indians invest a distinctive set of meanings that speak to their own experience, which they can read in a manner that affirms a way of life they value, or a fantasy they hold to.

In other words, values, not ethnicity, are the central issue. If a Native American film industry were to portray Native Americans with the same values that the Anglo movie industry projects onto cowboys, then Native Americans would identify with their own group. Thus, says Shively, Native Americans make cowboys "honorary Indians," for the cowboys express their values of bravery, autonomy, and toughness.

---

15. *Romantic love.* Americans feel that the only proper basis for marriage is romantic love. Songs, literature, mass media, and "folk beliefs" all stress this value. They especially love the theme that "love conquers all."

Value Clusters

As you can see, values are not independent units; some cluster together to form a larger whole. In the **value cluster** surrounding success, for example, we find hard work, education, efficiency, material comfort, and individualism bound up together. Americans are expected to go far in school, to work hard afterward, to be efficient, and then to attain a high level of material comfort, which, in turn, demonstrates success. Success is attributed to the individual's efforts; lack of success is blamed on his or her faults.

value cluster values that together form a larger whole

The many groups that compose the United States contribute to its culture. As the number of Latinos in the United States increases, Latinos are making a greater impact on music, art, and literature. This is also true of other areas of everyday life, such as this car-hopping contest in California. Cars are outfitted with bionic hydraulic systems, and contestants compete to see whose vehicle can hop the highest or shimmy the most erratically from tire to tire.

Value Contradictions and Social Change

Not all values fall into neat, integrated packages. Some even contradict one another. The value of group superiority contradicts freedom, democracy, and equality, producing a **value contradiction.** There simply cannot be full expression of freedom, democracy, and equality, along with racism and sexism. Something has to give. One way in which Americans sidestepped this contradiction in the past was to say that freedom, democracy, and equality applied only to some groups. The contradiction was bound to surface over time, however, and so it did with the Civil War and the women's liberation movement. *It is precisely at the point of value contradictions, then, that one can see a major force for social change in a society.*

Emerging Values

A value cluster of four interrelated core values—leisure, self-fulfillment, physical fitness, and youthfulness—-is emerging in the United States. A fifth core value—concern for the environment—is also emerging.

1. *Leisure.* The emergence of leisure as a value is reflected in a huge recreation industry—from computer games, boats, and motor homes to sports arenas, home entertainment systems, and luxury cruises.
2. *Self-fulfillment.* This value is reflected in the "human potential" movement, which emphasizes becoming "all one can be," and in books and talk shows that focus on "self-help," "relating," and "personal development."
3. *Physical fitness.* Physical fitness is not a new U.S. value, but its increased emphasis is moving it into this emerging cluster. This trend is evident in the emphasis on organic foods; obsessive concerns about weight and diet; the joggers, cyclists, and backpackers who take to the trails; and the many health clubs and physical fitness centers.
4. *Youthfulness.* While valuing youth and disparaging old age are not new, some note a new sense of urgency. They attribute this to the huge number of aging baby boomers, who, aghast at the physical changes that accompany their advancing years, attempt to deny their biological fate. An extreme view is represented by a physician who claims that "aging is not a normal life event, but a disease" (Cowley 1996). It is not surprising, then, that techniques for enhancing and maintaining a youthful appearance—from cosmetic surgery to Botox injections—have become popular. "Makeover" television shows are another reflection of this value.

This emerging value cluster is a response to fundamental changes in U.S. society. Americans used to be preoccupied with forging a nation and fighting for economic sur-

value contradiction values that contradict one another; to follow the one means to come into conflict with the other

Values, both those held by individuals and those that represent a nation or people, can undergo deep shifts. It is difficult for many of us to grasp the pride with which earlier Americans destroyed trees that took thousands of years to grow, are located only on one tiny speck of the globe, and that we today consider part of the nation's and world's heritage. But this is a value statement, representing current views. The pride expressed on these woodcutters' faces represents another set of values entirely.

vival. They now have come to a point in their economic development at which millions of people are freed from long hours of work, and millions more are able to retire from work at an age when they anticipate decades of life ahead of them. This value cluster centers on helping people to maintain their health and vigor during their younger years and enabling them to enjoy their years of retirement.

5. *Concern for the environment.* During most of U.S. history, the environment was viewed as something to be exploited—a wilderness to be settled, forests to be chopped down, rivers and lakes to be fished, and animals to be hunted. One result was the near extinction of the bison and the extinction in 1915 of the passenger pigeon, a bird previously so numerous that its annual migration would darken the skies for days. Today, Americans have developed a genuine and (we can hope) long term concern for the environment.

This emerging value of environmental concern is related to the current stage of U.S. economic development: People act on environmental concerns only after they meet their basic needs. At this point in their development, for example, the world's poor nations have a difficult time "affording" this value.

Culture Wars: When Values Clash

Changes in core values are met with strong resistance by the people who hold them dear. They see the change as a threat to their way of life, an undermining of both their present and their future. Efforts to change gender roles, for example, arouse intense controversy, as does support for the marriage of homosexuals. Alarmed at such onslaughts to their values, traditionalists fiercely defend historical family relationships and the gender roles they grew up with. Today's clash in values is so severe that the term *culture wars* has been coined to refer to it. Compared with the violence directed against the Mormons, however, today's reactions to such controversies are mild.

Values as Blinders

Just as values and their supporting beliefs paint a unique picture of reality, so they also form a view of what life *ought* to be like. Americans value individualism so highly, for example, that they tend to see everyone as free to pursue the goal of success. This value blinds them to the many circumstances that keep people from reaching this goal. The dire consequences of family poverty, parents' low education, and dead-end jobs tend to drop from sight. Instead, Americans cling to the notion that everyone can make it—if they put forth enough effort. And they "know" they are right, for every day, dangling before their eyes are enticing stories of individuals who have succeeded despite huge handicaps.

"Ideal" Versus "Real" Culture

Many of the norms that surround cultural values are followed only partially. Differences always exist between a group's ideals and what its members actually do. Consequently, sociologists use the term **ideal culture** to refer to the values, norms, and goals that a group considers ideal, worth aspiring to. Success, for example, is part of ideal culture. Americans glorify academic progress, hard work, and the display of material goods as signs of individual achievement. What people actually do, however, usually falls short of the cultural ideal. Compared with their abilities, for example, most people don't work as hard as they could or go as far as they could in school. Sociologists call the norms and values that people actually follow **real culture.**

Cultural Universals

With the amazing variety of human cultures around the world, are there any **cultural universals**—values, norms, or other cultural traits that are found everywhere?

To answer this question, anthropologist George Murdock (1945) combed through data that anthropologists had gathered on hundreds of groups around the world. He drew up a list of customs concerning courtship, marriage, funerals, games, laws, music, myths, incest taboos, and even toilet training. He found that although such activities are present in all cultures, *the specific customs differ from one group to another.* There is no universal form of the family, no universal way of toilet training children or of disposing of the dead. Similarly, games, songs, and stories differ from one culture to another.

Even incest is defined differently from group to group. For example, the Mundugumors of New Guinea extend the incest taboo so far that for each man, seven of every eight women are ineligible marriage partners (Mead 1935/1950). Other groups go in the opposite direction and allow some men to marry their own daughters (La Barre 1954). In certain circumstances, some groups *require* that brothers and sisters marry one another (Beals and Hoijer 1965). The Burundi of Africa even insist that, in order to remove a certain curse, a son must have sexual relations with his mother (Albert 1963). Such sexual relations are usually allowed only for special people (royalty) or in extraordinary situations (such as when a lion hunter faces a dangerous hunt). No society permits generalized incest for its members.

In short, although there are universal human activities (speech, music, storytelling, marrying, disposing of the dead, preparing food, and so on), there is no universally accepted way of doing any of them. Humans have no biological imperative that results in one particular form of behavior throughout the world. As indicated in the following Thinking Critically section, although a few sociologists take the position that genes significantly influence human behavior, almost all sociologists reject this view.

Thinking Critically

Are We Prisoners of Our Genes? Sociobiology and Human Behavior

A controversial view of human behavior, called **sociobiology** (also known as neo-Darwinism and evolutionary psychology), provides a sharp contrast to the perspective of this chapter, that hu-

---

ideal culture the ideal values and norms of a people; the goals held out for them

real culture the norms and values that people actually follow

cultural universal a value, norm, or other cultural trait that is found in every group

sociobiology a framework of thought that views human behavior as the result of natural selection and considers biological factors to be the fundamental cause of human behavior

man behavior is primarily due to culture. Sociobiologists (and their close cousins, evolutionary psychologists) believe that because of natural selection, the basic cause of human behavior is biology.

Charles Darwin (1859), who developed the idea of natural selection, pointed out that the genes of a species—the units that contain the individual's traits—are not distributed evenly among the offspring. The characteristics passed on to some members make it easier for them to survive their environment, increasing the likelihood that they will pass their genetic traits to the next generation. Over thousands of generations, the genetic traits that aid survival tend to become common in a species, while those that do not tend to disappear.

Natural selection explains not only the physical characteristics of animals, but also their behavior, for over countless generations, instincts emerged. Edward Wilson (1975), an insect specialist, claims that human behavior is also the result of natural selection. Human behavior, he asserts, is no different from the behavior of cats, dogs, rats, bees, or mosquitoes—it has been bred into *Homo sapiens* through evolutionary principles.

Wilson deliberately set out to create a storm of protest, and he succeeded. He went on to claim that religion, competition and cooperation, slavery and genocide, war and peace, envy and altruism—all can be explained by sociobiology. He provocatively added that because human behavior can be explained in terms of genetic programming, sociobiology will eventually absorb sociology—as well as anthropology and psychology.

Obviously, most sociologists find Wilson's position unacceptable. Not only is it a direct attack on their discipline but also it bypasses the essence of what sociologists focus on: humans developing their own cultures, their own unique ways of life. Sociologists do not deny that biology underlies human behavior—at least not in the sense that it takes a highly developed brain to develop human culture and abstract thought, and that there would be no speech if humans had no tongue or larynx.

But most sociologists find it difficult to believe that anyone would claim that genetic programming causes human behavior. Pigs act like pigs because they don't have a cerebral cortex, and instincts control their behavior. So it is for spiders, elephants, and so on (Howe et al. 1992). Humans, in contrast, possess a self and are capable of abstract thought. They discuss the reasons that underlie what they do. They develop purposes and goals. They immerse themselves in a world of symbols which allow them to consider, reflect, and make reasoned choices.

This controversy has turned into much more than simply an academic debate among scientists. Homosexuals, for example, have a personal interest in its outcome. If homosexuality is a lifestyle *choice,* then those who consider that lifestyle to be immoral will use this as a basis for excluding homosexuals from full social participation. If, however, homosexuality has a genetic basis, then choice as a reason for social exclusion is eliminated. Sociologist Peter Conrad (1997) expresses the dominant sociological position when he points out that not all homosexuals have Xq28, the so-called "gay gene," and some people who have this gene are not homosexual. This gene, then, does not determine behavior. Instead, we must look for *social* causes (Bearman and Bruckner 2002).

In short, sociobiologists and sociologists stand on opposite sides, the one looking at human behavior as determined by genetics, the other looking at human behavior as determined by social learning, by experiences in the human group. Sociologists point out that if humans were prisoners of their genes, we would not have developed such a variety of fascinating ways of life around the world—we would live in a monoculture of some sort.

Technology in the Global Village

The New Technology

The gestures, language, values, folkways, and mores that we have discussed—all are part of symbolic or nonmaterial culture. Culture, as you recall, also has a material aspect: a group's *things,* from its houses to its toys. Central to a group's material culture is its technology. In its simplest sense, **technology** can be equated with tools. In a broader sense, technology also includes the skills or procedures necessary to make and use those tools.

technology in its narrow sense, tools; its broader sense includes the skills or procedures necessary to make and use those tools

The adoption of new forms of communication by people who not long ago were cut off from events in the rest of the world is bound to change their *nonmaterial culture*. How do you think that this Tswana woman's thinking and views of the world are changing? (The Tswana are a South African tribe.)

We can use the term **new technology** to refer to an emerging technology that has a significant impact on social life. People develop minor technologies all the time. Most are slight modifications of existing technologies. Occasionally, however, they develop a technology that makes a major impact on human life. It is primarily to these that the term *new technology* refers. For people 500 years ago, the new technology was the printing press. For us, the new technology consists of computers, satellites, and the electronic media.

The sociological significance of technology goes far beyond the tool itself. *Technology sets the framework for a group's nonmaterial culture.* If a group's technology changes, so do people's ways of thinking and how they relate to one another. An example is gender relations. Through the centuries and throughout the world, it has been the custom (the nonmaterial culture of a group) for men to dominate women. Today, with instantaneous communications (the material culture), this custom has become much more difficult to maintain. For example, when women from many nations gathered in Beijing for a U.N. conference in 1995, satellites instantly transmitted their grievances around the globe. Such communications both convey and create discontent, as well as a feeling of sisterhood, motivating women to agitate for social change.

In today's world, the long-accepted idea that it is proper to withhold rights on the basis of someone's sex can no longer hold. What is usually invisible in this revolutionary change is the role of the new technology, which joins the world's nations into a global communications network.

Cultural Lag and Cultural Change

About three generations ago, sociologist William Ogburn (1922/1938), a functional analyst, coined the term **cultural lag.** By this, Ogburn meant that not all parts of a culture change at the same pace. When some part of a culture changes, other parts lag behind.

Ogburn pointed out that *a group's material culture usually changes first, with the nonmaterial culture lagging behind,* playing a game of catch-up. For example, when we get sick, we could type our symptoms into a computer and get a printout of our diagnosis and a recommended course of treatment. In fact, in some tests, computers outperform physicians. Yet our customs have not caught up with our technology, and we continue to visit the doctor's office.

Sometimes nonmaterial culture never catches up. Instead, we rigorously hold onto some outmoded form—one that once was needed, but that long ago was bypassed by new technology. A striking example is our nine-month school year. Have you ever wondered why it is nine months long, and why we take summers off? For most of us, this is "just the way it's always been," and we have never questioned it. But there is more to this custom than meets the eye, for it is an example of cultural lag.

In the late 1800s, when universal schooling came about, the school year matched the technology of the time, which was labor-intensive. Most parents were farmers, and for survival, they needed their children's help at the crucial times of planting and harvesting. Today, generations later, when few people farm and there is no need for the school year to be so short, we still live with this cultural lag.

Technology and Cultural Leveling

new technology the emerging technologies of an era that have a significant impact on social life

cultural lag Ogburn's term for human behavior lagging behind technological innovations

cultural diffusion the spread of cultural characteristics from one group to another

For most of human history, communication was limited and travel slow. Consequently, in their relative isolation, human groups developed highly distinctive ways of life as they responded to the particular situations they faced. The unique characteristics they developed that distinguished one culture from another tended to change little over time. The Tasmanians, who lived on a remote island off the coast of Australia, provide an extreme example. For thousands of years, they had no contact with other people. They were so isolated that they did not even know how to make clothing or fire (Edgerton 1992).

Except in such rare instances, humans have always had *some* contact with other groups. During these contacts, people learned from one another, adopting some part of the other's way of life. In this process, called **cultural diffusion,** groups are most open to changes in their technology or material culture. They usually are eager, for example, to adopt superior weapons and tools. In remote jungles in South America one can find metal cooking

Technological advances are now so rapid that the technology of one generation is practically unrecognizable by the next generation.

COCHRAN!

"COOL! A KEYBOARD THAT WRITES WITHOUT A PRINTER."

pots, steel axes, and even bits of clothing spun in mills in South Carolina. Although the direction of cultural diffusion today is primarily from the West to other parts of the world, cultural diffusion is not a one-way street—as bagels, woks, hammocks, and sushi bars in the United States attest.

With today's travel and communications, cultural diffusion is occurring rapidly. Air travel has made it possible to journey around the globe in a matter of hours. In the not-so-distant past, a trip from the United States to Africa was so unusual that only a few adventurous people made it, and newspapers would herald their feat. Today, hundreds of thousands make the trip each year.

The changes in communication are no less vast. Communication used to be limited to face-to-face speech, written messages that were passed from hand to hand, and visual signals such as smoke or light that was reflected from mirrors. Despite newspapers, people in some parts of the United States did not hear that the Civil War had ended until weeks and even months after it was over. Today's electronic communications transmit messages across the globe in a matter of seconds, and we learn almost instantaneously what is happening on the other side of the world. During Gulf War II, reporters traveled with U.S. soldiers, and for the first time in history, the public was able to view live video reports of battles and deaths as they occurred.

Travel and communication unite us to such an extent that there is almost no "other side of the world" anymore. One result is **cultural leveling,** a process in which cultures become similar to one another. The globalization of capitalism is bringing both technology and Western culture to the rest of the world. Japan, for example, has adopted not only capitalism but also Western forms of dress and music. These changes, which have been "superimposed" on Japanese culture, have transformed Japan into a blend of Western and Eastern cultures.

Cultural leveling is occurring rapidly around the world, as is apparent to any traveler. The Golden Arches of McDonald's welcome today's visitors to Tokyo, Paris, London, Madrid, Moscow, Hong Kong, and Beijing. In Mexico, the most popular piñatas are no longer donkeys but, instead, Mickey Mouse and Fred Flintstone (Beckett 1996). When I visited a jungle village in India—no electricity, no running water, and so remote that the only entrance was by a footpath—I saw a young man sporting a cap with the Nike emblem.

Shown here is a Masai Barbie Doll. Mattel Toys, the U.S. manufacturer, has modified Barbie to match Masai (Kenya) culture by dressing her in a traditional "shuka" dress, beads, shawl, headdress, and anklets. As objects diffuse from one culture to another, they are modified to meet the tastes of the adoptive culture. In this instance, the modification has been done intentionally as part of the globalization of capitalism. Now that Barbie is a Masai, can a Masai Ken be far behind?

cultural leveling the process by which cultures become similar to one another; refers especially to the process by which U.S. culture is being exported and diffused into other nations

Although the bridging of geography and culture by electronic signals and the exportation of Western icons do not in and of themselves mark the end of traditional cultures, the inevitable result is some degree of *cultural leveling,* some blander, less distinctive way of life—U.S. culture with French, Japanese, and Brazilian accents, so to speak. Although the "cultural accent" remains, something vital is lost forever.

Summary *and* Review

What Is Culture?

All human groups possess **culture**—language, beliefs, values, norms, and material objects that are passed from one generation to the next. **Material culture** consists of objects (art, buildings, clothing, tools). **Nonmaterial (or symbolic) culture** is a group's ways of thinking and their patterns of behavior. **Ideal culture** is a group's ideal values, norms, and goals. **Real culture** is their actual behavior, which often falls short of their cultural ideals. Pp. 36–37.

What are cultural relativism and ethnocentrism?

People are naturally **ethnocentric**; that is, they use their own culture as a yardstick for judging the ways of others. In contrast, those who embrace **cultural relativism** try to understand other cultures on those cultures' own terms. Pp. 37–39.

Components of Symbolic Culture

What are the components of nonmaterial culture?

The central component is **symbols**, anything to which people attach meaning and that they use to communicate with others. Universally, the symbols of nonmaterial culture are **gestures, language, values, norms, sanctions, folkways,** and **mores**. Pp. 39–42.

Why is language so significant to culture?

Language allows human experience to be goal-directed, cooperative, and cumulative. It also lets humans move beyond the present and share a past, future, and other common perspectives. According to the **Sapir-Whorf hypothesis,** language even shapes our thoughts and perceptions. Pp. 42–46.

How do values, norms, sanctions, folkways, and mores reflect culture?

All groups have **values,** standards by which they define what is desirable or undesirable, and **norms,** rules or expectations about behavior. Groups use **positive sanctions** to show approval of those who follow their norms, and **negative sanctions** to show disapproval of those who do not. Norms that are not strictly enforced are called **folkways,** while **mores** are norms to which groups demand conformity because they reflect core values. Pp. 46–48.

Many Cultural Worlds

How do subcultures and countercultures differ?

A **subculture** is a group whose values and related behaviors distinguish its members from the general culture. A **counterculture** holds some values that stand in opposition to those of the dominant culture. Pp. 48–49.

Values in U.S. Society

What are the core U.S. values?

Although the United States is a **pluralistic society,** made up of many groups, each with its own set of values, certain values dominate: achievement and success, individualism, activity and work, efficiency and practicality, science and technology, progress, material comfort, equality, freedom, democracy, humanitarianism, racism and group superiority, education, religiosity, and romantic love. Some values cluster together (**value clusters**) to form a larger whole. **Value contradictions** (such as equality and racism) indicate areas of tension, which are likely points of social change. Leisure, self-fulfillment, physical fitness, youthfulness, and concern for the environment are emerging core values. Core values do not change without opposition. Pp. 49–56.

Cultural Universals

Do cultural universals exist?

Cultural universals are values, norms, or other cultural traits that are found in all cultures. Although all human groups have customs concerning cooking, childbirth, funerals, and so on, because the forms these customs take vary from one culture to another, there are no cultural universals. Pp. 56–57.

Technology in the Global Village

How is technology changing culture?

William Ogburn coined the term **cultural lag** to describe how a group's nonmaterial culture lags behind its changing technology. With today's technological advances in travel and communications, **cultural diffusion** is occurring rapidly. This leads to **cultural leveling**, whereby many groups are adopting Western culture in place of their own customs. Much of the richness of the world's diverse cultures is being lost in the process. Pp. 57–59.

Thinking Critically
about Chapter 2

1. Do you favor ethnocentrism or cultural relativism? Explain your position.

2. Do you think that the language change in Miami, Florida, (discussed on page 45) is an indicator of the future of the United States? Why or why not?

3. Are you a member of any subcultures? Which one(s)? Why do you think that your group is a subculture? What is the your group's relationship to the mainstream culture?

Additional Resources

Companion Website www.ablongman.com/henslin8e

- *Content Select* Research Database for Sociology, with suggested key terms and annotated references
- Link to 2000 Census, with activities
- Flashcards of key terms and concepts
- Practice Tests
- Weblinks
- Interactive Maps

Where Can I Read More on This Topic?

Suggested readings for this chapter are listed at the back of this book.

Socialization

Simon Silva, *Orgullo de Familia*, 1997

The old man was horrified when he found out. Life never had been good since his daughter lost her hearing when she was just 2 years old. She couldn't even talk—just fluttered her hands around trying to tell him things. Over the years, he had gotten used to that. But now . . . he shuddered at the thought of her being pregnant. No one would be willing to marry her; he knew that. And the neighbors, their tongues would never stop wagging. Everywhere he went, he could hear people talking behind his back.

If only his wife were still alive, maybe she could come up with something. What should he do? He couldn't just kick his daughter out into the street.

After the baby was born, the old man tried to shake his feelings, but they wouldn't let loose. Isabelle was a pretty name, but every time he looked at the baby he felt sick to his stomach.

He hated doing it, but there was no way out. His daughter and her baby would have to live in the attic.

Unfortunately, this is a true story. Isabelle was discovered in Ohio in 1938 when she was about 6½ years old, living in a dark room with her deaf-mute mother. Isabelle couldn't talk, but she did use gestures to communicate with her mother. An inadequate diet and lack of sunshine had given Isabelle a disease called rickets. Her legs

were so bowed that as she stood erect the soles of her shoes came nearly flat together, and she got

> ## Her behavior toward strangers, especially men, was almost that of a wild animal, manifesting much fear and hostility.

about with a skittering gait. Her behavior toward strangers, especially men, was almost that of a wild animal, manifesting much fear and hostility. In lieu of speech she made only a strange croaking sound. (Davis 1940/2005:138–139)

When the newspapers reported this case, sociologist Kingsley Davis decided to find out what had happened to Isabelle after her discovery. We'll come back to that later, but first let's use the case of Isabelle to gain insight into human nature.

What Is Human Nature?

 For centuries, people have been intrigued with the question of what is human about human nature. How much of people's characteristics comes from "nature" (heredity) and how much from "nurture" (the **social environment,** contact with others)? One way to answer this question is to study identical twins who have been reared apart, such as those discussed in the Down-to-Earth Sociology box below. Another way is to examine children who have had little human contact. Let's consider such children.

Down-to-Earth Sociology

Heredity or Environment? The Case of Oskar and Jack, Identical Twins

IDENTICAL TWINS SHARE EXACTLY THE SAME GENETIC heredity. One fertilized egg divides to produce two embryos. If heredity determines personality—or attitudes, temperament, skills, and intelligence—then identical twins should be identical not only in their looks but also in these characteristics.

The fascinating case of Jack and Oskar helps us unravel this mystery. From their experience, we can see the far-reaching effects of the environment—how social experiences take precedence over biology.

Jack Yufe and Oskar Stohr are identical twins born in 1932 to a Jewish father and a Catholic mother. They were separated as babies after their parents divorced. Oskar was reared in Czechoslovakia by his mother's mother, who was a strict Catholic. When Oskar was a toddler, Hitler annexed this area of Czechoslovakia, and Oskar learned to love Hitler and to hate Jews. He joined the Hitler Youth (a sort of Boy Scout organization, except that this one was designed to instill the "virtues" of patriotism, loyalty, obedience—and hatred).

Jack's upbringing was a mirror image of Oskar's. Reared in Trinidad by his father, he learned loyalty to Jews and hatred of Hitler and the Nazis. After the war, Jack and his father moved to Israel. When he was 17, Jack joined a kibbutz, and later, served in the Israeli army.

In 1954, the two brothers met. It was a short meeting, and Jack had been warned not to tell Oskar that they were Jews. Twenty-five years later, in 1979, when they were 47 years old, social scientists at the University of Minnesota brought them together again. These researchers figured that because Jack and Oskar had the same genes, any differences they showed would have to be the result of their environment—their different social experiences.

Not only did Oskar and Jack hold different attitudes toward the war, Hitler, and Jews, but also their basic orienta-

The question of the relative influence of heredity and the environment on human behavior has fascinated and plagued researchers. Identical twins reared apart provide an opportunity to examine this relationship. However, almost all identical twins, including these girls, are reared together, frustrating efforts to separate heredity and environment.

tions to life were different. In their politics, Oskar was conservative, while Jack was more liberal. Oskar enjoyed leisure, while Jack was a workaholic. And, as you can predict, Jack was very proud of being a Jew. Oskar, who by this time knew that he was a Jew, wouldn't even mention it.

That would seem to settle the matter. But there was another side. The researchers also found that Oskar and Jack had both excelled at sports as children, but had difficulty with math. They also had the same rate of speech, and both liked sweet liqueur and spicy foods. Strangely, both flushed the toilet both before and after using it and enjoyed startling people by sneezing in crowded elevators.

for your Consideration

Heredity or environment? How much influence does each one have? The question is not yet settled, but at this point it seems fair to conclude that the *limits* of certain physical and mental abilities are established by heredity (such as ability at sports and aptitude for mathematics), while such basic orientations to life as attitudes are the result of the environment. We can put it this way: For some parts of life, the blueprint is drawn by heredity; but even here the environment can redraw those lines. For other parts, the individual is a blank slate, and it is up to the environment to determine what is written on that slate.

Sources: Based on Begley 1979; Chen 1979; Wright 1995; Segal 2000.

Feral Children

Over the centuries, people have occasionally found children living in the woods. Supposedly, these children could not speak; they bit, scratched, growled, and walked on all fours. They drank by lapping water, ate grass, tore ravenously at raw meat, and showed an insensitivity to pain and cold. These stories of what are called **feral children** sound like exaggerations, and it is easy to dismiss them as a type of folk myth.

Because of what happened in 1798, however, we can't be so sure. In that year, a child who walked on all fours and could not speak was found in the forests of Aveyron, France. "The wild boy of Aveyron," as this child became known, would have been simply another of those legends, except that French scientists took the child to a laboratory and studied him. Like the earlier informal reports, this child, too, gave no indication of feeling the cold. Most startling, though, the boy would growl when he saw a small animal, pounce on it, and devour it uncooked. Even today, the scientists' detailed reports make fascinating reading (Itard 1962).

Ever since I read Itard's account of this boy, I've been fascinated by feral children, especially the seemingly fantastic possibility that animals could rear human children. In 2002, I received a private report that a feral child had been found in the jungles of Cambodia. When I had the opportunity the following year to visit the child and interview his caregivers, I grabbed it. The boy's photo is on this page.

If animals really have raised children, the sociological question is: If we were untouched by society, would we be like feral children? By nature, would our behavior be like that of wild animals? Unable to study feral children, sociologists have studied children like Isabelle who were raised in isolation.

Isolated Children

Reports of isolated children are more recent and have been well documented. What can they tell us about human nature? We can first conclude that humans have no natural language, for Isabelle and others like her are unable to speak.

But maybe Isabelle was mentally impaired, and she could not progress through the usual stages of development. When Isabelle was given her first intelligence test, she scored practically zero. But after a few months of intensive language training, she was able to speak in short sentences. In about a year, she could write a few words, do simple addition, and retell stories after hearing them. Seven months later, she had a vocabulary of almost 2,000 words. In just two years, Isabelle reached the intellectual level that is normal for her age. She then went on to school, where she was "bright, cheerful, energetic . . . and participated in all school activities as normally as other children" (Davis 1940/2005:139).

As discussed in the previous chapter, language is the key to human development. Without language, people have no mechanism for developing thought. Unlike animals, humans have no instincts that take the place of language. If an individual lacks language, he or she lives in an isolated world—a world of internal silence, without shared ideas, lacking connections to others.

Without language, there can be no culture—no shared way of life—and culture is the key to what people become. Each of us possesses a biological heritage, but this heritage does not determine specific behaviors, attitudes, or values. It is our culture that superimposes the specifics of what we become onto our biological heritage.

Institutionalized Children

Other than language, what else is required for a child to develop into what we consider a healthy, balanced, intelligent human being? We find part of the answer in an intriguing experiment from the 1930s. Back then, life was shorter, and orphanages dotted the United States. Children reared in orphanages often had difficulty establishing close bonds with others—and they tended to have low IQs. "Common sense" (which we noted in Chapter 1 is unreliable) told everyone that the cause of mental retardation is biological ("They're

One of the reasons I went to Cambodia was to interview a feral child—the boy shown here—who supposedly had been raised by monkeys. When I arrived at the remote location where the boy was living, I was disappointed to find that the story was only partially true. During its reign of terror, the Khmer Rouge had shot and killed the boy's parents, leaving him, at about the age of two, abandoned on an island. Some months later, villagers found him in the care of monkeys. They shot the female monkey that was carrying the boy. Not quite a feral child—but the closest I'll ever come to one.

social environment the entire human environment, including direct contact with others

feral children children assumed to have been raised by animals, in the wilderness, isolated from other humans

just born that way"). Two psychologists, H. M. Skeels and H. B. Dye (1939), however, began to suspect a social cause.

For background on their experiment, Skeels (1966) provides this account of a "good" orphanage in Iowa during the 1930s, where he and Dye were consultants:

> Until about six months, they were cared for in the infant nursery. The babies were kept in standard hospital cribs that often had protective sheeting on the sides, thus effectively limiting visual stimulation; no toys or other objects were hung in the infants' line of vision. Human interactions were limited to busy nurses who, with the speed born of practice and necessity, changed diapers or bedding, bathed and medicated the infants, and fed them efficiently with propped bottles.

Perhaps, thought Skeels and Dye, the absence of stimulating social interaction was the problem, not some biological incapacity on the part of the children. To test their controversial idea, they selected thirteen infants whose mental retardation was so obvious that no one wanted to adopt them. They placed them in an institution for the mentally retarded. Each infant, then about 19 months old, was assigned to a separate ward of women ranging in mental age from 5 to 12 and in chronological age from 18 to 50. The women were pleased with this arrangement. Not only did they take care of the infants' physical needs—diapering, feeding, and so on—but also they loved to play with the children. They cuddled them and showered them with attention. They even competed to see which ward would have "its baby" walking or talking first. Each child had one woman who became

> particularly attached to him [or her] and figuratively "adopted" him [or her]. As a consequence, an intense one-to-one adult–child relationship developed, which was supplemented by the less intense but frequent interactions with the other adults in the environment. Each child had some one person with whom he [or she] was identified and who was particularly interested in him [or her] and his [or her] achievements. (Skeels 1966)

The researchers left a control group of twelve infants at the orphanage. These infants were also retarded, but they were considered higher in intelligence than the other thirteen. They received the usual care. Two and a half years later, Skeels and Dye tested all the children's intelligence. Their findings were startling: Those assigned to the retarded women had gained an average of 28 IQ points while those who remained in the orphanage had lost 30 points.

What happened after these children were grown? Did these initial differences matter? Twenty-one years later, Skeels and Dye did a follow-up study. Those in the control group who had remained in the orphanage had, on average, less than a third-grade education. Four still lived in state institutions, while the others held low-level jobs. Only two had married. In contrast, the average level of education for the thirteen individuals in the experimental group was twelve grades (about normal for that period). Five had completed one or more years of college. One had even gone to graduate school. Eleven had married. All thirteen were self-supporting or were homemakers (Skeels 1966). Apparently, then, one characteristic that we take for granted as being a basic "human" trait—high intelligence—depends on early, close relations with other humans.

A recent experiment in India confirms the Skeels and Dye research. Many of India's orphanages are similar to the ones that Skeels and Dye studied, dismal places where unattended children lie in bed all day.

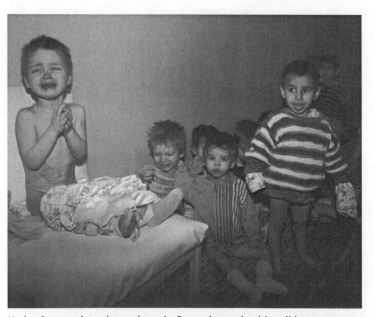

Under Communist rule, orphans in Romania received horrible treatment. (Some of the pictures are so gruesome that I prefer not to feature them in this text.) The children will carry emotional scars into adulthood. In severe cases, their treatment is likely to affect their ability to reason and to function as adults.

When experimenters added stimulating play and interaction to the children's activities, the children's motor skills improved and their IQs increased (Taneja et al. 2002).

Let's consider one other case, the story of Genie:

In 1970, California authorities found Genie, a 13-year-old girl who had been locked in a small room and tied to a chair since she was 20 months old. Apparently her father (70 years old when Genie was discovered) hated children, and probably had caused the death of two of Genie's siblings. Her 50-year-old mother was partially blind and frightened of her husband. Genie could not speak, did not know how to chew, was unable to stand upright, and could not straighten her hands and legs. On intelligence tests, she scored at the level of a 1-year-old. After intensive training, Genie learned to walk and use simple sentences (although they were garbled). As she grew up, her language remained primitive, she took anyone's property if it appealed to her, and she went to the bathroom wherever she wanted. At the age of 21, Genie went to live in a home for adults who cannot live alone. (Pines 1981)

IN SUM From Genie's pathetic story and from reports of institutionalized children, we can conclude that the basic human traits of intelligence and the ability to establish close bonds with others depend on early interaction with other humans. In addition, apparently there is a period prior to age 13 in which children must develop language and human bonding if they are to develop high intelligence and the ability to be sociable and follow social norms.

Deprived Animals

Finally, let's consider animals that have been deprived of normal interaction. In a series of experiments with rhesus monkeys, psychologists Harry and Margaret Harlow demonstrated the importance of early learning. The Harlows (1962) raised baby monkeys in isolation. They gave each monkey two artificial mothers, shown in the photo on this page. One "mother" was only a wire frame with a wooden head, but it did have a nipple from which the baby could nurse. The frame of the other "mother," which had no bottle, was covered with soft terrycloth. To obtain food, the baby monkeys nursed at the wire frame.

When the Harlows (1965) frightened the babies with a mechanical bear or dog, the babies did not run to the wire frame "mother." Instead, they would cling pathetically to their terrycloth "mother." The Harlows concluded that infant–mother bonding is not the result of feeding but, rather, to what they termed "intimate physical contact." To most of us, this phrase means cuddling.

The monkeys raised in isolation were never able to adjust to monkey life. Placed with other monkeys when they were grown, they didn't know how to participate in "monkey interaction"—to play and to engage in pretend fights—and the other monkeys rejected them. Neither did they know how to have sexual intercourse, despite futile attempts to do so. The experimenters designed a special device, which allowed some females to become pregnant. After giving birth, however, these monkeys were "ineffective, inadequate, and brutal mothers . . . [who] . . . struck their babies, kicked them, or crushed the babies against the cage floor."

In one of their many experiments, the Harlows isolated baby monkeys for different lengths of time. They found that when monkeys were isolated for shorter periods (about three months), they were able to overcome the effects of their isolation. Those isolated for six months or more, however, were unable to adjust to normal monkey life. As mentioned, they could not play or engage in pretend fights, and the other monkeys rejected them. In other words, the longer the period of isolation, the more difficult its effects

Like humans, monkeys need interaction to thrive. Those raised in isolation are unable to interact satisfactorily with others. In this photograph, we see one of the monkeys described in the text. Purposefully frightened by the experimenter, the monkey has taken refuge in the soft terrycloth draped over an artificial "mother."

are to overcome. In addition, a critical learning stage may exist: If that stage is missed, it may be impossible to compensate for what has been lost. This may have been the case with Genie.

Because humans are not monkeys, we must be careful about extrapolating from animal studies to human behavior. The Harlow experiments, however, support what we know about children who are reared in isolation.

IN SUM | **Society Makes Us Human.**   Apparently, babies do not develop "naturally" into human adults. Although their bodies grow, if children are reared in isolation, they become little more than big animals. Without the concepts that language provides, they can't experience or even grasp relationships between people (the "connections" we call brother, sister, parent, friend, teacher, and so on). And without warm, friendly interactions, they don't become "friendly" in the accepted sense of the term; nor do they cooperate with others. In short, it is through human contact that people learn to be members of the human community. This process by which we learn the ways of society (or of particular groups), called **socialization,** is what sociologists have in mind when they say "Society makes us human."

Socialization into the Self and Mind

At birth, we have no idea that we are separate beings. We don't even know that we are a he or she. How do we develop a **self,** our image of who we are? How do we develop our ability to reason? Let's see how this occurs.

Cooley and the Looking-Glass Self

Back in the 1800s, Charles Horton Cooley (1864–1929), a symbolic interactionist who taught at the University of Michigan, concluded that this unique aspect of "humanness" called the self is socially created. He said that *our sense of self develops from interaction with others.* Cooley (1902) coined the term **looking-glass self** to describe the process by which our sense of self develops. He summarized this idea in the following couplet:

> Each to each a looking-glass
> Reflects the other that doth pass.

The looking-glass self contains three elements:

1. *We imagine how we appear to those around us.* For example, we may think that others perceive us as witty or dull.
2. *We interpret others' reactions.* We come to conclusions about how others evaluate us. Do they like us for being witty? Do they dislike us for being dull?
3. *We develop a self-concept.* How we interpret others' reactions to us frames our feelings and ideas about ourselves. A favorable reflection in this *social mirror* leads to a positive self-concept; a negative reflection leads to a negative self-concept.

Note that the development of the self does *not* depend on accurate evaluations. Even if we grossly misinterpret how others think about us, those misjudgments become part of our self-concept. Note also that *although the self-concept begins in childhood, its development is an ongoing, lifelong process.* The three steps of the looking-glass self are a part of our everyday lives: As we monitor how others react to us, we continually modify the self. The self, then, is never a finished product—it is always in process, even into old age.

Mead and Role Taking

Another symbolic interactionist, George Herbert Mead (1863–1931), who taught at the University of Chicago, added that play is crucial to the development of a self. In play, children learn to **take the role of the other,** that is, to put themselves in someone else's

socialization the process by which people learn the characteristics of their group—the knowledge, skills, attitudes, values, and actions thought appropriate for them

self the unique human capacity of being able to see ourselves "from the outside"; the views we internalize of how others see us

looking-glass self a term coined by Charles Horton Cooley to refer to the process by which our self develops through internalizing others' reactions to us

taking the role of the other putting oneself in someone else's shoes; understanding how someone else feels and thinks and thus anticipating how that person will act

significant other an individual who significantly influences someone else's life

generalized other the norms, values, attitudes, and expectations of people "in general"; the child's ability to take the role of the generalized other is a significant step in the development of a self

shoes—to understand how someone else feels and thinks and to anticipate how that person will act.

Only gradually do children attain this ability (Mead 1934; Coser 1977). Psychologist John Flavel (1968) asked 8- and 14-year-olds to explain a board game to some children who were blindfolded and to others who were not. The 14-year-olds gave more detailed instructions to those who were blindfolded, but the 8-year-olds gave the same instructions to everyone. The younger children could not yet take the role of the other, while the older children could.

As they develop this ability, at first children are able to take only the role of **significant others,** individuals who significantly influence their lives, such as parents or siblings. By assuming their roles during play, such as dressing up in their parents' clothing, children cultivate the ability to put themselves in the place of significant others.

As the self gradually develops, children internalize the expectations of more and more people. The ability to take on roles eventually extends to being able to take the role of "the group as a whole." Mead used the term **generalized other** to refer to our perception of how people in general think of us.

Taking the role of others is essential if we are to become cooperative members of human groups—whether they be our family, friends, or co-workers. This ability allows us to modify our behavior by anticipating how others will react—something Genie never learned.

Learning to take the role of the other entails three stages (see Figure 3.1):

1. *Imitation.* Children under age 3 can only mimic others. They do not yet have a sense of self separate from others, and they can only imitate people's gestures and words. (This stage is actually not role taking, but it prepares the child for it.)
2. *Play.* During the second stage, from the age of about 3 to 6, children pretend to take the roles of specific people. They might pretend that they are a firefighter, a wrestler, a nurse, Supergirl, Xena, Spiderman, and so on. They also like costumes at this stage and enjoy dressing up in their parents' clothing, or tying a towel around their neck to "become" Spiderman or Wonder Woman.
3. *Games.* This third stage, organized play, or team games, coincides roughly with the early school years. The significance for the self is that to play these games the individual must be able to take multiple roles. One of Mead's favorite examples was that of a baseball game, in which each player must be able to take the role of all the other players. To play baseball, the child not only must know

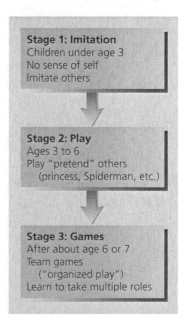

Figure 3.1 How We Learn to Take the Role of the Other: Mead's Three Stages

To help his students understand the term *generalized other,* Mead used baseball as an illustration. Why are team sports and organized games such excellent examples to use in explaining this concept?

Stage 1: Imitation
Children under age 3
No sense of self
Imitate others

Stage 2: Play
Ages 3 to 6
Play "pretend" others
   (princess, Spiderman, etc.)

Stage 3: Games
After about age 6 or 7
Team games
   ("organized play")
Learn to take multiple roles

SOCIALIZATION INTO THE SELF AND MIND **69**

his or her own role but also must be able to anticipate who will do what when the ball is hit or thrown.

Mead also said there were two parts of the self, the "I" and the "me." The "*I*" is *the self as subject,* the active, spontaneous, creative part of the self. In contrast, the "*me*" is *the self as object.* It is made up of attitudes we internalize from our interactions with others. Mead chose these pronouns because in English "I" is the active agent, as in "I shoved him," while "me" is the object of action, as in "He shoved me." Mead stressed that we are not passive in the socialization process. We are not like robots, passively absorbing the responses of others. Rather, our "I" is active. It evaluates the reactions of others and organizes them into a unified whole. Mead added that the "I" even monitors the "me," fine-tuning our actions to help us better match what others expect of us.

Mead also drew a conclusion that some find startling: *Not only the self but also the human mind is a social product.* Mead stressed that we cannot think without symbols. But where do these symbols come from? Only from society, which gives us our symbols by giving us language. If society did not provide the symbols, we would not be able to think, and thus would not possess what we call the mind. Mind, then, like language, is a product of society.

Mead analyzed *taking the role of the other* as an essential part of learning to be a full-fledged member of society. At first, we are able to take the role only of significant others, as this child is doing. Later we develop the capacity to take the role of the *generalized other,* which is essential not only for extended cooperation but also for the control of antisocial desires.

Piaget and the Development of Reasoning

An essential part of being human is the ability to reason. How do we learn this skill?

This question intrigued Jean Piaget (1896–1980), a Swiss psychologist who noticed that young children give similar wrong answers when they take intelligence tests. This might mean, he thought, that young children follow some sort of incorrect rule to figure out their answers. Perhaps children go through a natural process as they learn how to reason.

To find out, Piaget set up a laboratory where he could give children of different ages problems to solve (Piaget 1950, 1954; Flavel et al. 2002). After years of research, Piaget concluded that children go through four stages as they develop their ability to reason. (If you substitute "reasoning skills" for the term *operational* in the following explanations, Piaget's findings will be easier to understand.)

1. **The sensorimotor stage** (from birth to about age 2) During this stage, the infant's understanding is limited to direct contact with the environment—sucking, touching, listening, looking. Infants do not think in any sense that we understand. During the first part of this stage, they do not even know that their bodies are separate from the environment. Indeed, they have yet to discover that they have toes. Neither can infants recognize cause and effect. That is, they do not know that their actions cause something to happen.

2. **The preoperational stage** (from about age 2 to age 7) During this stage, children *develop the ability to use symbols.* However, they do not yet understand common concepts such as size, speed, or causation. Although they can count, they do not really understand what numbers mean. Nor do they yet have the ability to take the role of the other. Piaget asked preoperational children to describe a clay model of a mountain range. They did just fine. But when he asked them to describe how the mountain range looked from the perspective of a child who was sitting across from them, they couldn't do it. They could only repeat what they saw from their view.

3. **The concrete operational stage** (from the age of about 7 to 12) Although reasoning abilities are more developed, they remain *concrete.* Children can now understand numbers, causation, and speed, and they are able to take the role of the other and to participate in team games. Without concrete examples, however, they are unable to talk about concepts such as truth, honesty, or justice. They can explain why Jane's answer was a lie, but they cannot describe what truth itself is.

4. **The formal operational stage** (after the age of about 12) Children are now capable of abstract thinking. They can talk about concepts, come to conclusions based on general principles, and use rules to solve abstract problems. During this stage, children are likely to become young philosophers (Kagan 1984). If shown a photo of a slave, for example, a child at the concrete operational stage might

have said, "That's wrong!" However, a child at the formal operational stage is likely to add, "If our county was founded on equality, how could people have owned slaves?"

Global Aspects of the Self and Reasoning

Cooley's conclusions about the looking-glass self appear to be universal. So do Mead's conclusions about role taking and the mind as a social product, although researchers are finding that the self may develop earlier than Mead indicated. The stages of reasoning that Piaget identified are also probably universal, but researchers have found that the ages at which individuals enter the stages differ from one person to another, and that the stages are not as distinct as Piaget concluded (Flavel et al. 2002). Even during the sensorimotor stage, for example, children show early signs of reasoning, which may indicate an innate ability that is wired into the brain. Although Piaget's theory is being refined, his contribution remains: *A basic structure underlies the way we develop reasoning, and children all over the world begin with the concrete and move to the abstract.*

Interestingly, some people seem to get stuck in the concreteness of the third stage and never reach the fourth stage of abstract thinking (Kohlberg and Gilligan 1971; Suizzo 2000). College, for example, nurtures the fourth stage, and most people without this experience apparently have less ability for abstract thought. Social experiences, then, can modify these stages. Also, there is much that we don't yet know about how culture influences the way we think, a topic explored in the Cultural Diversity box below.

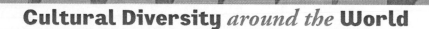

Cultural Diversity *around the* World

WHICH TWO OF THESE ITEMS GO together: a panda, a monkey, and a banana? Please answer before you read further.

You probably said the panda and the monkey. Both are animals, while the banana is a fruit. This is logical.

At least this is the logic of Westerners, and it is difficult for us to see how the answer could be anything else. Someone from Japan, however, is likely to reply that the monkey and the banana go together.

Why? Whereas Westerners typically see categories (animals and fruit), Asians typically see relationships (monkeys eat bananas).

In one study, Japanese and U.S. students were shown a picture of an aquarium that contained one big, fast-moving fish and several smaller fish, along with plants, a rock, and bubbles. Later, when the students were asked what they had seen, the Japanese students were 60 percent more likely to remember background elements. They also referred more to relationships, such as the "the little pink fish was in front of the blue rock."

The students were also shown 96 objects and asked which of them had been in the picture. The Japanese students did much better at remembering when the object was shown in its original surroundings. The U.S. students, in

Do You See What I See? Eastern and Western Ways of Perceiving and Thinking

The World

contrast, had not noticed the background.

Westerners pay more attention to the focal object, in this case the fish, while Asians are more attuned to the overall surroundings. The implications of this difference run deep: Easterners attribute less causation to actors and more to context, while Westerners minimize the context and place greater emphasis on individual actors.

Differences in how Westerners and Easterners perceive the world and think about it are just being uncovered. We know practically nothing about how these differences originate. *Because these initial findings indicate deep, culturally based, fundamental differences in perception and thinking,* this should prove to be a fascinating area of research.

for your Consideration

In our global village, differences in perception and thinking can have potentially devastating effects. Consider a crisis between the United States and North Korea. How might Easterners and Westerners see the matter differently? How might they attribute cause differently and, without knowing it, "talk past one another"?

Source: Based on Nisbett 2003.

Learning Personality, Morality, and Emotions

Vital for the type of people that we become are our personality, morality, and emotions. Let's look at how we learn these essential aspects of our being.

Freud and the Development of Personality

Along with the development of our mind and the self comes the development of our personality. Sigmund Freud (1856–1939) developed a theory of the origin of personality that has had a major impact on Western thought. Freud was a physician in Vienna in the early 1900s who founded *psychoanalysis,* a technique for treating emotional problems through long-term, intensive exploration of the subconscious mind. Let's look at his theory.

Freud believed that personality consists of three elements. Each child is born with the first element, an **id,** Freud's term for inborn drives that cause us to seek self-gratification. The id of the newborn is evident in its cries of hunger or pain. The pleasure-seeking id operates throughout life. It demands the immediate fulfillment of basic needs: attention, food, safety, sex, and so on.

The id's drive for immediate gratification, however, runs into a roadblock: primarily the needs of other people, especially those of the parents. To adapt to these constraints, a second component of the personality emerges, which Freud called the ego. The **ego** is the balancing force between the id and the demands of society that suppress it. The ego also serves to balance the id and the **superego,** the third component of the personality, more commonly called the *conscience.*

The superego represents *culture within us,* the norms and values we have internalized from our social groups. As the *moral* component of the personality, the superego provokes feelings of guilt or shame when we break social rules, or pride and self-satisfaction when we follow them.

According to Freud, when the id gets out of hand, we follow our desires for pleasure and break society's norms. When the superego gets out of hand, we become overly rigid in following those norms, finding ourselves bound in a straitjacket of rules that inhibit our lives. The ego, the balancing force, tries to prevent either the superego or the id from dominating. In the emotionally healthy individual, the ego succeeds in balancing these conflicting demands of the id and the superego. In the maladjusted individual, however, the ego fails to control the inherent conflict between the id and the superego. Either the id or the superego dominates this person, leading to internal confusion and problem behaviors.

Sociological Evaluation   Sociologists appreciate Freud's emphasis on socialization—that the social group into which we are born transmits norms and values that restrain our biological drives. Sociologists, however, object to the view that inborn and subconscious motivations are the primary reasons for human behavior. *This denies the central principle of sociology:* that factors such as social class (income, education, and occupation) and people's roles in groups underlie their behavior (Epstein 1988; Bush and Simmons 1990).

Feminist sociologists have been especially critical of Freud. Although what we just summarized applies to both females and males, Freud assumed that what is "male" is "normal." He even said that females are inferior, castrated males (Chodorow 1990; Gerhard 2000). It is obvious that sociologists need to research how we develop personality.

Kohlberg, Gilligan, and the Development of Morality

If you have observed young children, you know that they focus on immediate gratification and show little or no concern for others. ("Mine!" a 2-year-old will shout, as she grabs a toy from another child.) Yet, at a later age this same child will become considerate of others and concerned with moral issues. How does this change happen?

Kohlberg's Theory   Psychologist Lawrence Kohlberg (1975, 1984, 1986; Walsh 2000) concluded that we go through a sequence of stages as we develop morality. Building on Piaget's work, he found that children begin in the *amoral stage* I just described. For them,

id Freud's term for our inborn basic drives

ego Freud's term for a balancing force between the id and the demands of society

superego Freud's term for the conscience, the internalized norms and values of our social groups

there is no right or wrong, just personal needs to be satisfied. From about ages 7 to 10, children are in what Kohlberg called a *preconventional stage.* They have learned rules, and they follow them to stay out of trouble. They view right and wrong as what pleases or displeases their parents, friends, and teachers. Their concern is to avoid punishment. At about age 10, they enter the *conventional stage.* At this stage, morality means to follow the norms and values they have learned. In the *postconventional stage,* which Kohlberg says most people don't reach, individuals reflect on abstract principles of right and wrong and judge a behavior according to these principles.

Gilligan and Gender Differences in Morality   Carol Gilligan, another psychologist, grew uncomfortable with Kohlberg's conclusions. They didn't seem to match her own experience, and she noted that Kohlberg had used only boys in his studies. More women had become social scientists by this point, and they were questioning an assumption of male researchers—that female subjects were not necessary, for the results of research with boys would apply to girls as well.

Gilligan (1982, 1990) decided to find out if there were differences in how men and women looked at morality. After interviewing about 200 men and women, she concluded that women are more likely to evaluate morality in terms of *personal relationships.* They want to know how an action affects others. They are more concerned with personal loyalties and with the harm that might come to loved ones. Men, in contrast, tend to think more along the lines of *abstract principles* that define what is right or wrong. An act either matches or violates a code of ethics, and personal relationships have little to do with the matter.

Researchers tested Gilligan's conclusions. They found that *both* men and women use personal relationships and abstract principles when they make moral judgments (Wark and Krebs 1996). Because of this, Gilligan no longer supports her original position (Brannon 1999). The matter is not yet settled, however, for some researchers have found differences in how men and women make moral judgments (White 1999; Jaffee and Hyde 2000).

As with personality, in this vital area of human development, sociological research is also notably absent.

Socialization into Emotions

Emotions, too, are an essential aspect of who we become. Sociologists who research this area of our "humanness" find that emotions are not simply the results of biology. Like the mind, emotions also depend on socialization (Hochschild 1975; 1983; Reiser 1999; Barbalet 2002). This may sound strange. Don't all people get angry? Doesn't everyone cry? Don't we all feel guilt, shame, sadness, happiness, fear? What has socialization to do with emotions?

Global Emotions   At first, it may look as though socialization is not relevant. Paul Ekman (1980), an anthropologist, studied emotions in several countries. He concluded that everyone experiences six basic emotions: anger, disgust, fear, happiness, sadness, and surprise—and we all show the same facial expressions when we feel these emotions. A person from Zimbabwe, for example, could tell from just the look on an American's face that she is angry, disgusted, or fearful, and we could tell from the Zimbabwean's face that he is happy, sad, or surprised. Because we all show the same facial expressions when we experience these six emotions, Ekman concluded that they are built into our biology, "a product of our genes."

Expressing Emotions   The existence of universal facial expressions for these basic emotions does *not* mean that socialization has no effect on how we express them. Facial expressions are only one way in which we show emotions. Other ways vary with gender. For example, U.S. women are allowed to express their emotions more freely, while U.S. men are expected to be more reserved. To express sudden happiness, or a delighted surprise, for example, women are allowed to make "squeals of glee" in public places. Men are not. Such an expression would be a fundamental violation of their gender role.

Then there are culture, social class, and relationships. Consider culture. Two close Japanese friends who meet after a long separation don't shake hands or hug—they bow. Two Arab men will kiss. Social class is also significant, for it cuts across many other lines, even gender. Upon seeing a friend after a long absence, upper-class women and men are likely to be more reserved in expressing their delight than are lower-class women and men.

Relationships also make a big difference. We express our emotions more openly if we are with close friends, more guardedly if we are at a staff meeting with the corporate CEO. A good part of childhood socialization centers on learning these "norms of emotion"—how to express our emotions in a variety of settings.

What We Feel   The matter goes deeper than this. Socialization not only leads to different ways of expressing emotions, but it even affects *what* we feel (Clark 1997; Shields 2002). People in one culture may even learn to experience feelings that are unknown in another culture. For example, the Ifaluk, who live on the Western Caroline Islands of Micronesia, use the word *fago* to refer to the feelings they have when they see someone suffer. This comes close to what we call sympathy or compassion. But the Ifaluk also use this term to refer to what they feel when they are with someone who has high status, someone they highly respect or admire (Kagan 1984). To us, these are two distinct emotions, and they require separate terms.

For a glimpse of a culture in which emotions, values, and behaviors are shockingly different from those we expect, see the Down-to-Earth Sociology box below.

Down-to-Earth Sociology

Signs of the Times: Are We Becoming Ik?

ANTHROPOLOGIST COLIN TURNBULL (1972/1995) studied the Ik, a once-proud nomadic people in northern Uganda whose traditional hunting lands were seized by the government. Devastated by drought, hunger, and starvation, the Ik turned to extreme individualism in which selfishness, emotional numbness, and lack of concern for others reign supreme. Their society has become a passionless, numbed association of individuals, in which the only good is the pursuit of food.

Imagine, for a moment, that you are born into the Ik tribe. At the tender age of 3 or 4, your parents push you out of the hut. From then on, you are on your own. You can sleep in the village courtyard, and, with permission, you can sit in the doorway of your parents' house, but you may not lie down or sleep there.

There is no school. No church. Nothing from this point in your life that even comes close to what we call family. You join a group of children aged 3 to 7. The weakest soon die, for only the strongest survive. Later, you join a band of 8- to 12-year-olds. At 12 or 13, you split off by yourself.

You learn from what you see going on around you, and here you see coldness. The men hunt, but game is scarce. If they get anything, they refuse to bring it back to their families. They say, "Each of them is seeing what he can get for himself. Do you think they will bring any back for me?"

You also see cruelty. When blind Lo'ono trips and rolls to the bottom of the ravine, the adults laugh as she lies on her back, feebly thrashing her arms and legs. When Lolim begs his son to let him in, pleading that he is going to die in a few hours, Longoli drives him away. Lolim dies alone.

The Ik children learn their lesson well: Selfishness is good, survival is all that counts. But the children add a childish glee to the adults' dispassionate coldness. When blind Lolim took ill, the children teased him, stooping in front of him and laughing as he fell. His grandson crept up and drummed on the old man's bald head with a pair of sticks.

Then there was little Adupa, who managed, for a while, to maintain a sense of awe at what life had to offer. When Adupa found food, she would hold it in her hand, looking at it with wonder and delight. As she raised her hand to her mouth, the other children would jump on her, laughing as they took the food away from her and beat her.

for your Consideration

The Ik provide another example of the theme of this chapter, that characteristics we take to be uniquely human are not inherent in humanity. Rather, they arise from society. As such, they can be lost if the sense of identification (community) that lies at the basis of society breaks down.

It is easy to criticize members of another society if you don't have to walk in their shoes, so let's turn the critical lens on our own society. Consider how people are treated like things—discarded when they are no longer needed. Corporations fire older workers because they can pay younger ones less. They relocate factories to countrires where labor is cheaper, leaving hundreds and even thousands of workers without jobs. CEOs just shrug their shoulders and say, "That's business." For the sake of higher salaries, people move to other states, severing their ties with kin and community. Executives callously discard same-age spouses, the co-parent of their own children, in exchange for younger, more photogenic "trophy" mates.

Finally, consider how undervalued are the qualities we would wish for in friends and family—kindness, generosity, patience, tolerance, cooperation, and compassion. If a job requires such talents, it is low in pay and prestige (Maybury-Lewis 1995).

Research Needed Although Ekman identified only six emotions that are universal in feeling and facial expression, I suspect that other emotions are common to people around the world—and that everyone shows similar facial expressions when they experience them. I suggest that feelings of helplessness, despair, confusion, and shock are among these universal emotions. We need cross-cultural research to find out whether this is so. We also need research into how children learn to feel and express emotions.

Society Within Us: The Self and Emotions as Social Control

Much of our socialization is intended to turn us into conforming members of society. Socialization into the self and emotions is an essential part of this process, for both the self and our emotions mold our behavior. Although we like to think that we are "free," consider for a moment just some of the factors that influence how we act: the expectations of friends and parents, or neighbors and teachers; classroom norms and college rules; city, state, and federal laws. For example, if in a moment of intense frustration, or out of a devilish desire to shock people, you wanted to tear off your clothes and run naked down the street, what would stop you?

The answer is your socialization—*society within you*. Your experiences in society have resulted in a self that thinks along certain lines and feels particular emotions. This helps to keep you in line. Thoughts such as "Would I get kicked out of school?" and "What would my friends (parents) think if they found out?" represent an awareness of the self in relationship to others. So does the desire to avoid feelings of shame and embarrassment. Our *social mirror*, then—the result of being socialized into a self and emotions—sets up effective controls over our behavior. In fact, socialization into self and emotions is so effective that some people feel embarrassed just thinking about running nude in public!

IN SUM Socialization is essential for our development as human beings. From interaction with others, we learn how to think, reason, and feel. The net result is to shape our behavior—including our thinking and emotions—according to cultural standards. This is what sociologists mean when they refer to "*society within us.*"

Socialization into Gender

To channel our behavior—including our thinking and emotions—along expected avenues, society also uses **gender socialization.** By expecting different attitudes and behaviors from us *because* we are male or female, the human group nudges boys and girls in separate directions in life. This foundation of contrasting attitudes and behaviors is so thorough that, as adults, most of us act, think, and even feel according to our culture's guidelines of what is appropriate for our sex.

The significance of gender is emphasized throughout this book, and we focus specifically on gender in Chapter 11. For now, though, let's briefly consider some of the "gender messages" that we get from our family and the mass media.

Gender Messages in the Family

Our parents are the first significant others who teach us our role in this fundamental symbolic division of the world. Sometimes they do so consciously, perhaps by bringing into play pink and blue, colors that have no meaning in themselves but that are now associated with gender. Our parents' own gender orientations have become so firmly embedded that they do most of this teaching without being aware of what they are doing.

This is illustrated by a classic study done by psychologists Susan Goldberg and Michael Lewis (1969), whose results have been confirmed by other researchers (Fagot et al. 1985; Connors 1996).

gender socialization the ways in which society sets children onto different courses in life *because* they are male or female

Goldberg and Lewis asked mothers to bring their 6-month-old infants into their laboratory, supposedly to observe the infants' development. Covertly, however, they also observed the mothers. They found that the mothers kept their daughters closer to them. They also touched their daughters more and spoke to them more frequently than they did to their sons.

By the time the children were 13 months old, the girls stayed closer to their mothers during play, and they returned to their mothers sooner and more often than the boys did. When Goldberg and Lewis set up a barrier to separate the children from their mothers, who were holding toys, the girls were more likely to cry and motion for help; the boys, to try to climb over the barrier.

Goldberg and Lewis concluded that in our society mothers subconsciously reward daughters for being passive and dependent, and sons for being active and independent.

These lessons continue throughout childhood. On the basis of their sex, children are given different kinds of toys. Boys are more likely to get guns and "action figures" that destroy enemies. Girls are more likely to get dolls and jewelry. Some parents try to choose "gender neutral" toys, but kids know what is popular, and they feel left out if they don't have what the other kids have. The significance of toys in gender socialization can be summarized this way: Almost all parents would be upset if someone gave their son Barbie dolls.

Parents also let their preschool sons roam farther from home than their preschool daughters, and they subtly encourage the boys to participate in more rough-and-tumble play. They expect their sons to get dirtier and to be more defiant, their daughters to be daintier and more compliant (Gilman 1911/1971; Henslin 2005c). In large part, they get what they expect. Such experiences in socialization lie at the heart of the sociological explanation of male–female differences.

The family is a primary source of our socialization into gender. Shown here is a woman from the Kpelle tribe in Liberia as she pounds palm fruit. What gender messages do you think these children are learning from their mother?

We should note, however, that some sociologists would consider biology to be the cause, proposing that Goldberg and Lewis were simply observing innate differences in the children. In short, were the mothers creating those behaviors (the boys wanting to get down and play more, and the girls wanting to be hugged more), or were they responding to natural differences in their children? It is similarly the case with toys. In an intriguing experiment with monkeys, researchers discovered that male monkeys prefer cars and balls more than do female monkeys, who are more likely to prefer dolls and pots (Alexander and Hines 2002). We shall return to this controversial issue of nature versus nurture in Chapter 11.

Gender Messages from Peers

Sociologists stress how this sorting process that begins in the family is reinforced as the child is exposed to other aspects of society. Of those other influences, one of the most powerful is the **peer group**, individuals of roughly the same age who are linked by common interests. Examples of peer groups are friends, classmates, and "the kids in the neighbor-

76 CHAPTER 3 SOCIALIZATION

hood." Consider how girls and boys teach one another what it means to be a female or a male in U.S. society.

Let's eavesdrop on a conversation between two eighth-grade girls studied by sociologist Donna Eder (2005). You can see how these girls are reinforcing images of appearance and behavior that they think are appropriate for females:

CINDY: The only thing that makes her look anything is all the makeup . . .

PENNY: She had a picture, and she's standing like this. (Poses with one hand on her hip and one by her head)

CINDY: Her face is probably this skinny, but it looks that big 'cause of all the makeup she has on it.

PENNY: She's ugly, ugly, ugly.

Boys, of course, also reinforce cultural expectations of gender (Pascoe 2003). When sociologist Melissa Milkie (1994) studied junior high school boys, she found that much of their talk centered on movies and TV programs. Of the many images they saw, the boys would single out sex and violence. They would amuse one another by repeating lines, acting out parts, and joking and laughing at what they had seen.

If you know boys in their early teens, you've probably seen behavior like this. You may have been amused, or even have shaken your head in disapproval. As a sociologist, however, Milkie peered beneath the surface. She concluded that the boys were using media images to discover who they are as males. They had gotten the message: To be a "real" male is to be obsessed with sex and violence. Not to joke and laugh about murder and promiscuous sex would have marked a boy as a "weenie," a label to be avoided at all costs.

Gender Messages in the Mass Media

Another powerful influence is the **mass media,** forms of communication that are directed to large audiences. Let's look at how images in advertising, television, and video games reinforce **gender roles,** the behaviors and attitudes considered appropriate for our sex.

Advertising Advertising bombards us so greatly that the average U.S. child watches about 20,000 commercials a year (Witt 2000). Commercials aimed at children are more likely to show girls as cooperative and boys as aggressive. They also are more likely to show girls at home and boys in other locations (Larson 2001). Girls are also more likely to be portrayed as giggly and less capable at tasks (Browne 1998). When advertising directed at adults portrays men as dominant and rugged and women as sexy and submissive, it perpetuates similar stereotypes.

The result is a spectrum of stereotypical, culturally molded images. At one end of this spectrum are cowboys who roam the wide open spaces, while at the other end are scantily clad women, whose assets are intended to sell a variety of products, from automobiles to hamburgers. The portrayal of women with unrealistic physical assets makes women feel inadequate (Kilbourne 2003). This, of course, creates demand for an array of products that promise physical enhancement and romantic success.

Television Television reinforces stereotypes of the sexes. On prime-time television, male characters outnumber female characters. Male characters are also more likely to be portrayed in higher-status positions (Glascock 2001). Sports news also maintains traditional stereotypes. Sociologists who studied the content of televised sports news in Los Angeles found that women athletes receive little coverage (Messner et al. 2003). When they do, they are sometimes trivialized by men newscasters who focus on humorous events in

peer group a group of individuals of roughly the same age who are linked by common interests

mass media forms of communication, such as radio, newspapers, and television that are directed to mass audiences

gender role the behaviors and attitudes considered appropriate because one is a female or a male

Sports are a powerful agent of socialization. That suma wrestling teaches a form of masculinity should be apparent from this photo. What else do you think these boys are learning?

women's sports or turn the woman athlete into a sexual object. Newscasters even manage to emphasize breasts and bras and to engage in locker-room humor.

Stereotype-breaking characters, in contrast, are a sign of changing times. On comedies, women are more verbally aggressive than men (Glascock 2001). The path-breaking program, *Xena, Warrior Princess,* a television series imported from New Zealand, portrayed Xena as super dominant. The powers of the teenager *Buffy, The Vampire Slayer,* were also remarkable. On *Alias,* Sydney Bristow exhibits extraordinary strength. In cartoons, Kim Possible divides her time between cheerleading practice and saving the world from evil, while, also with tongue in cheek, the Powerpuff Girls are touted as "the most elite kindergarten crime-fighting force ever assembled." This new gender portrayal continues in a variety of programs, such as *Totally Spies.*

The gender messages on these programs are mixed. Girls are powerful, but they have to be skinny and gorgeous and wear the latest fashions, too. An impossible setup.

Video Games The popularity of video games has surged, and the average American now spends 75 hours a year playing video games (Dee 2003). Even one-fourth of 4- to 6-year-olds play them for an average of an hour a day (Rideout and Vandewater 2003). College students, especially men, relieve stress by escaping into video games (Jones 2003).

Although sociologists have begun to study how the sexes are portrayed in video games, their influence on the players' ideas of gender is unknown (Dietz 2000; Berger 2002). On the cutting edge of technology, some of these games reflect cutting-edge changes in sex roles, the topic of the Mass Media in Social Life box on the next page.

IN SUM All of us are born into a society in which "male" and "female" are significant symbols. Sorted into separate groups from early childhood, girls and boys learn different ideas of what to expect of themselves and of one another. These gender messages, first transmitted by the family, are reinforced by other social institutions. Each of us learns the meaning that our society associates with the sexes. These images become integrated into our views of the world, forming a picture of "how" males and females "are," and forcing an interpretation of the world in terms of gender. Because gender serves as a primary basis for **social inequality**—giving privileges and obligations to one group of people while denying them to another—gender images are especially important to understand.

Agents of Socialization

People and groups that influence our orientations to life—our self-concept, emotions, attitudes, and behavior—are called **agents of socialization.** We have already considered how three of these agents—the family, our peers, and the mass media—influence our ideas of gender. Now we'll look more closely at how agents of socialization prepare us to take our place in society. We shall first consider the family, then the neighborhood, religion, day care, school and peers, sports, and the workplace.

The Family

Around the world, the first group to have a major impact on us is our family. Our experiences in the family are so intense that they have a lifelong influence on us. They lay down our basic sense of self, establishing our initial motivations, values, and beliefs. The family gives us ideas about who we are and what we deserve out of life. It is in the family that we begin to think of ourselves as strong or weak, smart or dumb, good-looking or ugly—or somewhere in between. And as already noted, here we begin the lifelong process of defining ourselves as female or male.

Subtle Socialization To study this process, sociologists have observed parents and young children in public settings, where the act of observing does not interfere with the interaction. Researchers using this unobtrusive technique have noted what they call the *stroller effect* (Mitchell et al. 1992). When a child is in a stroller, the father is likely to be the one who pushes the stroller. If the child is out of the stroller, the mother is likely to push the empty stroller while the father carries the child. In this and countless ways,

social inequality a social condition in which privileges and obligations are given to some but denied to others

agents of socialization people or groups that affect our self-concept, attitudes, behaviors, or other orientations toward life

From Xena, Warrior Princess, to Lara Croft, Tomb Raider: Changing Images of Women in the Mass Media

The mass media reflect women's changing role in society. Portrayals of women as passive, as subordinate, or as mere background objects remain, but a new image has broken through. Although this new image exaggerates changes, it also illustrates a fundamental change in gender relations. As is mentioned in the text, Xena, the Warrior Princess is an outstanding example of this change.

Like books and magazines, video games are made available to a mass audience. And with digital advances, they have crossed the line from what is traditionally thought of as games to something that more closely resembles interactive movies. Costing an average of $10 million to produce and another $10 million to market, video games now have intricate subplots and use celebrity voices for the characters (Nussenbaum 2004).

Sociologically, what is significant is that the *content* of video games socializes their users. As they play, gamers are exposed not only to action but also to ideas and images. The gender images of video games communicate powerful messages, just as they do in other forms of the mass media.

Lara Croft, an adventure-seeking archeologist and star of *Tomb Raider* and its many sequels, is the essence of the new gender image. Lara is smart, strong, and able to utterly vanquish foes. With both guns blazing, she is the cowboy of the

The mass media not only reflect gender stereotypes but also they play a role in changing them. Sometimes they do both simultaneously. The images of Xena, Warrior Princess, and of Lara Croft not only reflect women's changing role in society, but also, by exaggerating the change, they mold new stereotypes.

twenty-first century, the term *cowboy* being purposefully chosen, as Lara breaks stereotypical gender roles and dominates what previously was the domain of men. She was the first female protagonist in a field of muscle-rippling, gun-toting macho caricatures (Taylor 1999).

Yet the old remains powerfully encapsulated in the new. As the photo on this page makes evident, Lara is a fantasy girl for young men of the digital generation. No matter her foe, no matter her predicament, Lara oozes sex. Her form-fitting outfits, which flatter her voluptuous physique, reflect the mental images of the men who fashioned this digital character.

Lara has caught young men's fancy to such an extent that they have bombarded corporate headquarters with questions about her personal life. Lara is the star of two movies and a comic book. There is even a Lara Croft candy bar.

for your Consideration

A sociologist who reviewed this text said, "It seems that for women to be defined as equal, we have to become symbolic males—warriors with breasts." Why is gender change mostly one-way—females adopting traditional male characteristics? To see why men get to keep their gender roles, these two questions should help: Who is moving into the traditional territory of the other? Do people prefer to imitate power or powerlessness?

Finally, consider just how far stereotypes have actually been left behind. The ultimate goal of the video game, after foes are vanquished, is to see Lara in a nightie.

---

parents send their children subtle gender messages. Most of the ways that parents teach their children about expected differences between men and women involve nonverbal cues, not specific instruction.

This photo captures an extreme form of family socialization. The father seems to be more emotionally involved in the goal—and in more pain—than his daughter, as he pushes her toward the finish line in the Teen Tours of America Kid's Triathlon.

The Family and Social Class   One of the main findings of sociologists concerns the way socialization depends on a family's social class. In a study of how working-class and middle-class parents rear their children, sociologist Melvin Kohn (1959, 1963, 1976, 1977; Kohn et al. 1986) found that working-class parents are mainly concerned that their children stay out of trouble. They also tend to use physical punishment. Middle-class parents, in contrast, focus more on developing their children's curiosity, self-expression, and self-control. They are more likely to reason with their children than to use physical punishment.

These findings were a sociological puzzle. Just why would working-class and middle-class parents rear their children so differently? Kohn knew that life experiences of some sort held the key, and he found that key in the world of work. Bosses usually tell blue-collar workers exactly what to do. Since blue-collar parents expect their children's lives to be like theirs, they stress obedience. At their work, in contrast, middle-class parents take more initiative. Expecting their children to work at similar jobs, middle-class parents socialize them into the qualities they have found valuable.

Kohn was still puzzled, for some working-class parents act more like middle-class parents, and vice versa. As Kohn probed this puzzle, the pieces fell into place. The key was the parents' type of job. Middle-class office workers, for example, are closely supervised, and Kohn found that they follow the working-class pattern of child rearing, emphasizing conformity. And some blue-collar workers, such as those who do home repairs, have a good deal of freedom. These workers follow the middle-class model in rearing their children (Pearlin and Kohn 1966; Kohn and Schooler 1969).

Working-class and middle-class parents also have different views of how children develop, which has interesting consequences for children's play (Lareau 2002). Working-class parents think of children as developing naturally, while middle-class parents think that children need a lot of guidance to develop correctly. As a result, working-class parents see their job as providing food, shelter, and comfort, with the child's development taking care of itself. They set limits ("Don't go near the railroad tracks"), and let their children play as they wish. Middle-class parents, in contrast, want their children's play to develop knowledge and social skills. For example, they may want them to play baseball, not for the enjoyment of playing ball, but to help them learn how to be team players.

The Neighborhood

As all parents know, some neighborhoods are better for their children than others. Parents try to move to those neighborhoods—if they can afford them. Their commonsense evaluations are borne out by sociological research. Children from poor neighborhoods are more likely to get in trouble with the law, to become pregnant, to drop out of school, and even to have worse mental health in later life (Wilson 1987; Brooks-Gunn et al. 1997; Sampson et al. 2001; Wheaton and Clarke 2003).

Sociologists have also documented that the residents of more affluent neighborhoods watch out for the children more than do the residents of poor neighborhoods (Sampson et al. 1999). This isn't because the adults in poor neighborhoods care less about children. Rather, the more affluent neighborhoods have less transition, so the adults are more likely to know the local children and their parents. This better equips them to help keep the children safe and out of trouble.

Religion

By influencing values, religion becomes a key component in people's ideas of right and wrong. Religion is so important to Americans that 65 percent belong to a local congregation, and during a typical week, two of every five Americans attend a religious service (*Statistical Abstract* 2003:Table 80). Religion is significant even for people who are reared in nonreligious homes—religious ideas pervade U.S. society, providing basic ideas of morality for us all.

The influence of religion extends to many areas of our lives. For example, participation in religious services teaches us not only beliefs about the hereafter but also ideas about what kinds of dress, speech, and manners are appropriate for formal occasions. Religion is so significant that we shall examine its influence in a separate chapter (Chapter 18).

Day Care

It is rare for social science research to make national news, but occasionally it does. This is what happened when researchers who had followed 1,300 children in ten cities from infancy into kindergarten reported their findings. They had observed the children both at home and at day care. (*Day care* was defined as any care other than by the mother—including care by other relatives and the father.) The researchers had also videotaped and made detailed notes on the children's interaction with their mothers (National Institute of Child Health and Human Development 1999; Guensburg 2001). What caught the media's attention? Children who spend more hours in day care have weaker bonds with their mothers. In addition, they are more likely to fight, to be cruel, and to be "mean." In contrast, children who spend less time in day care are more cooperative and more affectionate to their mothers. This holds true regardless of the quality of the day care, the family's social class, or whether the child is a girl or a boy.

This study was designed well, and its findings are without dispute. But how do we explain these findings? The cause could be time spent in day care. The researchers suggest that mothers who spend less time with their children are less responsive to their children's emotional needs because they are less familiar with their children's "signaling systems." But maybe the cause isn't day care. Perhaps mothers who put their children in day care for more hours are less sensitive to their children in the first place. Or perhaps employed mothers are less likely to meet their children's emotional needs because they are more tired and stressed than mothers who stay at home. From this study, we can't determine the cause of the weaker bonding and the behavioral problems.

These researchers also uncovered a positive side to day care. They found that children who spend more hours in day care score higher on language tests (Guensburg 2001). Other researchers have found similar improvement in language skills, especially for children from low-income homes, as well as those from dysfunctional families—those with alcoholic, inept, or abusive parents (Scarr and Eisenberg 1993). As is obvious, we need more studies to be able to understand the influences of day care. Although this longitudinal study is far from encouraging, it gives us no reason to conclude that day care is producing a generation of "mean but smart" children.

The School

Part of the **manifest function,** or *intended* purpose, of formal education is to transmit knowledge and skills, such as reading, writing, and arithmetic. The transmission of such skills is certainly part of socialization, but so are the schools' **latent functions,** its *unintended* consequences that help the social system. Let's look at this less visible aspect of education.

At home, children learn attitudes and values that match their family's situation in life. At school, they learn a broader perspective that helps prepare them to take a role in the world beyond the family. At home, for example, a child may have been the almost exclusive focus of doting parents, but in school, the child learns *universality*—that the same rules apply to everyone, regardless of who their parents are or how special they may be at home. The Cultural Diversity box on the next page explores how these new values and ways of looking at the world sometimes even replace those the child learns at home.

manifest functions the intended beneficial consequences of people's actions

latent functions unintended beneficial consequences of people's actions

Cultural Diversity *in the* United States

Caught Between Two Worlds

IT IS A STRUGGLE TO LEARN a new culture, for its behaviors and ways of thinking contrast with the ones already learned. This can lead to inner turmoil. One way to handle the conflict is to cut ties with your first culture. This, however, can create a sense of loss, perhaps one that is recognized only later in life.

Richard Rodriguez, a literature professor and essayist, was born to working-class Mexican immigrants. Wanting their son to be successful in their adopted land, his parents named him Richard instead of Ricardo. While his English-Spanish hybrid name indicates the parents' aspirations for their son, it was also an omen of the conflict that Richard would experience.

Like other children of Mexican immigrants, Richard's first language was Spanish—a rich mother tongue that introduced him to the world. Until the age of 5, when he began school, Richard knew only fifty words in English. He describes what happened when he began school:

The change came gradually but early. When I was beginning grade school, I noted to myself the fact that the classroom environment was so different in its styles and assumptions from my own family environment that survival would essentially entail a choice between both worlds. When I became a student, I was literally "remade"; neither I nor my teachers considered anything I had known before as relevant. I had to forget most of what my culture had provided, because to remember it was a disadvantage. The past and its cultural values became detachable, like a piece of clothing grown heavy on a warm day and finally put away.

As happened to millions of immigrants before him, whose parents spoke German, Polish, Italian, and so on, learning English eroded family and class ties and ate away at his ethnic roots. For him, language and education were not simply devices that eased the transition to the dominant culture. Instead, they slashed at the roots that had given him life.

To face conflicting cultures is to confront a fork in the road. Some turn one way and withdraw from the new culture—a clue that helps to explain why so many Latinos drop out of U.S. schools. Others go in the opposite direction. Cutting ties with their family and cultural roots, they wholeheartedly adopt the new culture.

Rodriguez took the second road. He excelled in his new language—so well, in fact, that he graduated from Stanford University and then became a graduate student in English at the University of California at Berkeley. He was even awarded a prestigious Fulbright fellowship to study English Renaissance literature at the British Museum.

But the past wouldn't let Rodriguez alone. Prospective employers were impressed with his knowledge of Renaissance literature. At job interviews, however, they would skip over the Renaissance training and ask him if he would teach the Mexican novel and be an adviser to Latino students. Rodriguez was also haunted by the image of his grandmother, the warmth of the culture he had left behind, and the language and thought to which he had become a stranger.

Richard Rodriguez represents millions of immigrants—not just those of Latino origin but those from other cultures, too—who want to be a part of life in the United States without betraying their past. They fear that to integrate into U.S. culture is to lose their roots. They are caught between two cultures, each beckoning, each offering rich rewards.

for your Consideration

I saw this conflict firsthand with my father, who did not learn English until after the seventh grade (his last in school). German was left behind, but broken English and awkward expressions remained for a lifetime. Then, too, there were the lingering emotional connections to old ways, as well as the suspicions, haughtiness, and slights of more assimilated Americans. His longing for security by grasping the past was combined with his wanting to succeed in the everyday reality of the new culture. Have you seen anything similar?

Sources: Based on Richard Rodriguez 1975, 1982, 1990, 1991, 1995.

Sociologists have also identified a *hidden curriculum* in our schools. This term refers to values that, although not explicitly taught, are part of a school's "message." For example, the stories and examples that are used to teach math and English may bring with them

Schools are one of the primary agents of socialization. One of their chief functions is to sort young people into the adult roles thought appropriate for them, and to teach them the attitudes and skills that match those roles. What sorts of attitudes and adult roles do you think these junior high school girls in Santa Monica, California, are being socialized into? Are these attitudes and roles functions or dysfunctions—or both?

lessons in patriotism, democracy, justice, and honesty. There is also a *corridor curriculum,* what students teach one another outside the classroom. Unfortunately, the corridor curriculum seems to center on racism, sexism, illicit ways to make money, and coolness (Hemmings 1999). You can determine for yourself which of these is functional and which is dysfunctional.

Conflict theorists point out that social class separates children into different worlds. Children born to wealthy parents go to private schools, where they learn skills and values that match their higher position. Children born to middle- and lower-class parents go to public schools. Here social class further refines the separation into distinct worlds. Children from blue-collar families learn that not many of "their kind" will become professionals or leaders, one of many reasons that children from blue-collar families are less likely to take college prep courses or to go to college. In short, schools around the world reflect and reinforce their nation's social class, economic, and political systems. We will return to this topic in the chapter on education (Chapter 17).

Peer Groups

As a child's experiences with agents of socialization broaden, the influence of the family lessens. Entry into school marks only one of many steps in this transfer of allegiance. One of the most significant aspects of education is that it exposes children to peer groups that help them resist the efforts of parents and schools to socialize them.

When sociologists Patricia and Peter Adler (1998), a husband and wife team, observed children at two elementary schools in Colorado, they saw how children separate themselves by sex and develop their own worlds with unique norms. The norms that made boys popular were athletic ability, coolness, and toughness. For girls, popularity was based on family background, physical appearance (clothing and use of makeup), and the ability to attract popular boys. In this children's subculture, academic achievement pulled in opposite directions: For boys, high grades lowered their popularity, but for girls, good grades increased their standing among peers.

You know from your own experience how compelling peer groups are. It is almost impossible to go against a peer group, whose cardinal rule seems to be "conformity or rejection." Anyone who doesn't do what the others want becomes an "outsider," a "nonmember," an "outcast." For preteens and teens just learning their way around in the world, it is not surprising that the peer group rules.

Gradeschool boys and girls prefer to play different games. When forced to play the same game, they like to divide by gender. Each sex develops its own norms and preferences. As you can see here, the boys are playing more vigorously and competitively with the ball, while the girls are being gentler and more cooperative. The origin of such differences, which show up early, are the subject of debate in sociology.

As a result, the standards of our peer groups tend to dominate our lives. If your peers, for example, listen to rap, heavy metal, rock and roll, country, or gospel, it is almost inevitable that you also prefer that kind of music. It is the same for other kinds of music, clothing styles, and dating standards. Peer influences also extend to behaviors that violate social norms. If your peers are college-bound and upwardly striving, that is most likely what you will be; but if they use drugs, cheat, and steal, you are likely to do so, too.

Sports and Competitive Success

Sports are another powerful socializing agent. Everyone recognizes that sports teach not only physical skills but also values. In fact, "teaching youngsters to be team players" is often given as the justification for financing organized sports.

The effects of sports on the self-image are not well understood. Boys learn that to achieve in sports is to gain stature in masculinity (Pascoe 2003). The more successful a boy is in sports, the more masculine he is considered to be and the more he achieves prestige among his peers. Sociologist Michael Messner (1990) points out that this encourages boys to develop *instrumental* relationships—those based on what you can get out of people. Other aspects of boys' socialization into competitive success have the same effect, and boys tend to relate instrumentally to girls. Girls, in contrast, are more likely to be socialized to construct their identities on meaningful relationships, not on competitive success. As sports become more important in the formation of female identities, we will have to see what effects they have on women.

The Workplace

Another agent of socialization that comes into play somewhat later in life is the workplace. Those initial jobs that we take in high school and college are much more than just a way to earn a few dollars. From the people we rub shoulders with at work, we learn not only a set of skills but also a perspective on the world.

Most of us eventually become committed to some particular line of work, often after trying out many jobs. This may involve **anticipatory socialization**, learning to play a role before entering it. Anticipatory socialization is a sort of mental rehearsal for some future activity. We may talk to people who work in a particular career, read novels about that type of work, or take a summer internship. This allows us to gradually identify with the role, to become aware of what would be expected of us. Sometimes this helps people avoid committing themselves to an unrewarding career, as with some of my students who tried

anticipatory socialization because one anticipates a future role, one learns parts of it now

student teaching, found that they couldn't stand it, and then moved on to other fields more to their liking.

An intriguing aspect of work as a socializing agent is that the more you participate in a line of work, the more the work becomes a part of your self-concept. Eventually you come to think of yourself so much in terms of the job that if someone asks you to describe yourself, you are likely to include the job in your self-description. You might say, "I'm a teacher," "I'm a nurse," or "I'm a sociologist."

Resocialization

What does a woman who has just become a nun have in common with a man who has just divorced? The answer is that they both are undergoing **resocialization;** that is, they are learning new norms, values, attitudes, and behaviors to match their new situation in life. In its most common form, resocialization occurs each time we learn something contrary to our previous experiences. A new boss who insists on a different way of doing things is resocializing you. Most resocialization is mild—-only a slight modification of things we have already learned.

Resocialization can also be intense. People who join Alcoholics Anonymous (AA), for example, are surrounded by reformed drinkers who affirm the destructive effects of excessive drinking. Some students experience an intense period of resocialization when they leave high school and start college—especially during those initially scary days before they start to fit in and feel comfortable. To join a cult or to begin psychotherapy is even more profound, for these events expose people to ideas that conflict with their previous ways of looking at the world. If these ideas "take," not only does the individual's behavior change but also he or she learns a fundamentally different way of looking at life.

Total Institutions

Relatively few of us experience the powerful agent of socialization that sociologist Erving Goffman (1961) called the **total institution.** He coined this term to refer to a place in which people are cut off from the rest of society and where they come under almost total control of the officials who run the place. Boot camp, prisons, concentration camps, convents, some religious cults, and some boarding schools, such as West Point, are total institutions.

A person entering a total institution is greeted with a **degradation ceremony** (Garfinkel 1956), an attempt to remake the self by stripping away the individual's current identity and stamping a new one in its place. This unwelcome greeting may involve fingerprinting, photographing, shaving the head, and banning the individual's *personal identity kit* (items such as jewelry, hairstyles, clothing, and other body decorations used to express individuality). Newcomers may be ordered to strip, undergo an examination (often in a humiliating, semi-public setting), and then to put on a uniform that designates their new status. (For prisoners, the public reading of the verdict and being led away in handcuffs by armed police are also part of the degradation ceremony.)

Total institutions are isolated from the public. The walls, bars, gates, and guards not only keep the inmates in but also keep outsiders out. Total institutions suppress preexisting statuses: Inmates learn that their previous roles such as spouse, parent, worker, or student mean nothing. The only thing that counts is their current role. Staff members control information and replace the norms of "the outside world" with their own rules, values, and interpretation of life. This helps the institution shape the inmates' ideas and "picture" of the world. Staff members, who control the rewards and punishments, closely supervise the day-to-day lives of the residents. Eating, sleeping, showering, recreation—all are standardized. Under conditions of deprivation, simple rewards for compliance such as sleep, a television program, a letter from home, extra food, or even a cigarette, are powerful incentives in controlling behavior.

No one leaves a total institution unscathed, for the experience brands an indelible mark on the individual's self and colors the way he or she sees the world. Boot camp, as described in the Down-to-Earth Sociology box on the next page, is brutal but swift. Prison,

resocialization the process of learning new norms, values, attitudes, and behaviors

total institution a place in which people are cut off from the rest of society and are almost totally controlled by the officials who run the place

degradation ceremony a term coined by Harold Garfinkel to describe an attempt to remake the self by stripping away an individual's self-identity and stamping a new identity in its place

Boot Camp as a Total Institution

THE BUS ARRIVES AT PARRIS ISLAND, South Carolina, at 3 A.M. The early hour is no accident. The recruits are groggy, confused. Up to a few hours ago, the young men were ordinary civilians. Now, as a sergeant sneeringly calls them "maggots," their heads are buzzed (25 seconds per recruit), and they are quickly thrust into the harsh world of Marine boot camp.

Buzzing the boys' hair is just the first step in stripping away their identity so that the Marines can stamp a new one in its place. The uniform serves the same purpose. There is a ban on using the first person "I." Even a simple request must be made in precise Marine style or it will not be acknowledged. ("Sir, Recruit Jones requests permission to make a head call, Sir.")

Every intense moment of the next eleven weeks reminds the recruits that they are joining a subculture of self-discipline. Here pleasure is suspect and sacrifice is good. As they learn the Marine way of talking, walking, and thinking, they are denied the diversions they once took for granted: television, cigarettes, cars, candy, soft drinks, video games, music, alcohol, drugs, and sex.

Lessons are bestowed with fierce intensity. When Sgt. Carey checks brass belt buckles, Recruit Robert Shelton nervously blurts, "I don't have one." Sgt. Carey's face grows red as his neck cords bulge. "I?" he says, his face just inches from the recruit. With spittle flying from his mouth, he screams, " 'I' is gone!"

"Nobody's an individual" is the lesson that is driven home again and again. "You are a team, a Marine. Not a civilian. Not black or white, not Hispanic or Indian or some hyphenated American—but a Marine. You will live like a Marine, fight like a Marine, and, if necessary, die like a Marine."

Each day begins before dawn with close–order formations. The rest of the day is filled with training in hand-to-hand combat, marching, running, calisthenics, Marine history, and—always—following orders.

Resocialization is often a gentle process. Usually we are gradually exposed to different ways of thinking and doing. Sometimes, however, resocialization can be swift and brutal, as it is during boot camp in the Marines. This private at Parris Island is learning a world vastly unlike the civilian world he left behind.

"An M-16 can blow someone's head off at 500 meters," Sgt. Norman says. "That's beautiful, isn't it?"

"Yes, sir!" shout the platoon's fifty-nine voices.

"Pick your nose!" Simultaneously 59 index fingers shoot into nostrils.

The pressure to conform is intense. Those who are sent packing for insubordination or suicidal tendencies are mocked in cadence during drills. ("Hope you like the sights you see / Parris Island casualty.") As lights go out at 9 P.M., the exhausted recruits perform the day's last task: The entire platoon, in unison, chants the virtues of the Marines.

Recruits are constantly scrutinized. Subperformance is not accepted, whether it be a dirty rifle or a loose thread on a uniform. The subperformer is shouted at, derided, humiliated. The group suffers for the individual. If a recruit is slow, the entire platoon is punished.

The system works.

One of the new Marines (until graduation, they are recruits, not Marines) says, "I feel like I've joined a new society or religion."

He has.

for your Consideration

Of what significance is the recruits' degradation ceremony? Why are recruits not allowed video games, cigarettes, or calls home? Why are the Marines so unfair as to punish an entire platoon for the failure of an individual? Use concepts in this chapter to explain why the system works.

Sources: Based on Garfinkel 1956; Goffman 1961; Ricks 1995; Dyer 2005.

---

in contrast, is brutal and prolonged. Neither recruit nor prisoner, however, has difficulty in pinpointing how the institution affected the self.

Socialization Through the Life Course

You are at a particular stage in your life now, and college is a good part of it. You know that you have more stages ahead of you as you go through life. These stages, from birth to death, are called the **life course** (Elder 1975; 1999). The sociological significance of the life course is twofold. First, as you pass through a stage, it affects your behavior and orientations. You simply don't think about life in the same way when you are 30, are married, and have a baby and a mortgage, as you do when you are 18 or 20, single, and in college. (Actually, you don't even see life the same as a freshman and as a senior.) Second, your life course differs by social location. Your social class, race-ethnicity, and gender, for example, map out distinctive worlds of experience. Consequently, the typical life course differs for males and females, the rich and the poor, and so on. To emphasize this major sociological point, in the sketch that follows I will stress the *historical* setting of people's lives. Because of your particular social location, your own life course may differ from this sketch, which is a composite of stages that others have suggested (Levinson 1978; Carr et al. 1995; Hunt 2005).

Childhood (from birth to about age 12)

Consider how different your childhood would have been if you had grown up in another historical time. Historian Philippe Ariès (1965) noticed that in European paintings from about 1000 A.D. children were always dressed in adult clothing. If they were not depicted stiffly posed, as in a family portrait, they were shown doing adult activities.

From this, Ariès drew a conclusion that sparked a debate among historians: He believed that during this time in Europe, childhood was not regarded as a special time of life. He said that adults viewed children as miniature adults, and put them to work at very early ages. At the age of 7, for example, a boy might leave home for good to learn to be a jeweler or a stonecutter. A girl, in contrast, stayed home until she married, but by the age of 7 she was expected to assume her daily share of the household tasks. Historians do not deny that these were the customs of that time, but some say that Aries' conclusion is ridiculous. They say that other evidence of that period indicates that childhood was viewed as a special time of life (Orme 2002).

Having children work like adults did not disappear with the Middle Ages. It is still common in the Least Industrialized Nations. The photo essay on pages 250–251 provides a startling example of this practice—reflecting not just different activities but also a view of children different from the one common in the Most Industrialized Nations.

life course the stages of our life as we go from birth to death

In contemporary Western societies such as the United States, children are viewed as innocent and in need of protection from adult responsibilities such as work and self-support. Ideas of childhood vary historically and cross-culturally. From paintings, such as this 1602 portrait of a Flemish family by Gortins Geldorp, some historians conclude that Europeans once viewed children as miniature adults who assumed adult roles at the earliest opportunity.

In earlier centuries, parents and teachers also considered it their moral duty to terrorize children to keep them in line. They would lock children in dark closets, frighten them with bedtime stories of death and hellfire, and force them to witness gruesome events. Consider this:

A common moral lesson involved taking children to visit the gibbet [an upraised post on which executed bodies were left hanging from chains], where they were forced to inspect rotting corpses hanging there as an example of what happens to bad children when they grow up. Whole classes were taken out of school to witness hangings, and parents would often whip their children afterwards to make them remember what they had seen. (DeMause 1975)

Industrialization transformed the way we perceive children. When children have the leisure to go to school, they come to be thought of as tender and innocent, as needing more adult care, comfort, and protection. Over time, such attitudes of dependency grow, and today we view children as needing gentle guidance if they are to develop emotionally, intellectually, morally, even physically. We take our view for granted—after all, it is only "common sense." Yet, as you can see, our view is not "natural," but is rooted in geography and history.

Technology can also change the nature of childhood. When television shows images of murder, rape, war, and other violence, children of a tender age learn about a world that used to be kept secret from them (Lee 2001).

IN SUM Childhood is more than biology. Everyone's childhood occurs at some point in history, and is embedded in particular social locations, especially social class and gender. *These social factors are as vital as our biology, for they determine what childhood will be like for us.* Although a child's *biological* characteristics (such as being small and dependent) are universal, the child's *social* experiences (what happens to that child because of what others expect of him or her) are not. Thus sociologists say that childhood varies from culture to culture.

Adolescence (ages 13–17)

Adolescence is not a "natural" age division. It is a social invention. In earlier centuries, people simply moved from childhood into young adulthood, with no stopover in between. The Industrial Revolution brought such an abundance of material surpluses, however, that for the first time in history, millions of people in their teens were able to remain outside the labor force. At the same time, education became a more important factor in achieving success. The convergence of these two forces in industrialized societies created a gap between childhood and adulthood. In the early 1900s, the term *adolescence* was coined to indicate this new stage in life (Hall 1904), one that has become renowned for inner turmoil.

To ground the self-identity and mark the passage of children into adulthood, tribal societies hold *initiation rites.* In the industrialized world, however, adolescents must "find" themselves on their own. As they attempt to carve out an identity that is distinct from both the "younger" world being left behind and the "older" world that is still out of range, adolescents develop their own subcultures, with distinctive clothing, hairstyles, language, gestures, and music. We usually fail to realize that contemporary society, not biology, created the period of inner turmoil that we call *adolescence.*

Transitional Adulthood (ages 18–29)

transitional adulthood a term that refers to a period following high school when young adults have not yet taken on the responsibilities ordinarily associated with adulthood; also called *adultolescence*

If society invented adolescence, can it also invent other periods of life? As Figure 3.2 illustrates, this is actually happening now. Postindustrial societies are adding a period of extended youth to the life course, which sociologists call **transitional adulthood** (also known as *adultolescence*). After high school, millions of young adults go to college, where they postpone adult responsibilities. They are mostly freed from the control of their parents, yet they don't have to support themselves. Even after college, many return home, so they

In many societies, manhood is not bestowed upon males simply because they reach a certain age. Manhood, rather, signifies a standing in the community that must be achieved. Shown here is an initiation ceremony in Indonesia, where boys, to lay claim to the status of manhood, must jump over this barrier.

can live cheaply while they establish themselves in a career—and, of course, continue to "find themselves." During this time, people are "neither psychological adolescents nor sociological adults" (Keniston 1971). At some point during this period of extended youth, young adults gradually ease into adult responsibilities. They take a full-time job, become serious about a career, engage in courtship rituals, get married—and go into debt.

The Middle Years (ages 30–65)

The Early Middle Years (ages 30–49)   During their early middle years, most people are more sure of themselves and of their goals in life. As with any point in the life course, however, the self can receive severe jolts—in this case from such circumstances as divorce or being fired. It may take years for the self to stabilize after such ruptures.

The early middle years pose a special challenge for many U.S. women, who have been given the message, especially by the media, that they can "have it all." They can be superworkers, superwives, and supermoms—all rolled into one. The reality, however, usually consists of conflicting pressures—too little time and too many demands. Something has to give. Attempts to resolve this dilemma are often compounded by another hard reality—that during gender socialization, their husbands learned that child care and housework are not "masculine." In short, adjustments continue in this and all phases of life.

The Later Middle Years (ages 50–65)   During the later middle years, health issues and mortality begin to loom large

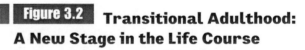

Figure 3.2   Transitional Adulthood: A New Stage in the Life Course

Who has completed the transition?

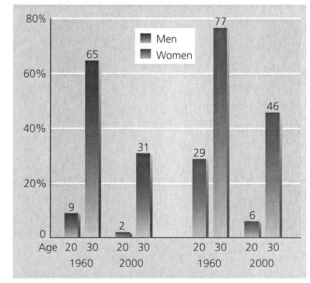

The data show the percent who have completed the transition to adulthood, as measured by leaving home, finishing school, getting married, having a child, and being financially independent.

Source: Furstenberg, et al. 2004.

SOCIALIZATION THROUGH THE LIFE COURSE   **89**

as people feel their bodies change, especially if they watch their parents become frail, fall ill, and die. The consequence is a fundamental reorientation in thinking—*from time since birth to time left to live* (Neugarten 1976). With this changed orientation, people attempt to evaluate the past and come to terms with what lies ahead. They compare what they have accomplished with how far they had hoped to go. Many people also find themselves caring not only for their own children but also for their aging parents. Because of this set of burdens, which is often crushing, people in the later middle years sometimes are called the "sandwich generation."

Life during this stage isn't stressful for everyone. Many find late middle age to be the most comfortable period of their lives. They enjoy job security and a standard of living higher than ever before; they have a bigger house (one that may even be paid for), newer cars, and longer and more exotic vacations. The children are grown, the self is firmly planted, and fewer upheavals are likely to occur.

As they anticipate the next stage of life, however, most people do not like what they see.

The Older Years (about age 65 on)

The Early Older Years In industrialized societies, the older years begin around the mid-60s. This, too, is recent, for in agricultural societies, when most people died early, old age was thought to begin at around age 40. Industrialization brought about improved nutrition and public health, which prolonged life. Today, people in good health who are over the age of 65 often experience this period not as old age, but as an extension of the middle years. People who continue to work or to do things they enjoy are less likely to perceive themselves as old (Neugarten 1977). Although frequency of sex declines, most men and women in their 60s and 70s are sexually active (Denney and Quadagno 1992).

Because we have a self and can reason abstractly, we can contemplate death. Initially, we regard death as a vague notion, a remote possibility. But as people see their friends die and observe their own bodies no longer functioning as before, the thought of death becomes less abstract. Increasingly during this stage in the life course, people feel that "time is closing in" on them.

The Later Older Years As with the preceding periods of life except the first one, there is no precise beginning point to this last stage. For some, the 75th birthday may mark entry into this period of life. For others, that marker may be the 80th or even the 85th birthday. For most, this stage is marked by growing frailty and illness; for all who reach this stage, it is ended by death. For some, the physical decline is slow, and a rare few manage to see their 100th birthday mentally alert and in good physical health.

The Sociological Significance of the Life Course

The sociological significance of the life course is that it does not merely represent biology, things that naturally occur to all of us as we add years to our lives. Rather, *social* factors influence our life course. As you just saw, *when* you live makes a huge difference in the course that your life takes. And with today's rapid social change, the difference in historical time does not have to be vast. Being born just ten years earlier or later may mean that you experience war or peace, an expanding economy or a depression—and those factors vitally affect what happens to you not just during childhood but throughout your life.

Your *social location,* such as social class, gender, and race, is also highly significant. Your experience of society's events will be similar to that of people who share your social location, but different from that of people who do not. If you are poor, for example, you likely will feel older faster than most wealthy people for whom life is much less demanding. Individual factors—such as your health, or marrying early or entering college late—may throw your life course "out of sequence," making it atypical.

This January 1937 photo from Sneedville, Tennessee, shows Eunice Johns, age 9, and her husband, Charlie Johns, age 22. The groom gave his wife a doll as a wedding gift. The new husband and wife planned to build a cabin, and, as Charlie Johns phrased it, "go to housekeepin'."

This photo illustrates the cultural relativity of life stages, which we sometimes mistake as fixed. It also is interesting from a symbolic interactionist perspective—that of changing definitions—for while our sensibilities are shocked by such marriages, even though they were not common, they once were taken for granted.

For all these reasons, this sketch of the life course may not adequately reflect your own past, present, and future. As sociologist C. Wright Mills (1959) would say, because employers are beating a path to your door, or failing to do so, you are more inclined to marry, to buy a house, and to start a family—or to postpone these life course events, perhaps indefinitely. In short, changing times change lives, steering the life course into different directions.

Are We Prisoners of Socialization?

From our discussion of socialization, you might conclude that sociologists think of people as robots: The socialization goes in, and the behavior comes out. People cannot help what they do, think, or feel, for everything is simply a result of their exposure to socializing agents.

Sociologists do *not* think of people in this way. Although socialization is powerful, and profoundly affects us all, we each have a self. Established in childhood and continually modified by later experience, the self is dynamic. It is not a sponge that passively absorbs influences from the environment, but, rather, a vigorous, essential part of our being that allows us to act on our environment.

Indeed, it is precisely because individuals are not robots that their behavior is so hard to predict. The countless reactions of other people merge in each of us. As discussed earlier, even identical twins do not receive identical reactions from others. As the self develops, each person internalizes or "puts together" these innumerable reactions, producing a unique whole called the *individual*. Each unique individual uses his or her own mind to reason and to make choices in life.

In this way, *each of us is actively involved in the construction of the self.* For example, although our experiences in the family lay down the basic elements of our personality, including fundamental orientations to life, we are not doomed to keep those orientations if we do not like them. We can purposely expose ourselves to groups and ideas that we prefer. Those experiences, in turn, will have their own effects on our self. In short, although socialization is powerful, within the limitations of the framework laid down by our social location we can change even the self. And that self—along with the options available within society—is the key to our behavior.

Summary *and* Review

What Is Human Nature?

How much of our human characteristics come from "nature" (heredity) and how much from "nurture" (the social environment)?

Observations of isolated, institutionalized, and **feral children** help to answer this question, as do experiments with monkeys that were raised in isolation. Language and intimate social interaction—aspects of "nurture"—are essential to the development of what we consider to be human characteristics. Pp. 64–68.

Socialization into the Self and Mind

How do we acquire a self?

Humans are born with the *capacity* to develop a **self**, but the self must be socially constructed; that is, its contents depend on social interaction. According to Charles Horton Cooley's concept of the **looking-glass self**, our self develops as we internalize others' reactions to us. George Herbert Mead identified the ability to **take the role of the other** as essential to the development of the self. Mead concluded that even the mind is a social product. Pp. 68–70.

How do children develop reasoning skills?

Jean Piaget identified four stages that children go through as they develop the ability to reason: (1) *sensorimotor,* in which understanding is limited to sensory stimuli such as touch and sight; (2) *preoperational,* the ability to use symbols; (3) *concrete operational,* in which reasoning ability is more complex but not yet capable of complex abstractions; and (4) *formal operational,* or abstract thinking. Pp. 70–71.

How do sociologists evaluate Freud's psychoanalytic theory of personality development?

Freud viewed personality development as the result of our **id** (inborn, self-centered desires) clashing with the demands of society. The **ego** develops to balance the id and the **superego,** the conscience. Sociologists, in contrast, do not examine inborn or subconscious motivations, but, instead, how *social* factors—social class, gender, religion, education, and so forth—underlie personality development. P. 72.

How do people develop morality?

Children are born without morality, and, according to Kohlberg, they go through four stages in learning it: amoral, preconventional, conventional, and postconventional. As they make moral decisions, both men and women use personal relationships and abstract principles. Pp. 72–73.

How does socialization influence emotions?

Socialization influences not only *how we express our emotions,* but also *what emotions we feel.* Socialization into emotions is one of the means by which society produces conformity. Pp. 73–75.

Socialization into Gender

How does gender socialization affect our sense of self?

Gender socialization—sorting males and females into different roles—is a primary means of controlling human behavior. Children receive messages about gender even in infancy. A society's ideals of sex-linked behaviors are reinforced by its social institutions. Pp. 75–78.

Agents of Socialization

What are the main agents of socialization?

The **agents of socialization** include family, the neighborhood, religion, day care, school, **peer groups,** sports, the **mass media,** and the workplace. Each has its particular influences in socializing us into becoming full-fledged members of society. Pp. 78–85.

Resocialization

What is resocialization?

Resocialization is the process of learning new norms, values, attitudes, and behavior. Most resocialization is voluntary, but some, as with residents of **total institutions,** is involuntary. Pp. 85–86.

Socialization Through the Life Course

Does socialization end when we enter adulthood?

Socialization occurs throughout the life course. In industrialized societies, the **life course** can be divided into childhood, adolescence, young adulthood, the middle years, and the older years. The West is adding a new stage, transitional adulthood. Life course patterns vary by social location such as history, gender, race-ethnicity, and social class, as well as by individual experiences such as health and age at marriage. Pp. 86–91.

Are We Prisoners of Socialization?

Although socialization is powerful, we are not merely the sum of our socialization experiences. Just as socialization influences human behavior, so humans act on their environment and influence even their self concept. P. 91.

Thinking Critically

about **Chapter 3**

1. What two agents of socialization have influenced you the most? Can you pin-point their influence on your attitudes, beliefs, values, or other orientations to life?

2. Summarize your views of gender. What in your socialization has led you to have these views?

3. What is your location in the life course? How does the text's summary of that location match your experiences? Explain the similarities and differences.

Additional Resources

Companion Website www.ablongman.com/henslin8e

- *Content Select* Research Database for Sociology, with suggested key terms and annotated references
- Link to 2000 Census, with activities
- Flashcards of key terms and concepts

- Practice Tests
- Weblinks
- Interactive Maps

Where Can I Read More on This Topic?

Suggested readings for this chapter are listed at the back of this book.

Social Structure and Social Interaction

Jacob Lawrence, *Street Scene (Boy with Kite)*, 1962

My curiosity had gotten the better of me. When the sociology convention finished, I climbed aboard the first city bus that came along. I didn't know where the bus was going, and I didn't know where I was going to spend the night.

"Maybe I overdid it this time," I thought, as the bus began winding down streets I had never seen before. Actually, this was my first visit to Washington, D.C., so everything was unfamiliar to me. I had no destination, no plans, not even a map. I carried no billfold, just a driver's license shoved into my jeans for emergency identification, some pocket change, and a $10 bill tucked into my socks. My goal was simple: If I saw something interesting, I would get off and check it out.

"Nothing but the usual things," I mused, as we passed row after row of apartment buildings and stores. I could see myself riding buses the entire night. Then something caught my eye. Nothing spectacular—just groups of people clustered around a large circular area where several streets intersected.

I climbed off the bus and made my way to what turned out to be Dupont Circle. I took a seat on a sidewalk bench and began to observe what was going on around me. As the scene came into focus, I noted several streetcorner men drinking and joking with one another. One of the men broke from his companions and sat down next to me. As we talked, I mostly listened.

As night fell, the men said that they wanted to get another bottle of wine. I contributed. They counted their money and asked if I wanted to go with them.

Although I felt my stomach churning—a combination of hesitation and fear—I heard a confident "Sure!"

> **Suddenly one of the men jumped up, smashed the empty bottle against the sidewalk, and . . .**

come out of my mouth. As we left the circle, the three men began to cut through an alley. "Oh, no," I thought. "This isn't what I had in mind."

I had but a split second to make a decision. I found myself continuing to walk with the men, but holding back half a step so that none of the three was behind me. As we walked, they passed around the remnants of their bottle. When my turn came, I didn't know what to do. I shuddered to think about the diseases lurking within that bottle. I made another quick decision. In the semidarkness I faked it, letting only my thumb and forefinger touch my lips and nothing enter my mouth.

When we returned to Dupont Circle, the men passed around their new bottle of Thunderbird. I couldn't fake it in the light, so I passed, pointing at my stomach to indicate that I was having digestive problems.

Suddenly one of the men jumped up, smashed the emptied bottle against the sidewalk, and thrust the jagged neck outward in a menacing gesture. He glared straight ahead at another bench, where he had spotted someone with whom he had some sort of unfinished business. As the other men told him to cool it, I moved slightly to one side of the group—ready to flee, just in case.

Levels of Sociological Analysis

On this sociological adventure, I almost got myself in over my head. Fortunately, it turned out all right. The man's "enemy" didn't look our way, the broken bottle was set down next to the bench "just in case he needed it," and my introduction to a life that up until then I had only read about continued until dawn.

Sociologists Elliot Liebow (1967/1999), Mitchell Duneier (1999), and Elijah Anderson (1978, 1990, 2006) have written fascinating accounts about men like my companions from that evening. Although streetcorner men may appear to be disorganized—simply coming and going as they please and doing whatever feels good at the moment—sociologists have analyzed how, like us, these men are influenced by the norms and beliefs of our society. This will become more apparent as we examine the two levels of analysis that sociologists use.

Macrosociology and Microsociology

The first level, **macrosociology**, focuses on broad features of society. Sociologists who use this approach analyze such things as social class and how groups are related to one another. If macrosociologists were to analyze streetcorner men, for example, they would stress that these men are located at the bottom of the U.S. social class system. Their low status means that many opportunities are closed to them: The men have few job skills, little education, hardly anything to offer an employer. As "able-bodied" men, however, they are not eligible for welfare, even for a two-year limit, so they hustle to survive. As a consequence, they spend their lives on the streets.

Conflict theory and functionalism, both of which focus on the broader picture, are examples of this macrosociological approach. In these theories, the goal is to examine the large-scale social forces that influence people.

The second level, **microsociology**, examines **social interaction,** what people do when they come together. Sociologists who use this approach to study streetcorner men are likely to focus on the men's rules or "codes" for getting along; their survival strategies ("hustles"); how they divide up money, wine, or whatever other resources they have; their relationships with girlfriends, family, and friends; where they spend their time and what they do there; their language; their pecking order; and so on. With its focus on face-to-face interaction, symbolic interactionism is an example of microsociology.

Sociologists use both macro and micro levels of analysis to study social life. Those who use *macrosociology* to analyze the homeless—or any human behavior—focus on broad aspects of society, such as the economy and social classes. Sociologists who use the *microsociological approach* analyze how people interact with one another. This photo illustrates social structure—the disparities between power and powerlessness are amply evident. It also illustrates the micro level— the isolation of these homeless men.

Because each approach has a different focus, macrosociology and microsociology yield distinctive perspectives, and both are needed to gain a fuller understanding of social life. We cannot adequately understand streetcorner men, for example, without using *macrosociology*. It is essential that we place the men within the broad context of how groups in U.S. society are related to one another—for, just as with ourselves, the social class of these men helps to shape their attitudes and behavior. Nor can we adequately understand these men without *microsociology*, for their everyday situations also form a significant part of their lives—as they do for all of us.

Let's look in more detail at how these two approaches in sociology work together to help us understand social life. As we examine them more closely, you may find yourself feeling more comfortable with one approach than the other. This is what happens with sociologists. For reasons of personal background and professional training, sociologists find themselves more comfortable with one approach and tend to use it in their research. Both approaches, however, are necessary to understand life in society.

The Macrosociological Perspective: Social Structure

Why did the street people in the opening vignette act as they did, staying up all night drinking wine, prepared to use a lethal weapon? Why don't *we* act like this? Social structure helps us answer such questions.

The Sociological Significance of Social Structure

To better understand human behavior, we need to understand *social structure,* the framework of society that was already laid out before you were born. **Social structure** refers to the typical patterns of a group, such as its usual relationships between men and women or students and teachers. *The sociological significance of social structure is that it guides our behavior.*

Because this term may seem vague, let's consider how you experience social structure in your own life. As I write this, I do not know your race-ethnicity. I do not know your religion. I do not know whether you are young or old, tall or short, male or female. I do not know whether you were reared on a farm, in the suburbs, or in the inner city. I do not know whether you went to a public high school or to an exclusive prep school. But I do know that you are in college. And this, alone, tells me a great deal about you.

From this one piece of information, I can assume that the social structure of your college is now shaping what you do. For example, let's suppose that today you felt euphoric over some great news. I can be fairly certain (not absolutely, mind you, but relatively certain) that when you entered the classroom, social structure overrode your mood. That is, instead of shouting at the top of your lungs and joyously throwing this book into the air, you entered the classroom in a fairly subdued manner and took your seat.

The same social structure influences your instructor, even if he or she, on the one hand, is facing a divorce or has a child dying of cancer, or, on the other, has just been awarded a promotion or a million-dollar grant. The instructor may feel like either retreating into seclusion or celebrating wildly, but most likely he or she will conduct class in the usual manner. In short, social structure tends to override personal feelings and desires.

Just as social structure influences you and your instructor, so it also establishes limits for street people. They, too, find themselves in a specific location in the U.S. social structure—although it is quite different from yours or your instructor's. Consequently, they are affected differently. Nothing about their social location leads them to take notes or to lecture. Their behaviors, however, are as logical an outcome of where they find themselves in the social structure as are your own. In their position in the social structure, it is just as "natural" to drink wine all night as it is for you to stay up studying all night for a crucial examination. It is just as "natural" for you to nod and say, "Excuse me," when you enter a crowded classroom late and have to claim a desk on which someone has already placed books as it is for them to break off the head of a wine bottle and glare at an enemy.

macrosociology analysis of social life that focuses on broad features of society, such as social class and the relationships of groups to one another; usually used by functionalists and conflict theorists

microsociology analysis of social life that focuses on social interaction; typically used by symbolic interactionists

social interaction people's interaction with one another

social structure the framework that surrounds us, consisting of the relationships of people and groups to one another, which gives direction to and sets limits on behavior

In short, people learn their behaviors and attitudes because of their location in the social structure (whether they be privileged, deprived, or in between), and they act accordingly. This is equally true of street people and ourselves. *The differences in behavior and attitudes are due not to biology (race, sex, or any other supposed genetic factors), but to people's location in the social structure.* Switch places with street people and watch your behaviors and attitudes change!

To better understand social structure, read the Down-to-Earth Sociology box on football below.

Because social structure so crucially affects who we are and what we are like, let's look more closely at its major components: culture, social class, social status, roles, groups, and social institutions.

Down-to-Earth Sociology

College Football as Social Structure

TO GAIN A BETTER IDEA OF WHAT *social structure* is, think of college football (see Dobriner 1969a). You probably know the various positions on the team: center, guards, tackles, ends, quarterback, running backs, and the like. Each is a *status;* that is, each is a social position. For each of these statuses, there is a *role;* that is, each of these positions has certain expectations attached to it. The center is expected to snap the ball, the quarterback to pass it, the guards to block, the tackles to tackle or block, the ends to receive passes, and so on. Those role expectations guide each player's actions; that is, the players try to do what their particular role requires.

Let's suppose that football is your favorite sport and you never miss a home game at your college. Let's also suppose that you graduate, get a great job, and move across the country. Five years later, you return to your campus for a nostalgic visit. The climax of your visit is the biggest football game of the season. When you get to the game, you might be surprised to see a different coach, but you are not surprised that each playing position is occupied by people you don't know, for all the players you knew have graduated, and their places have been filled by others.

This scenario mirrors *social structure,* the framework around which a group exists. In football, that framework consists of the coaching staff and the eleven playing positions. The game does not depend on any particular individual, but, rather, on *social statuses,* the positions that the individuals occupy. When some-

one leaves a position, the game can go on because someone else takes over that position or status and plays the role. The game will continue even though not a single individual remains from one period of time to the next. Notre Dame's football team endures today even though Knute Rockne, the Gipper, and his teammates are long dead.

Even though you may not play football, you nevertheless live your life within a clearly established social structure. The statuses that you occupy and the roles you play were already in place before you were born. You take your particular positions in life, others do the same, and society goes about its business. Although the specifics change with time, the game—whether of life or of football—goes on.

Figure 4.1 **Team Positions (Statuses) in Football**

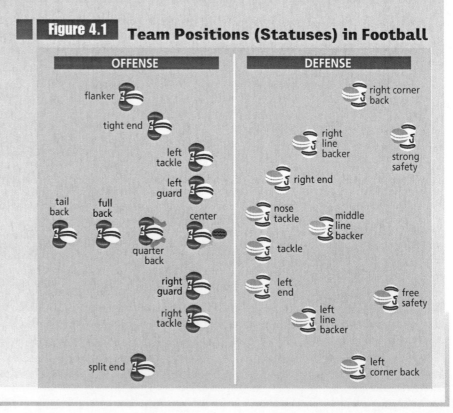

Culture

In Chapter 2, we considered culture's far-reaching effects on our lives. At this point, let's simply summarize its main impact. Sociologists use the term *culture* to refer to a group's language, beliefs, values, behaviors, and even gestures. Culture also includes the material objects that a group uses. Culture is the broadest framework that determines what kind of people we become. If we are reared in Chinese, Arab, Russian, or U.S. culture, we will grow up to be like most Chinese, Arabs, Russians, or Americans. On the outside, we will look and act like them; and on the inside, we will think and feel like them.

Social Class

To understand people, we must examine the social locations that they hold in life. Especially significant is *social class,* which is based on income, education, and occupational prestige. Large numbers of people who have similar amounts of income and education and who work at jobs that are roughly comparable in prestige make up a **social class.** It is hard to overemphasize this aspect of social structure, for our social class influences not only our behaviors but even our ideas and attitudes. We have this in common, then, with the street people described in the opening vignette—we both are influenced by our location in the social class structure. Theirs may be a considerably less privileged position, but it has no less influence on their lives. Social class is so significant that we shall spend an entire chapter (Chapter 10) on this topic.

Social Status

When you hear the word *status,* you are likely to think of prestige. These two words are welded together in people's minds. As you saw in the box on football, however, sociologists use **status** in a different way—to refer to the *position* that someone occupies. That position may carry a great deal of prestige, as in the case of a judge or an astronaut, or it may bring little prestige, as in the case of a convenience store clerk or a waitress. The status may also be looked down on, as in the case of a streetcorner man, an ex-convict, or a thief.

All of us occupy several positions at the same time. You may simultaneously be a son or daughter, a worker, a date, and a student. Sociologists use the term **status set** to refer to all the statuses or positions that you occupy. Obviously your status set changes as your particular statuses change. For example, if you graduate from college and take a full-time job, get married, buy a home, have children, and so on, your status set changes to include the positions of worker, spouse, homeowner, and parent.

Like other aspects of social structure, statuses are part of our basic framework of living in society. The example given earlier of students and teachers who come to class and do what others expect of them despite their particular moods illustrates how statuses affect our actions—and those of the people around us. Our statuses—whether daughter or son, worker or date—serve as guides for our behavior.

Ascribed and Achieved Statuses   An **ascribed status** is involuntary. You do not ask for it, nor can you choose it. You inherit some ascribed statuses at birth such as your race-ethnicity, sex, and the social class of your parents, as well as your statuses as female or male, daughter or son, niece or nephew, and granddaughter or grandson. Others, such as teenager and senior citizen, are related to the life course discussed in Chapter 3, and are given to you later in life.

Achieved statuses, in contrast, are voluntary. These you earn or accomplish. As a result of your efforts you become a student, a friend, a spouse, a rabbi, minister, priest, or nun. Or, for lack of effort (or for efforts that others fail to appreciate), you become a school dropout, a former friend, an ex-spouse, or a defrocked rabbi, priest, or nun. In other words, achieved statuses can be either positive or negative; both college president and bank robber are achieved statuses.

Each status provides guidelines for how we are to act and feel. Like other aspects of social structure, statuses set limits on what we can and cannot do. Because social statuses are an essential part of the social structure, they are found in all human groups.

social class according to Weber, a large group of people who rank close to one another in wealth, power, and prestige; according to Marx, one of two groups: capitalists who own the means of production or workers who sell their labor

status the position that someone occupies in society or in a social group

status set all the statuses or positions that an individual occupies

ascribed statuses positions an individual either inherits at birth or receives involuntarily later in life

achieved statuses positions that are earned, accomplished, or involve at least some effort or activity on the individual's part

Master statuses are those that overshadow our other statuses. Shown here is Stephen Hawking, who is suffering from Lou Gehrig's disease. For many, his master status is that of a person with disabilities. Because Hawking is one of the greatest physicists who has ever lived, however, his outstanding achievements have given him another master status, that of world-class physicist in the ranking of Einstein.

status symbols items used to identify a status

master status a status that cuts across the other statuses that an individual occupies

status inconsistency ranking high on some dimensions of social class and low on others

role the behaviors, obligations, and privileges attached to a status

Status Symbols   People who are pleased with their particular social status often want others to recognize that they occupy that status. To elicit this recognition, they use **status symbols,** signs that identify a status. For example, people wear wedding rings to announce their marital status; uniforms, guns, and badges to proclaim that they are police officers (and to not so subtly let you know that their status gives them authority over you); and "backward" collars to declare that they are Lutheran ministers or Roman Catholic or Episcopal priests.

Some social statuses are negative, and so, therefore, are their status symbols. The scarlet letter in Nathaniel Hawthorne's book by the same title is one example. Another is the CONVICTED DUI (Driving Under the Influence) bumper sticker that some U.S. courts require convicted drunk drivers to display if they wish to avoid a jail sentence.

All of us use status symbols to announce our statuses to others and to help smooth our interactions in everyday life. You might consider what your own status symbols communicate. For example, how does your clothing announce your statuses of sex, age, and college student?

Master Statuses   A **master status** is one that cuts across the other statuses that you hold. Some master statuses are ascribed. An example is your sex. Whatever you do, people perceive you as a male or as a female. If you are working your way through college by flipping burgers, people see you not only as a burger flipper and a student but also as a *male* or *female* burger flipper and a *male* or *female* college student. Other master statuses are race and age.

Some master statuses are achieved. If you become very, very wealthy (and it doesn't matter whether your wealth comes from a successful invention or from winning the lottery—it is still *achieved* as far as sociologists are concerned), your wealth is likely to become a master status. For example, people might say, "She is a very rich burger flipper"—or, more likely, "She's very rich, and she used to flip burgers!"

Similarly, people who become disfigured find, to their dismay, that their condition becomes a master status. For example, a person whose face is scarred from severe burns will be viewed through this unwelcome master status regardless of his or her occupation or accomplishments. The same is true for people with disabilities. Those who are confined to wheelchairs can attest to how their handicap overrides all their other statuses and determines others' perceptions of everything they do.

Although our statuses usually fit together fairly well, some people have a contradiction or mismatch between their statuses. This is known as **status inconsistency** (or discrepancy). A 14-year-old college student is an example. So is a 40-year-old married woman who is dating a 19-year-old college sophomore.

These examples reveal an essential aspect of social statuses: Like other components of social structure, they come with built-in *norms* (that is, expectations) that guide our behavior. When statuses mesh well, as they usually do, we know what to expect of people. This helps social interaction to unfold smoothly. Status inconsistency, however, upsets our expectations. If you met someone mentioned in the preceding examples, how should you act? Are you supposed to treat the 14-year-old as you would a young teenager, or as you would your college classmate? Do you react to the married woman as you would to the mother of your friend, or as you would to a classmate's date?

Roles

All the world's a stage
And all the men and women merely players.
They have their exits and their entrances;
And one man in his time plays many parts . . .
(William Shakespeare, *As You Like It,* Act II, Scene 7)

Like Shakespeare, sociologists see roles as essential to social life. When you were born, **roles**—the behaviors, obligations, and privileges attached to a status—were already set up for you. Society was waiting with outstretched arms to teach you how it expected you to act as a boy or a girl. And whether you were born poor, rich, or somewhere in between, that, too, attached certain behaviors, obligations, and privileges to your statuses.

The difference between role and status is that you *occupy* a status, but you *play* a role (Linton 1936). For example, being a son or daughter is your status, but your expectations of receiving food and shelter from your parents—as well as their expectations that you show respect to them—are part of your role. Or, again, your status is student, but your role is to attend class, take notes, do homework, and take tests.

Roles are like a fence. They allow us a certain amount of freedom, but for most of us that freedom doesn't go very far. Suppose that a woman decides that she is not going to wear dresses—or a man that he will not wear suits and ties—regardless of what anyone says. In most situations, they'll stick to their decision. When a formal occasion comes along, however, such as a family wedding or a funeral, they are likely to cave in to norms that they find overwhelming. Almost all of us follow the guidelines for what is "appropriate" for our roles. Most of us are little troubled by such constraints, for our socialization is so thorough that we usually *want* to do what our roles indicate is appropriate.

The sociological significance of roles is that they lay out what is expected of people. As individuals throughout society perform their roles, those roles mesh together to form this thing called *society.* As Shakespeare put it, people's roles provide "their exits and their entrances" on the stage of life. In short, roles are remarkably effective at keeping people in line— telling them when they should "enter" and when they should "exit," as well as what to do in between.

Groups

A **group** consists of people who regularly interact with one another. Ordinarily, the members of a group share similar values, norms, and expectations. Just as social class, statuses, and roles influence our actions, so, too, the groups to which we belong are powerful forces in our lives. In fact, *to belong to a group is to yield to others the right to make certain decisions about our behavior.* If we belong to a group, we assume an obligation to act according to the expectations of other members of that group.

Although this principle holds true for all groups, some groups wield influence over only small segments of our behavior. For example, if you belong to a stamp collector's club, the group's influence may center on your display of knowledge about stamps, and perhaps your attendance at meetings. Other groups, in contrast, such as the family, control many aspects of our behavior. When parents say to their 15-year-old daughter, "As long as you are living under my roof, you had better be home by midnight," they show their expectation that their children, as members of the family, will conform to their ideas about many aspects of life, including their views on curfew. They are saying that as long as the daughter wants to remain a member of the household, her behavior must conform to their expectations.

Let's look in greater detail at the next component of social structure, social institutions.

Social Institutions

At first glance, the term *social institution* may seem to have little relevance to your personal life. The term seems so cold and abstract. In fact, however, **social institutions**—the ways that each society develops to meet its basic needs—vitally affect your life. By weaving the fabric of society, social institutions shape our behavior. They even color our thoughts. How can this be? Look at what social institutions are: the family, religion, education, economics, medicine, politics, law, science, the military, and the mass media.

In industrialized societies, social institutions tend to be more formal; in tribal societies, they are more informal. Education in industrialized societies, for example, is highly structured, while in tribal societies it usually consists of informally learning what adults do. Figure 4.2 on the next page summarizes the basic social institutions. Note that each institution has its own groups, statuses, values, and norms. Social institutions are so significant that Part IV of this book focuses on them.

group people who have something in common and who believe that what they have in common is significant; also called a social group

social institution the organized, usual, or standard ways by which society meets its basic needs

Figure 4.2 **Social Institutions in Industrial and Postindustrial Societies**

Social Institution	Basic Needs	Some Groups or Organizations	Some Statuses	Some Values	Some Norms
Family	Regulate reproduction, socialize and protect children	Relatives, kinship groups	Daughter, son, father, mother, brother, sister, aunt, uncle, grandparent	Sexual fidelity, providing for your family, keeping a clean house, respect for parents	Have only as many children as you can afford, be faithful to your spouse
Religion	Concerns about life after death, the meaning of suffering and loss; desire to connect with the Creator	Congregation, synagogue, mosque, denomination, charity	Priest, minister, rabbi, imam, worshipper, teacher, disciple, missionary, prophet, convert	Reading and adhering to holy texts such as the Bible, the Koran, and the Torah; honoring God	Attend worship services, contribute money, follow the teachings
Education	Transmit knowledge and skills across the generations	School, college, student senate, sports team, PTA, teachers' union	Teacher, student, dean, principal, football player, cheerleader	Academic honesty, good grades, being "cool"	Do homework, prepare lectures, don't snitch on classmates
Economics	Produce and distribute goods and services	Credit unions, banks, credit card companies, buying clubs	Worker, boss, buyer, seller, creditor, debtor, advertiser	Making money, paying bills on time, producing efficiently	Maximize profits, "the customer is always right," work hard
Medicine	Heal the sick and injured, care for the dying	AMA, hospitals, pharmacies, insurance companies, HMOs	Doctor, nurse, patient, pharmacist, medical insurer	Hippocratic oath, staying in good health, following doctor's orders	Don't exploit patients, give best medical care available
Politics	Allocate power, determine authority, prevent chaos	Political party, congress, parliament, monarchy	President, senator, lobbyist, voter, candidate, spin doctor	Majority rule, the right to vote as a sacred trust	One vote per person, voting as a privilege and a right
Law	Maintain social order	Police, courts, prisons	Judge, police officer, lawyer, defendant, prison guard	Trial by one's peers, innocence until proven guilty	Give true testimony, follow the rules of evidence
Science	Master the environment	Local, state, regional, national, and international associations	Scientist, researcher, technician, administrator, journal editor	Unbiased research, open dissemination of research findings, originality	Follow scientific method, be objective, disclose findings, don't plagiarize
Military	Protection from enemies, support of national interests	Army, navy, air force, marines, coast guard, national guard	Soldier, recruit, enlisted person, officer, prisoner, spy	To die for one's country is an honor, obedience unto death	Be ready to go to war, obey superiors, don't question orders
Mass Media (an emerging institution)	Disseminate information, mold public opinion, report events	TV networks, radio stations, publishers, association of bloggers	Journalist, newscaster, author, editor, publisher, blogger	Timeliness, accuracy, large audiences, freedom of the press	Be accurate, fair, timely, and profitable

The Sociological Significance of Social Institutions

To understand social institutions is to realize how profoundly social structure affects our lives. Much of the influence of social institutions lies beyond our ordinary awareness. For example, because of our economic institution, it is common to work eight hours a day for five days every week. There is nothing normal or natural about this pattern, however. Its regularity is only an arbitrary arrangement for dividing work and leisure. Yet this one aspect of a single social institution has far-reaching effects, not only in terms of how people structure their time and activities but also in terms of how they deal with family and friends, and how they meet their personal needs.

Each of the other social institutions also has far-reaching effects on our lives. Our social institutions establish the context in which we live, shaping our behavior and coloring our thoughts. Social institutions are so significant that if they were different, we would be different people. We certainly could not remain the same, for social institutions influence our orientations to the social world, and even to life itself.

An Example: The Mass Media as an Emerging Social Institution

Far beyond serving simply as sources of information, the mass media influence our attitudes toward social issues, the ways that we view other people, and even our self-concept. Because the media significantly shape public opinion, all totalitarian governments attempt to maintain tight control over them.

The mass media are relatively new in human history, owing their origins to the invention of the printing press in the 1400s. This invention had profound consequences on all social institutions. The printing of the Bible altered religion, for instance, while the publication of political broadsides and newspapers altered politics. From these beginnings, a series of inventions—from radio and movies to television and the microchip—has made the media an increasingly powerful force.

One of the most significant questions we can ask about this social institution is: Who controls it? That control, which in totalitarian countries is obvious, is much less visible in democratic nations. Functionalists might conclude that the media in a democratic nation represent the varied interests of the many groups that make up that nation. Conflict theorists, in contrast, see the matter quite differently: The mass media—at least a country's most influential newspapers and television stations—represent the interests of the political elite. They give coverage to mildly dissenting opinions, but they stand solidly behind the government. The most obvious example is the positive treatment that the media give to the inauguration of a president.

Since the mass media are so influential in our lives today, the answer to this question of who controls the media is of more than passing interest. This matter is vital to our understanding of contemporary society.

The mass media are a major influence in contemporary life. Until 1436, when Johann Gutenberg invented movable type, printing was a slow process, and printed materials were expensive. Today, printed materials are common and often cheap. "Cheap" has a double meaning, with its second meaning illustrated in this photo.

Comparing Functionalist and Conflict Perspectives

Just as the functionalist and conflict perspectives of the mass media differ, so do their views of the nature of social institutions. Let's compare these views.

The Functionalist Perspective Functionalists stress that no society is without social institutions. This is because social institutions perform vital functions for society. A group may be too small to have people who specialize in education, but it will have its own established ways of teaching skills and ideas to the young. It may be too small to have a military, but it will have some mechanism of self-defense. To survive, every society must meet its basic needs (or **functional requisites**). According to functionalists, that is the purpose of social institutions.

What are those basic needs? Functionalists identify five *functional requisites* that each society must fulfill if it is to survive (Aberle et al. 1950; Mack and Bradford 1979).

1. *Replacing members.* If a society does not replace its members, it cannot continue to exist. Because reproduction is so fundamental to a society's existence, and because every society has a vital need to protect infants and children, all groups have developed some version of the family. The family gives the newcomer to society a sense of belonging by providing a "lineage," an account of how he or she is

functional requisites the major tasks that a society must fulfill if it is to survive

Functionalist theorists have identified five *functional requisites* for the survival of a society. One, providing a sense of purpose, is often met through religious groups. To most people, snake handling, as in this church service in Jolo, West Virginia, is nonsensical. From a functional perspective, however, it makes a great deal of sense. Can you identify its sociological meanings?

related to others. The family also functions to control people's sex drive and to maintain orderly reproduction.

2. *Socializing new members.* Each baby must be taught what it means to be a member of the group into which it is born. To accomplish this, each human group develops devices to ensure that its newcomers learn the group's basic expectations. As the primary "bearer of culture," the family is essential to this process, but other social institutions, such as religion and education, also help meet this basic need.

3. *Producing and distributing goods and services.* Every society must produce and distribute basic resources, from food and clothing to shelter and education. Consequently, every society establishes an *economic* institution, a means of producing goods and services along with routine ways of distributing them.

4. *Preserving order.* Societies face two threats of disorder: one internal, the potential for chaos, and the other external, the possibility of attack. To defend themselves against external conquest, they develop a means of defense, some form of the military. To protect themselves from internal threat, they develop a system of policing themselves, ranging from formal organizations of armed groups to informal systems of gossip.

5. *Providing a sense of purpose.* Every society must get people to yield self interest in favor of the needs of the group. To convince people to sacrifice personal gains, societies instill a sense of purpose. Human groups develop many ways to implant such beliefs, but a primary one is religion, which attempts to answer questions about ultimate meaning. Actually, all of a society's institutions are involved in meeting this functional requisite; the family provides one set of answers about the sense of purpose, the school another, and so on. To see how essential a sense of purpose is to social life, recall the Ik (page 74), who lost it.

The Conflict Perspective   Although conflict theorists agree that social institutions were originally designed to meet basic survival needs, they do not view social institutions as working harmoniously for the common good. On the contrary, conflict theorists stress that powerful groups control society's institutions, manipulating them in order to maintain their own privileged position of wealth and power (Useem 1984; Domhoff 1999a, b, 2002).

Conflict theorists point out that a fairly small group of people has garnered the lion's share of the nation's wealth. Members of this elite sit on the boards of major corporations and the country's most prestigious universities. They make strategic campaign contributions to influence (or control) the nation's lawmakers, and it is they who make the major decisions in this society: to go to war or to refrain from war; to increase or to decrease taxes; to raise or to lower interest rates; and to pass laws that favor or impede moving capital, technology, and jobs out of the country.

Feminist sociologists (both women and men) have used conflict theory to gain a better understanding of how social institutions affect gender relations. Their basic insight is that gender is also an element of social structure, not simply a characteristic of individuals. In other words, throughout the world, social institutions divide males and females into separate groups, each with unequal access to society's resources.

IN SUM   Functionalists view social institutions as working together to meet universal human needs. Conflict theorists, in contrast, regard social institutions as having a single primary purpose—to preserve the social order. They interpret this as preserving the wealthy and powerful in their privileged positions.

Changes in Social Structure

As you can see, this enveloping system that we call social structure powerfully affects our lives. This means that as social structure changes, so, too, do our orientations to life. Our culture is not static. It is continuously evolving as it responds to changing values, to new technology, and to contact with cultures around the world. As our culture changes, so do we. Similarly, as our economy responds to globalization, it grows or stagnates. This opens or closes opportunities, changing our lives, sometimes brutally so. New groups such as the Department of Homeland Security come into being, wielding extraordinary power over us. In short, the corner in life that we occupy is not something independent, but it is pushed and pulled and stretched in different directions as social structure changes.

What Holds Society Together?

With its many, often conflicting, groups and its extensive social change, how does society manage to hold together? Let's examine two answers that sociologists have proposed. You will see that both past and present societies are based on social solidarity, but the types of solidarity differ remarkably.

Mechanical and Organic Solidarity Sociologist Emile Durkheim (1893/1933) found the key to **social integration**—the degree to which members of a society are united by shared values and other social bonds—in what he called **mechanical solidarity.** By this term, Durkheim meant that people who perform similar tasks develop a shared consciousness. Think of a farming community in which everyone is involved in planting, cultivating, and harvesting. Members of this group have so much in common that they know how most others feel about life. Societies with mechanical solidarity tolerate little diversity in thinking and attitudes, for their unity depends on similar thinking.

As societies get larger, their **division of labor** (how they divide up work) becomes more specialized. Some people mine gold, others turn it into jewelry, while still others sell it. This division of labor makes people depend on one another—for the work of each person contributes to the welfare of the whole.

Because this form of solidarity is based on interdependence, Durkheim called it **organic solidarity.** To see why he used this term, think about how you depend on your teacher to guide you through this introductory course in sociology. At the same time, your teacher needs you and other students in order to have a job. You and your teacher are *like organs in the same body.* (The "body" in this case is the college or university.) Although each of you performs different tasks, you depend on one another. This creates a form of unity.

The change to organic solidarity produced a new basis for solidarity—not similar views, but separate activities that contribute to the overall welfare of the group. As a result, modern societies can tolerate many differences among people and still manage to work as a whole. You will see that both past and present societies are based on social solidarity, but the types of solidarity differ remarkably.

Gemeinschaft and Gesellschaft Ferdinand Tönnies (1887/1988) also analyzed this fundamental change. Tönnies used the term *Gemeinschaft* (Guh-MINE-shoft), or "intimate community," to describe village life, the type of society in which everyone knows everyone else. He noted that in the society that was emerging, the village's personal ties, kinship connections, and lifelong friendships were being crowded out by short-term relationships, individual accomplishments, and self-interest. Tönnies called this new type of society *Gesellschaft* (Guh-ZELL-shoft), or "impersonal association." He did not mean that we no longer have intimate ties to family and friends, but, rather, that these ties have shrunk in importance. Contracts, for example, replace handshakes, and work doesn't center on friends and family, but on strangers and short-term acquaintances.

How Relevant Are These Concepts Today? I know that *Gemeinschaft, Gesellschaft,* and *mechanical* and *organic solidarity* are strange terms and that Durkheim's and Tönnies' observations must seem like a dead issue. The concern these sociologists expressed, however—that their world was changing from a community in which people are united by close ties and shared ideas and feelings to an anonymous association built around impersonal, short-term contacts—is still very real. In large part, this same concern explains the rise of Islamic fundamentalism (Volti 1995). Islamic leaders fear that Western values will uproot their traditional culture, that cold rationality will replace warm, personal relationships among families and clans. They fear, rightly so, that this will change even

social integration the degree to which members of a group or a society feel united by shared values and other social bonds; also known as *social cohesion*

mechanical solidarity Durkheim's term for the unity (a shared consciousness) that people feel as a result of performing the same or similar tasks

division of labor the splitting of a group's or a society's tasks into specialties

organic solidarity the interdependence that results from the division of labor—people needing others to fulfill their jobs

Gemeinschaft a type of society in which life is intimate; a community in which everyone knows everyone else and people share a sense of togetherness

Gesellschaft a type of society that is dominated by impersonal relationships, individual accomplishments, and self-interest

Warm, more intimate relationships of *Gemeinschaft* society are apparent in this restaurant in Salzburg, Austria. The more impersonal relationships of *Gesellschaft* soceity are evident in this café in London, where, ignoring one another, the customers engage in electronic interactions.

their views on life and morality. Although the terms may sound strange, even obscure, you can see that the ideas remain a vital part of today's world.

IN SUM Whether the terms are *Gemeinschaft* and *Gesellschaft* or *mechanical solidarity* and *organic solidarity,* they indicate that as societies change, so do people's orientations to life. *The sociological point is that social structure sets the context for what we do, feel, and think, and ultimately, then, for the kind of people we become.* As you read the Cultural Diversity box on the next page, which describes one of the few remaining *Gemeinschaft* societies in the United States, think of how fundamentally different you would be had you been reared in an Amish family.

The Microsociological Perspective: Social Interaction in Everyday Life

Whereas the macrosociological approach stresses the broad features of society, the microsociological approach has a narrower focus. Microsociologists examine *face-to-face interaction*—what people do when they are in one another's presence. Let's examine some of the areas of social life that microsociologists study.

Symbolic Interaction

For symbolic interactionists, the most significant part of life in society is social interaction. Symbolic interactionists are especially interested in the symbols that people use. They want to know how people look at things and how this, in turn, affects their behavior and orientations to life. Of the many areas of social life that microsociologists study, let's look at stereotyping, personal space, touching, and eye contact.

Cultural Diversity *in the* United States

The Amish: *Gemeinschaft* Community in a *Gesellschaft* Society

In Ferdinand Tönnies' term, the United States is a *Gesellschaft* society. Impersonal associations pervade our everyday life. Local, state, and federal governments regulate many activities. Corporations hire and fire people not on the basis of personal relationships, but on the basis of the bottom line. And, perhaps even more significantly, millions of Americans do not even know their neighbors.

Within the United States, a handful of small communities exhibits characteristics that depart from those of the mainstream society. One such community is the Old Order Amish, followers of a sect that broke away from the Swiss-German Mennonite church in the 1600s, and settled in Pennsylvania around 1727. Today, about 150,000 Old Order Amish live in the United States. About 75 percent live in just three states: Pennsylvania, Ohio, and Indiana. The largest concentration, about 22,000, reside in Lancaster County, Pennsylvania. The Amish, who believe that birth control is wrong, have doubled in population in just the past two decades.

Because Amish farmers use horses instead of tractors, most of their farms are one hundred acres or less. To the five million tourists who pass through Lancaster County each year, the rolling green pastures, white farmhouses, simple barns, horse-drawn buggies, and clotheslines hung with somber-colored garments convey a sense of peace and innocence reminiscent of another era. Although just sixty-five miles from Philadelphia, "Amish country" is a world away.

Amish life is based on separation from the world—an idea taken from Christ's Sermon on the Mount—and obedience to the church's teachings and leaders. This rejection of worldly concerns, writes sociologist Donald Kraybill in *The Riddle of Amish Culture* (1989), "provides the foundation of such Amish values as humility, faithfulness, thrift, tradition, communal goals, joy of work, a slow-paced life, and trust in divine providence."

The *Gemeinschaft* of village life that has been largely lost to industrialization remains a vibrant part of Amish life. The Amish make their decisions in weekly meetings, where, by consensus, they follow a set of rules, or *Ordnung*, to guide their behavior. Religion and discipline are the glue that holds the Amish together. Brotherly love and the welfare of the community are paramount values. In times of birth, sickness, and death, neighbors pitch in with the chores. In these ways, they maintain the bonds of intimate community.

The Amish are bound by other ties, including language (a dialect of German known as Pennsylvania Dutch), plain clothing, often black, whose style has remained unchanged for almost 300 years, and church-sponsored schools. Nearly all Amish marry, and divorce is forbidden. The family is a vital ingredient in Amish life; all major events take place in the home, including weddings, births, funerals, and church services. Amish children attend church schools, but only until the age of 13. (In 1972, the Supreme Court ruled that Amish parents had the right to take their children out of school after the eighth grade.) To go to school beyond the eighth grade would expose them to values and "worldly concerns" that would drive a wedge between the children and their community. The Amish believe that violence is bad, even personal self-defense, and they register as conscientious objectors during times of war. They pay no social security, and they receive no government benefits.

The Amish cannot resist all change, of course. Instead, they try to adapt to change in ways that will least disrupt their core values. Because urban sprawl has driven up the price of farmland, about half of Amish men work at jobs other than farming, most in farm-related businesses or in woodcrafts. They go to great lengths to avoid leaving the home. The Amish believe that when a husband works away from home, all aspects of life change—from the marital relationship to the care of the children—certainly an astute sociological insight. They also believe that if a man receives a paycheck, he will think that his work is of more value than his wife's. For the Amish, intimate, or *Gemeinschaft*, society is essential for maintaining their way of life.

Sources: Hostetler 1980; Aeppel 1996; Kephart and Zellner 2001; Kraybill 1989, 2002; Dawley 2003; Savells 2005.

Stereotypes in Everyday Life You are familiar with how strong first impressions are and the way they "set the tone" for interaction. When you first meet someone, you cannot help but notice certain features, especially the person's sex, race-ethnicity, age, and clothing. Despite your best intentions, your assumptions about these characteristics shape your first impressions. They also affect how you act toward that person—and, in turn, how that person acts toward you. These fascinating aspects of our social interaction are discussed in the Down-to-Earth Sociology box on the next page.

Personal Space   We all surround ourselves with a "personal bubble" that we go to great lengths to protect. We open the bubble to intimates—to our friends, children, parents, and so on—but we're careful to keep most people out of this space. In the hall, we might walk with our books clasped in front of us (a strategy often chosen by females). When we stand in line, we make certain there is enough space so we don't touch the person in front of us and aren't touched by the person behind us.

At times, we extend our personal space. In the library, for example, you may place your coat on the chair next to you—claiming that space for yourself even though you aren't using it. If you want to really extend your space, you might even spread books in front of the other chairs, keeping the whole table to yourself by giving the impression that others have just stepped away.

The amount of space that people prefer varies from one culture to another. South Americans, for example, like to be closer when they speak to others than do people reared in the United States. Anthropologist Edward Hall (1959; Hall and Hall 2005) recounts a conversation with a man from South America who had attended one of his lectures.

> He came to the front of the class at the end of the lecture. . . . We started out facing each other, and as he talked I became dimly aware that he was standing a little too close and that I was beginning to back up. Fortunately I was able to suppress my first impulse and remain stationary because there was nothing to communicate aggression in his behavior except the conversational distance. . . .
>
> By experimenting I was able to observe that as I moved away slightly, there was an associated shift in the pattern of interaction. He had more trouble expressing himself. If I shifted to where I felt comfortable (about twenty-one inches), he looked somewhat puzzled and hurt, almost as though he were saying, "Why is he acting that way? Here I am doing everything I can to talk to him in a friendly manner and he suddenly withdraws. Have I done anything wrong? Said something I shouldn't?" Having ascertained that distance had a direct effect on his conversation, I stood my ground, letting him set the distance.

As you can see, despite Hall's extensive knowledge of other cultures, he still felt uncomfortable in this conversation. He first interpreted the invasion of his personal space as possible aggression, for people get close (and jut out their chins and chests) when they are hostile. But when he realized that this was not the case, Hall resisted his impulse to move.

Social space is one of the many aspects of social life studied by sociologists who have a micro-sociological focus. What do you see in common in these two photos?

Down-to-Earth Sociology

Beauty May Be Only Skin Deep, But Its Effects Go On Forever: Stereotypes in Everyday Life

MARK SNYDER, A PSYCHOLOGIST, wondered whether **stereotypes**—our assumptions of what people are like—might be self-fulfilling. He came up with an ingenious way to test this idea. He (1993) gave college men a Polaroid snapshot of a woman (supposedly taken just moments before) and told them that he would introduce them to her after they talked with her on the telephone. Actually, the photographs—showing either a pretty or a homely woman—had been prepared before the experiment began. The photo was not of the woman the men would talk to.

Stereotypes came into play immediately. As Snyder gave each man the photograph, he asked him what he thought the woman would be like. The men who saw the photograph of the attractive woman said that they expected to meet a poised, humorous, outgoing woman. The men who had been given a photo of the unattractive woman described her as awkward, serious, and unsociable.

The men's stereotypes influenced the way they spoke to the women on the telephone, who did not know about the photographs. The men who had seen the photograph of a pretty woman were warm, friendly, and humorous. This, in turn, affected the women they spoke to, for they responded in a warm, friendly, outgoing manner. And the men who had seen the photograph of a homely woman? On the phone, they were cold, reserved, and humorless, and the women they spoke to became cool, reserved, and humorless. Keep in mind that the women did not know that their looks had been eval-

uated—and that the photographs were not even of them. In short, stereotypes tend to produce behaviors that match the stereotype. This principle is illustrated in Figure 4.3.

Although beauty might be only skin deep, its consequences permeate our lives (Katz 2005). Beauty bestows an advantage in everyday interaction, but it also has other effects. For one, if you are physically attractive, you are likely to make more money. Researchers in both Holland and the United States found that advertising firms with better-looking executives have higher revenues (Bosman et al. 1997; Pfann et al. 2000). The reason? The researchers suggest that people are more willing to associate with individuals whom they perceive as good-looking.

for your Consideration

Stereotypes have no single, inevitable effect. They are not magical. People can resist stereotypes and change outcomes. However, these studies do illustrate that stereotypes deeply influence how we react to one another.

Instead of beauty, consider gender and race-ethnicity. How do they affect those who do the stereotyping and those who are stereotyped?

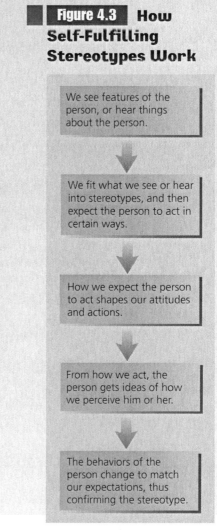

Figure 4.3 How Self-Fulfilling Stereotypes Work

We see features of the person, or hear things about the person.

⬇

We fit what we see or hear into stereotypes, and then expect the person to act in certain ways.

⬇

How we expect the person to act shapes our attitudes and actions.

⬇

From how we act, the person gets ideas of how we perceive him or her.

⬇

The behaviors of the person change to match our expectations, thus confirming the stereotype.

Physical attractiveness underlies much of our social interaction in everyday life. The experiment reviewed in this box illustrates how college men modified their interactions with women on the basis of attractiveness. How do you think women would modify their interactions if they were to meet the two men in these photographs? How about men? Would they change their interactions in the same way?

After Hall (1969; Hall and Hall 2005) analyzed situations like this, he observed that North Americans use four different "distance zones."

1. *Intimate distance.* This is the zone that the South American unwittingly invaded. It extends to about 18 inches from our bodies. We reserve this space for lovemaking, comforting, protecting, wrestling, hugging, and intimate touching.
2. *Personal distance.* This zone extends from 18 inches to 4 feet. We reserve it for friends and acquaintances and ordinary conversations. This is the zone in which Hall would have preferred speaking with the South American.
3. *Social distance.* This zone, extending out from us about 4 to 12 feet, marks impersonal or formal relationships. We use this zone for such things as job interviews.
4. *Public distance.* This zone, extending beyond 12 feet, marks even more formal relationships. It is used to separate dignitaries and public speakers from the general public.

Touching   Not only does frequency of touching differ across cultures, but so does the meaning of touching within a culture. In general, higher-status individuals do more touching. Thus you are much more likely to see teachers touch students and bosses touch secretaries than the other way around. Apparently it is considered unseemly for lower-status individuals to put their hands on superiors.

An experiment with surgery patients illustrates how touching can have different meanings. The nurse, whose job it was to tell patients about their upcoming surgery, purposely touched the patients twice, once briefly on the arm when she introduced herself, and then for a full minute on the arm during the instruction period. When she left, she also shook the patient's hand (Thayer 1988).

Men and women reacted differently. Touching soothed the women patients. It lowered their blood pressure both before the surgery and for more than an hour afterward. The men's blood pressure increased, however. The experimenters suggest that the men found it harder to acknowledge dependency and fear. Instead of a comfort, the touch was a threatening reminder of their vulnerability. Perhaps. But the men could have taken the touching as a suggestion of sexual intimacy. We don't know the answer. For this, we need more research.

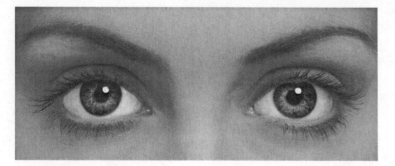

"Eye encounters" are a fascinating aspect of everyday life. We use fleeting eye contact for most of our interactions, such as those with clerks or people we pass in the hall between classes. Just as we reserve our close personal space for intimates, so, too, we reserve lingering eye contact for them.

Eye Contact   One way that we protect our personal bubble is by controlling eye contact. Letting someone gaze into our eyes—unless the person is our eye doctor—can be taken as a sign that we are attracted to that person, and even as an invitation to intimacy. A chain of supermarkets in Illinois, wanting to become "the friendliest store in town," ordered their checkout clerks to make direct eye contact with each customer. Women clerks complained that men customers were taking their eye contact the wrong way, as an invitation to intimacy. Management said they were exaggerating. The clerks' reply was, "We know the kind of looks we're getting back from men," and they refused to make direct eye contact with them.

Let's now turn to dramaturgy, a special area of symbolic interactionism.

Dramaturgy: The Presentation of Self in Everyday Life

It was their big day, two years in the making. Jennifer Mackey wore a white wedding gown adorned with an 11-foot train and 24,000 seed pearls that she and her mother had sewn onto the dress. Next to her at the altar in Lexington, Kentucky, stood her intended, Jeffrey Degler, in black tie. They said their vows, then turned to gaze for a moment at the four hundred guests. That's when groomsman Daniel Mackey collapsed. As the shocked organist struggled to play Mendelssohn's "Wedding March," Mr. Mackey's unconscious body was dragged away, his feet striking—loudly—every step of the altar stairs.

"I couldn't believe he would die at my wedding," the bride said. (Hughes 1990)

Sociologist Erving Goffman (1922–1982) added a new twist to microsociology when he developed **dramaturgy** (or dramaturgical analysis). By this term he (1959) meant that social life is like a drama or a stage play: Birth ushers us onto the stage of everyday life, and our socialization consists of learning to perform on that stage. The self that we studied in the previous chapter lies at the center of our performances. We have ideas of how we want others to think of us, and we use our roles in everyday life to communicate those ideas. Goffman called these efforts to manage the impressions that others receive of us **impression management**.

Everyday life, said Goffman, involves playing our assigned roles. We have **front stages** on which to perform them, as did Jennifer and Jeffrey. (By the way, Daniel Mackey didn't really die—he had just fainted.) But we don't have to look at weddings to find front stages. Everyday life is filled with them. Where your teacher lectures is a front stage. So are the places you go out to with your friends. So is a barbecue. In fact, you spend most of your time on front stages, for a front stage is wherever you deliver your lines. We also have **back stages,** places where we can retreat and let our hair down. When you close the bathroom or bedroom door for privacy, for example, you are entering a back stage.

In *dramaturgy*, a specialty within sociology, social life is viewed as similar to the theater. In our everyday lives, we all are actors like those in this cast of *The George Lopez Show*. We, too, perform roles, use props, and deliver lines to fellow actors—who, in turn, do the same.

The same setting can serve as both a back and a front stage. For example, when you get into your car and look over your hair in the mirror or check your makeup, you are using the car as a back stage. But when you wave at friends or if you give that familiar gesture to someone who has just cut in front of you in traffic, you are using your car as a front stage.

Everyday life brings with it many roles. The same person may be a student, a teenager, a shopper, a worker, and a date, as well as a daughter or a son. Although a role lays down the basic outline for a performance, it also allows a great deal of flexibility. The particular emphasis or interpretation that we give a role, our "style," is known as **role performance.** Consider your role as son or daughter. You may play the role of ideal daughter or son—being respectful, coming home at the hours your parents set, and so forth. Or this description may not even come close to your particular role performance.

Ordinarily, our statuses are sufficiently separated that we find minimal conflict between them. Occasionally, however, what is expected of us in one status (our role) is incompatible with what is expected of us in another status. This problem, known as **role conflict**, is illustrated in Figure 4.4 on the next page, in which family, friendship, student, and work roles come crashing together. Usually, however, we manage to avoid role conflict by segregating our statuses, which in some instances requires an intense juggling act.

Sometimes the *same* status contains incompatible roles, a conflict known as **role strain.** Suppose that you are exceptionally well prepared for a particular class assignment. Although the instructor asks an unusually difficult question, you find yourself knowing the answer when no one else does. If you want to raise your hand, yet don't want to make your fellow students look bad, you will experience role strain. As illustrated in Figure 4.4, the difference between role conflict and role strain is that role conflict is conflict *between roles,* while role strain is conflict *within* a role.

A fascinating characteristic of roles is that *we tend to become the roles we play.* That is, roles become incorporated into the self-concept, especially roles for which we prepare long and hard and that become part of our everyday lives. When sociologist Helen Ebaugh (1988), who had been a nun, studied *role exit,* she interviewed people who had left

dramaturgy an approach, pioneered by Erving Goffman, in which social life is analyzed in terms of drama or the stage; also called *dramaturgical analysis*

impression management people's efforts to control the impressions that others receive of them

front stage where performances are given

back stage where people rest from their performances, discuss their presentations, and plan future performances

role performance the ways in which someone performs a role within the limits that the role provides; showing a particular "style" or "personality"

role conflict conflicts that someone feels *between* roles because the expectations attached to one role are incompatible with the expectations of another role

role strain conflicts that someone feels *within* a role

Figure 4.4 Role Strain and Role Conflict

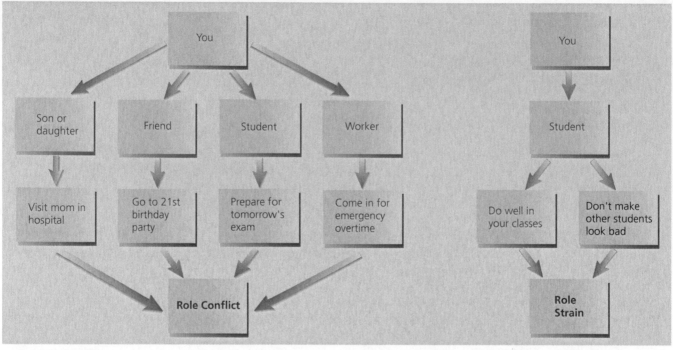

Source: By the author.

marriages, police work, the military, medicine, and religious vocations. She found that the role had become so intertwined with the individual's self-concept that leaving it threatened the person's identity. The question these people struggled with was "Who am I, now that I am not a nun (or physician, wife, colonel, and so on)?" Even years after leaving these roles, many continue to perform them in their dreams.

A statement by one of my respondents illustrates how roles that become part of the person linger after the individual leaves them:

> After I left the ministry, I felt like a fish out of water. Wearing that backward collar had become a part of me. It was especially strange on Sunday mornings when I'd listen to someone else give the sermon. I knew that I should be up there preaching. I felt as though I had left God.

To communicate information about the self, we use three types of **sign-vehicles:** the social setting, our appearance, and our manner. The *social setting* is the place where the action unfolds. This is where the curtain goes up on your performance, where you find yourself on stage playing parts and delivering lines. A social setting might be an office, dorm, living room, church, gym, or bar. It is wherever you interact with others. Your social setting includes *scenery,* the furnishings you use to communicate messages, such as desks, blackboards, scoreboards, couches, and so on.

The second sign-vehicle is *appearance,* or how we look when we play our roles. Appearance includes *props,* which are like scenery except that they decorate the person rather than the setting. The teacher has books, lecture notes, and chalk, while the football player wears a costume called a uniform. Although few of us carry around a football, we all use makeup, hairstyles, and clothing to communicate messages about ourselves. Props and other aspects of appearance give us cues that help us navigate everyday life: By letting us know what to expect from others, props tell us how we should react. Think of the messages that props communicate. Some people use clothing to say they are college students, others to say they are older adults. Some use clothing to say they are clergy, others to say they are prostitutes. Similarly, people choose brands of cigarettes, liquor, and automobiles to convey messages about the self.

sign-vehicles the term used by Goffman to refer to how people use social setting, appearance, and manner to communicate information about the self

Both individuals and organizations do *impression management*, trying to communicate messages about the self (or organization) that best meets their goals. At times, these efforts fail.

Even our body is a prop, its shape proclaiming messages about the self. The messages that are attached to various shapes change over time, but, as explored in the Mass Media box on the next page, thinness currently screams desirability.

The third sign-vehicle is *manner*, the attitudes we show as we play our roles. We use manner to communicate information about our feelings and moods. If we show anger or indifference, sincerity or good humor, for example, we indicate to others what they can expect of us as we play our roles.

We become so used to the roles we play in everyday life that we tend to think we are "just doing" things, not that we are like actors on a stage who manage impressions. Yet every time we dress for school, or for any other activity, we are preparing for impression management. Have you ever noticed how your very casually dressed classmates tend to change their appearance on the day they are scheduled to make a report to the class? No one asks them to do so, but their role has changed, and they dress for their slightly modified part. Similarly, you may have noticed that when teenagers want to impress the opposite sex, they stand before a mirror for hours as they comb and recomb their hair, and then change and rechange their clothing until they "get it just right."

Despite our best efforts to manage impressions, however, we sometimes fail. One of my favorite television scenes took place on an old TV show, *The Days and Nights of Molly Dodd*. In this particular episode, Molly Dodd tried to impress a date. She went to the "powder room," a backstage fix-up place reserved for women, where she did the usual things. Satisfied that she looked good, she made her grand entrance, walking confidently, an expectant smile on her face—all the while trailing a long piece of toilet paper from her shoe. The scene is humorous because it highlights an incongruity of elements, which creates *embarrassment*. In dramaturgical terms, embarrassment is a feeling we get when our performance fails.

If we show ourselves to be good role players, we get positive recognition from others. To accomplish this, said Goffman, we often use **teamwork**—two or more people working together to make certain that a performance goes off as planned. When a performance doesn't come off quite right, we use **face-saving behavior.** We may ignore flaws in someone's performance, which Goffman defines as *tact*. Suppose your teacher is about to make an important point. Suppose also that her lecturing has been outstanding and the class is hanging on every word. Just as she pauses for emphasis, her stomach lets out a loud growl. She might then use a *face-saving technique* by remarking, "I was so busy preparing for class that I didn't get breakfast this morning." It is more likely, however, that both class and teacher will simply ignore the sound, both giving the impression that no one heard a thing—a face-saving technique called *studied nonobservance*. This allows the teacher to make the point, or as Goffman would say, it allows the performance to go on.

Before closing this section, we should note that impression management is not limited to individuals. Families, businesses, colleges, sports teams—in fact, probably all groups—try to manage impressions. So do governments. When on September 11, 2001, terrorists hijacked four commercial airliners and flew three of them into the World Trade Center in New York City and the Pentagon in Washington, D.C., the president was in Florida, speaking at a grade school. For his safety, the Secret Service rushed him into hiding, first to a military base in Louisiana, then to another base in Nebraska. President Bush first addressed the nation from these secluded locations. To assure the people that the

teamwork the collaboration of two or more people to manage impressions jointly

face-saving behavior techniques used to salvage a performance that is going sour

mass Media in social life

You Can't Be Thin Enough: Body Images and the Mass Media

An ad for Kellogg's Special K cereal shows an 18-month-old girl wearing nothing but a diaper. She has a worried look on her face. A bubble caption over her head has her asking, "Do I look fat?" (Krane et al. 2001)

When you stand before a mirror, do you like what you see? To make your body more attractive, do you watch your weight or work out? You have ideas about what you should look like. Where did you get them?

TV and magazine ads keep pounding home the message that our bodies aren't good enough, that we've got to improve them. The way to improve them, of course, is to buy the advertised products: wigs, hairpieces, hair transplants, padded brassieres, diet pills, and exercise equipment. Muscular hulks show off machines that magically produce "six-pack abs" and incredible biceps—in just a few minutes a day. Female movie stars effortlessly go through their own tough workouts without even breaking into a sweat. Women and men get the feeling that attractive members of the opposite sex will flock to them if they purchase that wonder-working workout machine.

All of us contrast the reality we see when we look in the mirror with our culture's ideal body types. Mary Kate Olsen, a top U.S. actress, represents an ideal body type that has developed in some parts of Western culture. These cultural images often make it difficult for large people to maintain positive images of their bodies. These twins in Los Angeles, California, have struggled against dominant cultural images.

Although we try to shrug off such messages, knowing that they are designed to sell products, the messages still get our attention. They penetrate our thinking and feelings, helping to shape ideal images of how we "ought" to look. Those models so attractively clothed and coiffed as they walk down the runway, could they be any thinner? For women, the message is clear: You can't be thin enough. The men's message is also clear: You can't be strong enough.

Woman or man, your body isn't good enough. It sags where it should be firm. It bulges where it should be smooth. It sticks out where it shouldn't, and it doesn't stick out enough where it should.

And—no matter what your weight— it's too much. You've got to be thinner.

Exercise takes time, and getting in shape is painful. Once you do get in shape, if you slack off it seems to take only a few days for your body to sag into its previous slothful, drab appearance. You can't let up, you can't exercise enough, and you can't diet enough.

---

government was still in control, it wouldn't do for the president to speak while in hiding. He had to get back to Washington. The perceived danger to the president was ruled less important than his presence in the White House, and Bush was flown to Washington, escorted by U.S. Air Force F-16 fighter jets. That same evening, he addressed the American people from within the symbol of power: the Oval office.

Ethnomethodology: Uncovering Background Assumptions

As discussed in Chapter 1, symbolic interactionists stress that the events of life do not come with built-in meanings. Rather, we give meaning to things by classifying them. When we place objects and events into the categories provided by our culture, we are doing more than naming things—we are interpreting our world.

But who can continue at such a torrid pace, striving for what are unrealistic cultural ideals? A few people, of course, but not many. So liposuction is appealing. Just lie there, put up with a little discomfort, and the doctor will vacuum the fat right out of you. Surgeons can transform flat breasts into super breasts overnight. They can lower receding hairlines and smooth furrowed brows. They remove lumps with their magical tummy tucks, and can take off a decade with their rejuvenating skin peels, face lifts, and Botox injections.

With the impossibly shaped models at *Victoria's Secret* as the standard to which they hold themselves, even teens call the plastic surgeon. Anxious lest their child violate peer ideals and trail behind in her race for popularity, parents foot the bill. Some parents pay $25,000 just to give their daughters a flatter tummy (Gross 1998).

With peer pressure to alter the body already intense, surgeons keep stoking the fire. A sample ad: "No Ifs, Ands or Butts. You Can Change Your Bottom Line in Hours!" Some surgeons even offer gift certificates—so you can give your loved ones liposuction or botox injections along with their greeting card (Dowd 2002).

The thinness craze has moved to the East. Glossy magazines in Japan and China are filled with skinny models and crammed with ads touting diet pills and diet teas. In China, where famine used to abound, a little extra padding was valued as a sign of good health. Today, the obsession is thinness (Rosenthal 1999; Prystay and Fowler 2003). Not-so-subtle ads scream that fat is bad. Some teas come with a package of diet pills. Weight-loss machines, with electrodes attached to acupuncture pressure points, not only reduce fat but also build breasts—or so the advertisers claim.

Not limited by our rules, advertisers in Japan and China push a soap that supposedly "sucks up fat through the skin's pores" (Marshall 1995). What a dream product! After all, even though our TV models smile as they go through their paces, those exercise machines do look like a lot of hard work.

Then there is the other bottom line: Attractiveness does pay off. Economists studied physical attractiveness and earnings. The result? "Good-looking" men and women earn the most, "average-looking" men and women earn more than "plain" people, and the "ugly" are paid a "pittance" (Hamermesh and Biddle 1994). Consider obese women: Their net worth is less than half that of their slimmer sisters ("Fat is a Financial Issue" 2000). "Attractive" women have another cash advantage: They attract and marry higher-earning men.

More popularity *and* more money? Maybe you can't be thin enough after all. Maybe those exercise machines are a good investment. If only we could catch up with the Japanese and develop a soap that would suck the fat right out of our pores. You can practically hear the jingle now.

for your Consideration

What image do you have of your body? How do cultural expectations of "ideal" bodies underlie your image? Can you recall any advertisement or television program that has affected your body image?

What is considered ideal body size differs with historical periods and from one ethnic group to another. The women who posed for 16th century European painters, for example, appear to be "thicker" than the so-called "ideal" young women of today. Why do you think that this difference exists?

Most advertising and television programs that focus on weight are directed at women. Women are more concerned than men about weight, more likely to have eating disorders, and more likely to be dissatisfied with their bodies (Honeycutt 1995; Stinson 2001). Do you think that the targeting of women in advertising creates these attitudes and behaviors? Or do you think that these attitudes and behaviors would exist even if there were no such ads? Why?

Certainly one of the strangest words in sociology is *ethnomethodology*. To better understand this term, consider the word's three basic components. *Ethno* means folk or people; *method* means how people do something; *ology* means "the study of." Putting them together, then, *ethno/method/ology* means "the study of how people do things." Specifically, **ethnomethodology** is the study of how people use commonsense understandings to make sense of life.

Let's suppose that during a routine office visit, your doctor remarks that your hair is rather long, then takes out a pair of scissors and starts to give you a haircut. You would feel strange about this, for your doctor would be violating **background assumptions**—your ideas about the way life is and the way things ought to work. These assumptions, which lie at the root of everyday life, are so deeply embedded in our consciousness that we are seldom aware of them, and most of us fulfill them unquestioningly. Thus, your doctor does not offer you a haircut, even if he or she is good at cutting hair and you need one!

ethnomethodology the study of how people use background assumptions to make sense out of life

background assumptions deeply embedded common understandings of how the world operates and of how people ought to act

All of us have *background assumptions,* deeply ingrained expectations of how the world operates. They lay the groundwork for what we expect will happen in our interactions. How do you think the *background assumptions* of these two people differ?

The founder of ethnomethodology, sociologist Harold Garfinkel, conducted some interesting exercises designed to uncover our background assumptions. Garfinkel (1967) asked his students to act as though they did not understand the basic rules of social life. Some tried to bargain with supermarket clerks; others would inch close to people and stare directly at them. They were met with surprise, bewilderment, even anger. In one exercise Garfinkel asked students to act as though they were boarders in their own homes. They addressed their parents as "Mr." and "Mrs.," asked permission to use the bathroom, sat stiffly, were courteous, and spoke only when spoken to. As you can imagine, the other family members didn't know what to make of this (Garfinkel 1967):

> They vigorously sought to make the strange actions intelligible and to restore the situation to normal appearances. Reports (by the students) were filled with accounts of astonishment, bewilderment, shock, anxiety, embarrassment, and anger, and with charges by various family members that the student was mean, inconsiderate, selfish, nasty, or impolite. Family members demanded explanations: What's the matter? What's gotten into you? . . . Are you sick? . . . Are you out of your mind or are you just stupid?

In another exercise, Garfinkel asked students to take words and phrases literally. When a student asked his girlfriend what she meant when she said that she had a flat tire, she said:

> What do you mean, "What do you mean?"? A flat tire is a flat tire. That is what I meant. Nothing special. What a crazy question!

Another conversation went like this:

> **ACQUAINTANCE:** How are you?
> **STUDENT:** How am I in regard to what? My health, my finances, my schoolwork, my peace of mind, my . . . ?
> **ACQUAINTANCE** (red in the face): Look! I was just trying to be polite. Frankly, I don't give a damn how you are.

Students who are asked to break background assumptions can be highly creative. The young children of one of my students were surprised one morning when they came down for breakfast to find a sheet spread across the living room floor. On it were dishes, silverware, lit candles—and bowls of ice cream. They, too, wondered what was going on, but they dug eagerly into the ice cream before their mother could change her mind.

This is a risky assignment to give students, however, for breaking some background assumptions can make people suspicious. When a colleague of mine gave this assignment, a couple of his students began to wash dollar bills in a laundromat. By the time they put the bills in the dryer, the police had arrived.

IN SUM Ethnomethodologists explore *background assumptions,* the taken-for-granted ideas about the world that underlie our behavior. Most of these assumptions, or basic rules of social life, are unstated. We learn them as we learn our culture, and we violate them only with risk. Deeply embedded in our minds, they give us basic directions for living everyday life.

The Social Construction of Reality

Symbolic interactionists stress how our ideas help determine our reality. In what has become known as *the definition of the situation,* or the **Thomas theorem,** sociologists W. I. and Dorothy S. Thomas said "If people define situations as real, they are real in their consequences." Consider the following incident:

> On a visit to Morocco, in northern Africa, I decided to buy a watermelon. When I indicated to the street vendor that the knife he was going to use to cut the watermelon was dirty (encrusted with filth would be more apt), he was very obliging. He immediately bent down and began to swish the knife in a puddle on the street. I shuddered as I looked at the passing burros that were freely urinating and defecating as they went by. Quickly, I indicated by gesture that I preferred my melon uncut after all.

For that vendor, germs did not exist. For me, they did. And each of us acted according to our definition of the situation. My perception and behavior did not come from the fact that germs are real but *because I grew up in a society that teaches they are real.* Microbes, of course, *objectively* exist, and whether or not germs are part of our thought world makes no difference to whether we are infected by them. Our behavior, however, does not depend on the *objective* existence of something but, rather, on our *subjective interpretation,* on what sociologists call our *definition of reality.* In other words, it is not the reality of microbes that impresses itself on us, but society that impresses the reality of microbes on us.

Let's consider another example. Do you remember the identical twins, Oskar and Jack, who grew up so differently? As discussed on page 64, Jack was reared in Trinidad and learned to hate Hitler, while Oskar was reared in Germany and learned to love Hitler. Thus what Hitler meant to Oskar and Jack (and what he means to us) depends not on Hitler's acts, but, rather, on how we view his acts—that is, on our definition of the situation.

This is the **social construction of reality.** Our society, or the social groups to which we belong, holds particular views of life. From our groups (the *social* part of this process), we learn specific ways of looking at life—whether that be our view of Hitler or Saddam Hussein (they're good, they're evil), germs (they exist, they don't exist), or *anything else in life.* In short, through our interaction with others, we *construct reality;* that is, we learn ways of interpreting our experiences in life.

Gynecological Examinations To better understand the social construction of reality, let's consider an extended example.

To do research on vaginal examinations, I interviewed a gynecological nurse, Mae Biggs, who had been present at about 14,000 examinations. I focused on how the medical profession constructs social reality in order to define this examination as nonsexual (Henslin and Biggs 1971/2005). It became apparent that the pelvic examination unfolds much as a stage play does. I will use "he" to refer to the physician because only male physicians were part of this study. Perhaps the results would be different with women gynecologists.

Thomas theorem William I. and Dorothy S. Thomas' classic formulation of the definition of the situation: "If people define situations as real, they are real in their consequences."

social construction of reality the use of background assumptions and life experiences to define what is real

Scene 1 (the patient as person) In this scene, the doctor maintains eye contact with his patient, calls her by name, and discusses her problems in a professional manner. If he decides that a vaginal examination is necessary, he tells a nurse, "Pelvic in room 1." By this statement, he is announcing that a major change will occur in the next scene.

Scene 2 (from person to pelvic) This scene is the depersonalizing stage. In line with the doctor's announcement, the patient begins the transition from a "person" to a "pelvic." The doctor leaves the room, and a female nurse enters to help the patient make the transition. The nurse prepares the "props" for the coming examination and answers any questions the woman might have.

What occurs at this point is essential for the social construction of reality, for *the doctor's absence removes even the suggestion of sexuality.* To undress in front of him could suggest either a striptease or intimacy, thus undermining the reality so carefully being defined, that of nonsexuality.

The patient also wants to remove any hint of sexuality in the coming interaction, and during this scene she may express concern about what to do with her panties. Some mutter to the nurse, "I don't want him to see these." Most women solve the problem by either slipping their panties under their other clothes or placing them in their purse.

Scene 3 (the person as pelvic) This scene opens when the doctor enters the room. Before him is a woman lying on a table, her feet in stirrups, her knees tightly together, and her body covered by a drape sheet. The doctor seats himself on a low stool before the woman, tells her, "Let your knees fall apart" (rather than the sexually loaded "Spread your legs"), and begins the examination.

The drape sheet is crucial in this process of desexualization, for it *dissociates the pelvic area from the person:* Leaning forward and with the drape sheet above his head, the physician can see only the vagina, not the patient's face. Thus dissociated from the individual, the vagina is dramaturgically transformed into an object of analysis. If the doctor examines the patient's breasts, he also dissociates them from her person by examining them one at a time, with a towel covering the unexamined breast. Like the vagina, each breast becomes an isolated item dissociated from the person.

In this third scene, the patient cooperates in being an object, becoming, for all practical purposes, a pelvis to be examined. She withdraws eye contact from the doctor, and usually from the nurse, is likely to stare at the wall or at the ceiling, and avoids initiating conversation.

Scene 4 (from pelvic to person) In this scene, the patient becomes "repersonalized." The doctor has left the examining room; the patient dresses and fixes her hair and makeup. Her reemergence as a person is indicated by such statements to the nurse as, "My dress isn't too wrinkled, is it?" indicating a need for reassurance that the metamorphosis from "pelvic" back to "person" has been completed satisfactorily.

Scene 5 (the patient as person) In this final scene, the patient is once again treated as a person rather than as an object. The doctor makes eye contact with her and addresses her by name. She, too, makes eye contact with the doctor, and the usual middle-class interaction patterns are followed. She has been fully restored.

IN SUM To an outsider to our culture, the custom of women going to a male stranger for a vaginal examination might seem bizarre. But not to us. We learn that pelvic examinations are nonsexual. To sustain this definition requires teamwork—the doctors, nurse, and patient working together to *socially construct reality.*

It is not just pelvic examinations or our views of microbes that make up our definitions of reality. Rather, *our behavior depends on how we define reality.* Our definitions (or constructions) provide the basis for what we do and how we feel about life. To understand human behavior, then, we must know how people define reality.

The Need for Both Macrosociology and Microsociology

As was noted earlier, both microsociology and macrosociology make vital contributions to our understanding of human behavior.

Our understanding of social life would be vastly incomplete without one or the other. The photo essay on the next two pages should help to make clear why we need *both* perspectives.

To illustrate this point, let's consider two groups of high school boys studied by sociologist William Chambliss (1973/2005). Both groups attended Hanibal High School. In one group were eight middle-class boys who came from "good" families and were perceived by the community as "going somewhere." Chambliss calls this group the "Saints." The other group consisted of six lower-class boys who were seen as headed down a dead-end road. Chambliss calls this group the "Roughnecks."

Boys in both groups skipped school, got drunk, and did a lot of fighting and vandalism. The Saints were actually somewhat more delinquent, for they were truant more often and engaged in more vandalism. Yet the Saints had a good reputation, while the Roughnecks were seen by teachers, the police, and the general community as no good and headed for trouble.

The boys' reputations carried crucial consequences. Seven of the eight Saints went on to graduate from college. Three studied for advanced degrees: One finished law school and became active in state politics, one finished medical school, and one went on to earn a Ph.D. The four other college graduates entered managerial or executive training programs with large firms. After his parents divorced, one Saint failed to graduate from high school on time and had to repeat his senior year. Although this boy tried to go to college by attending night school, he never finished. He was unemployed the last time Chambliss saw him.

In contrast, only four of the Roughnecks finished high school. Two of these boys did exceptionally well in sports and received athletic scholarships to college. They both graduated from college and became high school coaches. Of the two others who graduated from high school, one became a small-time gambler and the other disappeared "up north," where he was last reported to be driving a truck. The two who did not complete high school were sent to state penitentiaries for separate murders.

To understand what happened to the Saints and the Roughnecks, we need to grasp *both* social structure and social interaction. Using *macrosociology,* we can place these boys within the larger framework of the U.S. social class system. This reveals how opportunities open or close to people depending on their social class and how people learn different goals as they grow up in different groups. We can then use *microsociology* to follow their everyday lives. We can see how the Saints manipulated their "good" reputations to skip classes and how their access to automobiles allowed them to protect those reputations by transferring their troublemaking to different communities. In contrast, the Roughnecks, who did not have cars, were highly visible. Their lawbreaking, which was limited to a small area, readily came to the attention of the community. Microsociology also reveals how their respective reputations opened doors of opportunity to the first group of boys while closing them to the other.

Thus we need both kinds of sociology, and both are stressed in the following chapters.

When a **Tornado Strikes:**

Social Organization Following a Natural Disaster

a s I was watching television on March 20, 2003, I heard a report that a tornado had hit Camilla, Georgia. "Like a big lawn mower," the report said, it had cut a path of destruction through this little town. In its fury, the tornado had left behind six dead and about 200 injured.

From sociological studies of natural disasters, I knew that immediately after the initial shock the survivors of natural disasters work together to try to restore order to their disrupted lives. I wanted to see this restructuring process first hand. The next morning, I took off for Georgia.

These photos, taken the day after the tornado struck, tell the story of people who are in the midst of trying to put their lives back together. I was impressed at how little time people spend commiserating about their misfortune and how quickly they take practical steps to restore their lives.

As you look at these photos, try to determine why you need both microsociology and macrosociology to understand what occurs after a natural disaster.

After making sure that their loved ones are safe, one of the next steps people take is to recover their possessions. The cooperation that emerges among people, as documented in the sociological literature on natural disasters, is illustrated here.

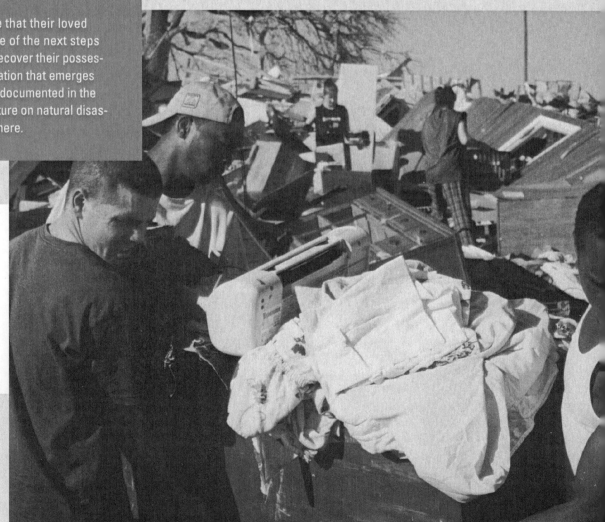

© James M. Henslin,
all photos

▲ In addition to the inquiring sociologist, television news teams also were interviewing survivors and photographing the damage. This was the second time in just three years that a tornado had hit this neighborhood.

◄ The owners of this house invited me inside to see what the tornado had done to their home. In what had been her dining room, this woman is trying to salvage whatever she can from the rubble. She and her family survived by taking refuge in the bathroom. They had been there only five seconds, she said, when the tornado struck.

No building or social institution escapes a tornado as it follows its path of destruction. Just the night before, members of this church had held evening worship service. After the tornado, someone mounted a U.S. flag on top of the cross, symbolic of the church members' patriotism and religiosity —and of their enduring hope.

Personal relationships are essential in putting lives together. Consequently, reminders of these relationships are one of the main possessions that people attempt to salvage. This young man, having just recovered the family photo album, is eagerly reviewing the photos.

Formal organizations also help the survivors of natural disasters recover. In this neighborhood, I saw representatives of insurance companies, the police, the fire department, and an electrical co-op. The Salvation Army brought meals to the neighborhood.

For children, family photos are not as important as toys. This girl has managed to salvage a favorite toy, which will help anchor her to her previous life.

A sign of the times. Like electricity and gas, cable television also has to be restored as soon as possible.

Introductory Sociology 1

Summary *and* Review

Levels of Sociological Analysis

What two levels of analysis do sociologists use?

Sociologists use macrosociological and microsociological levels of analysis. In **macrosociology,** the focus is placed on large-scale features of social life, while in **microsociology,** the focus is on **social interaction.** Functionalists and conflict theorists tend to use a macrosociological approach, while symbolic interactionists are more likely to use a microsociological approach. Pp. 96–97.

The Macrosociological Perspective: Social Structure

How does social structure influence our behavior?

The term **social structure** refers to the social envelope that surrounds us and establishes limits on our behavior. Social structure consists of culture, social class, social statuses, roles, groups, and social institutions. Together, these serve as foundations for how we view the world.

Our location in the social structure underlies our perceptions, attitudes, and behaviors. Culture lays the broadest framework, while **social class** divides people according to income, education, and occupational prestige. Each of us receives **ascribed statuses** at birth; later we add **achieved statuses.** Our behaviors and orientations are further influenced by the **roles** we play, the **groups** to which we belong, and our experiences with social institutions. These components of society work together to help maintain social order. Pp. 97–101.

Social Institutions

What are social institutions?

Social institutions are the standard ways that a society develops to meet its basic needs. As summarized in Figure 4.2 (page 102), industrialized societies have ten social institutions—the family, religion, education, economics, medicine, politics, law, science, the military, and the mass media. From the functionalist perspective, social institutions meet universal group needs, or **functional requisites.** Conflict theorists stress how society's elites use social institutions to maintain their privileged positions. Pp. 101–105.

What holds society together?

According to Emile Durkheim, in agricultural societies people are united by **mechanical solidarity** (similar views and feelings). With industrialization comes **organic solidarity** (people depend on one another to do their more specialized jobs). Ferdinand Tönnies pointed out that the informal means of control of *Gemeinschaft* (small, intimate) societies are replaced by formal mechanisms in *Gesellschaft* (larger, more impersonal) societies. Pp. 105–106.

The Microsociological Perspective: Social Interaction in Everyday Life

What is the focus of symbolic interactionism?

In contrast to functionalists and conflict theorists, who as macrosociologists focus on the "big picture," symbolic interactionists tend to be microsociologists who focus on face-to-face social interaction. Symbolic interactionists analyze how people define their worlds, and how their definitions, in turn, influence their behavior. P. 106.

How do stereotypes affect social interaction?

Stereotypes are assumptions of what people are like. When we first meet people, we classify them according to our perceptions of their visible characteristics. Our ideas about those characteristics guide our behavior toward them. Our behavior, in turn, may influence them to behave in ways that reinforce our stereotypes. Pp. 107–108, 109.

Do all human groups share a similar sense of personal space?

In examining how people use physical space, symbolic interactionists stress that we surround ourselves with a "personal bubble," one that we carefully protect. People from different cultures use "personal bubbles" of varying sizes, so the answer to the question is no. Americans typically use four different "distance zones"—intimate, personal, social, and public. Pp. 108, 110.

What is dramaturgy?

Erving Goffman developed **dramaturgy** (or dramaturgical analysis), in which everyday life is analyzed in terms of the stage. At the core of this analysis is **impression management,** our attempts to control the impressions we make on others. For this, we use the **sign-vehicles** of setting, appearance, and manner. Our performances often call for **teamwork** and **face-saving behavior.** Pp. 110–117.

What is the social construction of reality?

The phrase the **social construction of reality** refers to how we construct our views of the world, which, in turn, underlie our actions. **Ethnomethodology** is the study of how people make sense of everyday life. Ethnomethodologists try to uncover **background assumptions,** our basic ideas about the way life is. Pp. 117–119.

The Need for Both Macrosociology and Microsociology

Why are both levels of analysis necessary?

Because each focuses on different aspects of the human experience, both microsociology and macrosociology are necessary for us to understand social life. P. 119.

Thinking Critically
about Chapter 4

1. The major components of social structure are culture, social class, social status, roles, groups, and social institutions. Use social structure to explain why Native Americans have such a low rate of college graduation. (See Table 12.2 on page 346.)

2. Dramaturgy is a form of microsociology. Use dramaturgy to analyze a situation with which you are intimately familiar (such as interaction with your family or friends, or even interaction in one of your college classes).

3. To illustrate why we need both macrosociology and microsociology to understand social life, use an example from your own life.

Additional Resources

Companion Website www.ablongman.com/henslin8e

- *Content Select* Research Database for Sociology, with suggested key terms and annotated references
- Link to 2000 Census, with activities
- Flashcards of key terms and concepts
- Practice Tests
- Weblinks
- Interactive Maps

Where Can I Read More on This Topic?

Suggested readings for this chapter are listed at the back of this book.

Societies to Social Networks

CHAPTER
6

OUTLINE

Bernard Bonhomme, *Group of People,* 1999

When Kody Scott joined the L.A. Crips, his initiation had two parts. Here's the first:

"How old is you now anyway?"

"Eleven, but I'll be twelve in November."

I never saw the blow to my head come from Huck. Bam! And I was on all fours . . . Kicked in the stomach, I was on my back counting stars in the blackness. Grabbed by the collar, I was made to stand again. A solid blow to my chest exploded pain on the blank screen that had now become my mind. Bam! Another, then another. Blows rained on me from every direction . . .

Up until this point not a word had been spoken. . . . Then I just started swinging, with no style or finesse, just anger and the instinct to survive. . . . (This) reflected my ability to represent the set [gang] in hand-to-hand combat. The blows stopped abruptly . . . My ear was bleeding, and my neck and face were deep red . . .

Scott's beating was followed immediately by the second part of his initiation. For this, he received the name *Monster*, which he carried proudly:

"Give Kody the pump" [12-gauge pump action shotgun] . . . Tray Ball spoke with the calm of a football coach. "Tonight we gonna rock they world." . . .

Kody, you got eight shots, you don't come back to the car unless they all are gone.

Hand slaps were passed around the room . . . "Kody, you got eight shots, you don't come back to the car unless they all are gone."

"Righteous," I said, eager to show my worth. . . .

Hanging close to buildings, houses, and bushes, we made our way, one after the other, to within spitting distance of the Bloods. . . . Huck and Fly stepped from the shadows simultaneously and were never noticed until it was too late. Boom! Boom! Heavy bodies hitting the ground, confusion, yells of dismay, running, . . . By my sixth shot I had advanced past the first fallen bodies and into the street in pursuit of those who had sought refuge behind cars and trees. . . .

Back in the shack we smoked more pot and drank more beer. I was the center of attention for my acts of aggression. . . .

Tray Ball said. "You got potential, 'cause you eager to learn. Bangin' [being a gang member] ain't no part-time thang, it's full-time, it's a career. It's bein' down when ain't nobody else down with you. It's gettin' caught and not tellin'. Killin' and not caring, and dyin' without fear. It's love for your set and hate for the enemy. You hear what I'm sayin'?"

Kody adds this insightful remark:

Though never verbally stated, death was looked upon as a sort of reward, a badge of honor,

(continued)

especially if one died in some heroic capacity for the hood . . . The supreme sacrifice was to "take a bullet for a homie" [fellow gang member]. The set functioned as a religion. Nothing held a light to the power of the set. If you died on the trigger you surely were smiled upon by the Crip God.

Excerpts from Scott 1994:8–13, 103.

As society—the largest and most complex type of group—changes, so, too, do the groups, activities, and, ultimately, the type of people who form that society. This photo of Stacy Keibler and Torrie Wilson in Madison Square Garden captures some of the changes that U.S. society has been undergoing in recent years. What social changes can you identify from this photo?

Groups are the essence of life in society. We become who we are because of our membership in human groups. As we saw in Chapter 3, even our minds are a product of society, or, more specifically phrased, of the groups to which we belong.

In this chapter, we'll consider how groups influence our lives—and even the power that groups wield over us. Although none of us wants to think that we could participate in killings such as those recounted in our opening vignette, don't bet on it. You are going to read some surprising things about groups in this chapter.

Societies and Their Transformation

To better understand **groups**—people who interact with one another and who think of themselves as belonging together—let's first look at the big picture. The largest and most complex group that sociologists study is **society**, which consists of people who share a culture and a territory. Society, which surrounds us, sets the stage for our life experiences. Not only does it lay the broad framework for our behavior but also it influences the ways we think and feel. Since our society is so significant in our lives, let's look at how it developed. In Figure 6.1, you can see that technology is the key to understanding the broad, sweeping changes that have produced our society. As we summarize these changes, picture yourself as a member of each society. Consider how your life—even your thoughts and values—would be different in each society.

Hunting and Gathering Societies

Societies with the fewest social divisions are called **hunting and gathering societies.** As the name implies, these groups depend on hunting animals and gathering plants for their survival. In some, the men do the hunting, and the women the gathering. In others, both men and women (and children) gather plants, the men hunt large animals, and both men and women hunt small animals. Beyond this basic division of labor by sex, there are few social divisions. The groups usually have a **shaman,** an individual thought to be able to influence spiritual forces, but shamans, too, must help obtain food. Although these groups give greater prestige to the men hunters, the women gatherers contribute more food to the group, perhaps even four-fifths of their total food supply (Bernard 1992).

In addition to gender, the major unit of organization is the family. Most group members are related by ancestry or marriage. Because the family is the only distinct social institution in these societies, it fulfills functions that are divided among modern society's many specialized institutions. The family distributes food to its members, educates its children (especially in survival skills), nurses its sick, and provides for virtually all other needs.

Because an area cannot support a large number of people who hunt animals and gather plants (they do not plant—they only gather what is already there), hunting and gathering societies are small. They usually consist of only twenty-five to forty people. These groups are nomadic, moving from one place to another as the food supply of an area gives out. They place high value on sharing food, which is essential to their survival. Because of disease, drought, and pestilence, children have only about a fifty-fifty chance of surviving childhood (Lenski and Lenski 1987).

Of all societies, hunters and gatherers are the most egalitarian. Because what they hunt and gather is perishable and they have no money, the people accumulate few personal possessions. Consequently, no one becomes wealthier than anyone else. There are no rulers, and most decisions are arrived at through discussion. Because their needs are basic and they do not work to store up material possessions, hunters and gatherers have the most leisure of all human groups (Sahlins 1972; Lorber 1994; Volti 1995).

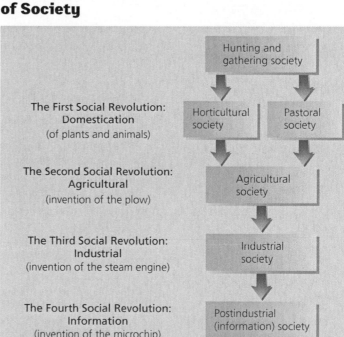

Figure 6.1 The Social Transformations of Society

The First Social Revolution: Domestication (of plants and animals)

The Second Social Revolution: Agricultural (invention of the plow)

The Third Social Revolution: Industrial (invention of the steam engine)

The Fourth Social Revolution: Information (invention of the microchip)

The Fifth Social Revolution?: Bioeconomic (decoding of human genome system?)

Hunting and gathering society → Horticultural society / Pastoral society → Agricultural society → Industrial society → Postindustrial (information) society → Emerging → Biotech society?

Source: By the author.

All human groups were once hunters and gatherers, and until several hundred years ago such societies were common. Their demise came when other groups took over the regions in which they moved about in their search for food. Today, fewer than 300 hunter-gatherer groups remain; they include the pygmies of central Africa, the aborigines of Australia, and groups in South America represented by the photo below (Stiles 2003). These groups seem doomed to a similar fate, and it is likely that their way of life will soon disappear from the human scene (Lenski and Lenski 1987).

The simplest forms of societies are called hunting and gathering societies. Members of these societies have adapted well to their environments, and they have more leisure than the members of other societies. Shown here is a member of the Kayapó tribe in the rainforest of Brazil.

group people who have something in common and who believe that what they have in common is significant; also called a *social group*

society people who share a culture and a territory

hunting and gathering society a human group that depends on hunting and gathering for its survival

shaman the healing specialist of a tribe who attempts to control the spirits thought to cause a disease or injury; commonly called a witch doctor

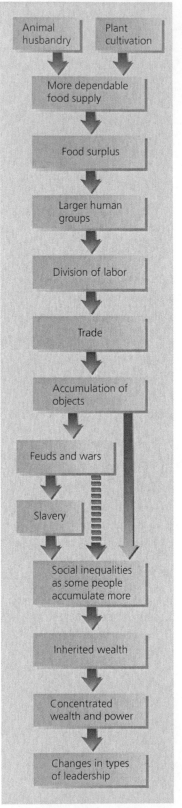

Figure 6.2 **Consequences of Animal Domestication and Plant Cultivation**

Animal husbandry

Plant cultivation

More dependable food supply

Food surplus

Larger human groups

Division of labor

Trade

Accumulation of objects

Feuds and wars

Slavery

Social inequalities as some people accumulate more

Inherited wealth

Concentrated wealth and power

Changes in types of leadership

Source: By the author.

Pastoral and Horticultural Societies

About ten thousand years ago, some groups found that they could tame and breed some of the animals they hunted—primarily goats, sheep, cattle, and camels. Others discovered that they could cultivate plants. As a result, hunting and gathering societies branched into two directions, each with different means of acquiring food.

The key to understanding the first branching is the word *pasture;* **pastoral** (or herding) **societies** are based on the *pasturing of animals.* Pastoral societies developed in arid regions, where low rainfall made it impractical to build life around growing crops. Groups that took this turn remained nomadic, for they followed their animals to fresh pasture. The key to understanding the second branching is the word *horticulture,* or plant cultivation. **Horticultural** (or gardening) **societies** are based on the *cultivation of plants by the use of hand tools.* Because they no longer had to abandon an area as the food supply diminished, these groups developed permanent settlements.

We can call the domestication of animals and plants the *first social revolution.* As shown in Figure 6.1 on page 149, it transformed human society. Although the **domestication revolution** was gradual, occurring over thousands of years, it represented a fundamental break with the past and changed human history. The more dependable food supply ushered in changes that touched almost every aspect of human life. Groups became larger because the more dependable food supply supported more people. With more food than was needed for survival, no longer was it necessary for everyone to produce food. This allowed groups to develop a *division of labor,* and some people began to specialize in making jewelry, tools, weapons, and so on. This led to a surplus of objects, which, in turn, stimulated trade. With trading, groups began to accumulate objects they prized, such as gold, jewelry, and utensils.

Figure 6.2 illustrates how these changes set the stage for *social inequality.* Some families (or clans) acquired more goods than others. This led to feuds and war, for groups now possessed animals, pastures, croplands, jewelry, and other material goods to fight about. War, in turn, opened the door to slavery, for people found it convenient to let their captives do their drudge work. Social inequality remained limited, however, for the surplus itself was limited. As individuals passed their possessions on to their descendants, wealth grew more concentrated. So did power. At some point during this period, some individuals became chiefs, leaders of groups.

Note the primary pattern that runs through this transformation of group life: the change *from fewer to more possessions and from greater to lesser equality.* Where people were located *within* a society became vital for determining what happened to them in life. Again, Figure 6.2 summarizes how these changes led to social inequality.

Agricultural Societies

When the plow was invented about five or six thousand years ago, social life was once again changed forever. Compared with hoes and digging sticks, the use of animals to pull plows was immensely efficient. As the earth was plowed, more nutrients were returned to the soil, making the land more productive. The food surplus of the **agricultural revolution** was unlike anything ever seen in human history. It allowed even more people to engage in activities other than farming. In this new **agricultural society,** people developed cities and what is popularly known as "culture," such as philosophy, art, music, literature, and architecture. Accompanied by the inventions of the wheel, writing, and numbers, the changes were so profound that this period is sometimes referred to as "the dawn of civilization."

The tendency toward social inequality of previous societies was only a forerunner of what was to come. *Inequality became a fundamental feature of life in society.* Some people managed to gain control of the growing surplus resources. To protect their expanding privileges and power, this elite surrounded itself with armed men. They even levied taxes on others, who now had become their "subjects." As conflict theorists point out, this concentration of resources and power—along with the oppression of people not in power—was the forerunner of the state.

No one knows exactly how it happened, but during this period females also became subject to males. Sociologist Elise Boulding (1976) theorizes that this change occurred because men were in charge of plowing and the cows. She suggests that when metals were developed, men took on the new job of attaching the metal as tips to the wooden plows and doing the plowing. As a result,

> the shift of the status of the woman farmer may have happened quite rapidly, once there were two male specializations relating to agriculture: plowing and the care of cattle. This situation left women with all the subsidiary tasks, including weeding and carrying water to the fields. The new fields were larger, so women had to work just as many hours as they did before, but now they worked at more secondary tasks. . . . This would contribute further to the erosion of the status of women.

This explanation, however, creates more questions than it answers. Why, for example, did men take over metal work and plowing? Why didn't women? It also does not account for why men control societies in which women are in charge of the cattle. In short, we are left in the dark as to why and how men became dominant, a reason likely to remain lost in human history.

Industrial Societies

In the 1700s, another invention turned society upside down. The **Industrial Revolution** began in 1765 when the steam engine was first used to run machinery in Great Britain. Before this, people used a few machines (such as wind and water mills) to harness nature, but most machines depended on human and animal power. The resulting **industrial society** is defined by sociologist Herbert Blumer (1990) as one in which goods are produced by machines powered by fuels, instead of by the brute force of humans or animals.

With the steam engine, social inequality took another leap. This new technology was far more efficient than anything that preceded it. Just as its surplus was greater, so also were its effects on social life. Those who first used the steam engine accumulated such wealth that in many instances their riches outran the imagination of royalty. Gaining an early position in the markets, the early industrialists were able not only to control the means of production (factories, machinery, tools) but also to dictate people's working conditions. The breakdown of feudal society also helped them to control the workers. Masses of people were thrown off the lands that their ancestors had farmed as tenants for centuries. Having become homeless, these landless peasants moved to the cities. There they faced the choice of stealing, starving, or working for near-starvation wages (Chambliss 1964; Michalowski 1985).

Workers had no legal right to safe working conditions, nor the right to unionize. Employment was a private contract between the employer and the individual worker. If workers banded together to protest or to ask for higher wages, they were fired. If they returned to the factory, they were arrested for trespassing on private property. Strikes were illegal, and strikers were savagely beaten by the employer's private security force. On some occasions during the early 1900s, U.S. strikers were shot by private police, and even by the National Guard.

Against these odds, workers gradually won their fight for better working conditions. Wealth then spread to larger segments of society. Eventually, home ownership became common, as did the ownership of automobiles and an incredible variety of consumer goods. Today's typical worker in advanced industrial societies enjoys a high standard of living in

The sociological significance of the social revolutions discussed in the text is that the type of society in which we live determines the kind of people we become. It is obvious, for example, that the orientations to life of this worker would differ markedly from those of the man shown on page 149.

The machinery that ushered in industrial society was met with ambivalence. On one hand, it brought a multitude of welcomed goods. On the other hand, factory time clocks and the incessant production line made people slaves to the very machines they built. The idea of machines dominating workers is illustrated by this classic scene of Charlie Chaplin's in *Modern Times*.

pastoral society a society based on the pasturing of animals

horticultural society a society based on cultivating plants by the use of hand tools

domestication revolution the first social revolution, based on the domestication of plants and animals, which led to pastoral and horticultural societies

agricultural revolution the second social revolution, based on the invention of the plow, which led to agricultural societies

agricultural society a society based on large-scale agriculture; plows drawn by animals are the source of food production

Industrial Revolution the third social revolution, occurring when machines powered by fuels replaced most animal and human power

industrial society a society based on the harnessing of machines powered by fuels

terms of material conditions, health care, longevity, and access to libraries and education. Such gains go far beyond what early social reformers could have imagined.

As industrialization progressed, it reversed the pattern set earlier, and equality began to increase. Indicators of greater equality include better housing and a vast increase in consumer goods, the abolition of slavery, the shift from monarchies to more representative political systems, the right to be tried by a jury of one's peers and to cross-examine witnesses, the right to vote, the right to travel, and greater rights for women and minorities.

It is difficult to overstate the sociological principle that the type of society we live in is the fundamental reason for why we become who we are. To see how industrial society affects your life, note that you would not be taking this course if it were not for industrialization. Clearly you would not have a computer, car, cell phone, DVD player, television, or your type of clothing or home. You wouldn't even have electric lights. And on a much deeper level, you would not feel the same about life, or have your particular aspirations for the future. Actually, no aspect of your life would be the same; you would be locked into the attitudes and views that come with an agricultural or horticultural way of life.

Postindustrial (Information) Societies

If you were to choose one word that characterizes our society, what would it be? Of the many candidates, the word *change* would have to rank high among them. The primary source of the sweeping changes that are transforming our lives is the technology centering around the microchip. The change is so vast that sociologists say that a new type of society has emerged. They call it the **postindustrial** (or **information**) **society.**

What are the main characteristics of this new society? Unlike the industrial society, its hallmark is not raw materials and manufacturing. Rather, its basic component is *information.* Teachers pass on knowledge to students, while lawyers, physicians, bankers, pilots, and interior decorators sell their specialized knowledge of law, the body, money, aerodynamics, and color schemes to clients. Unlike the factory workers of an industrial society, these individuals don't *produce* anything. Rather, they transmit or use information to provide services that others are willing to pay for.

The United States was the first country to have more than 50 percent of its work force in service industries such as education, health, research, the government, counseling, banking, investments, insurance, sales, law, and the mass media. Australia, New Zealand, western Europe, and Japan soon followed. This trend away from manufacturing and toward selling information and services shows no sign of letting up.

The changes have been so profound that they have led to a *fourth social revolution.* The microchip is transforming established ways of life, uprooting old perspectives and replacing them with new ones. This new technology allows us to work at home, and while we ride in cars, trucks, and airplanes, to talk to others in distant cities and even to people on the other side of the globe. This tiny device lets us peer farther into the remote recesses of space than ever before. It is changing our shopping patterns as we spend billions of dollars on Internet purchases. And because of it, millions of children spend countless hours battling virtual video villains. For a review of other changes, see the section on the computer in Chapter 22 (pages 665–669).

Biotech Societies: Is a New Type of Society Emerging?

Can you believe these new products (Elias 2001)?

- Tobacco that fights cancer. ("Yes, smoke your way to health!")
- Corn that fights herpes and is a contraceptive. ("Corn flakes in the morning—and safe sex all day!")
- Goats whose milk contains spider silk (to make fishing lines and body armor) ("Got milk? The best bulletproofing.")
- Animals that are part human: Human genes have been inserted into their genes, so they produce medicines for humans—and creamier mozzarella cheese. (You can write your own jingle for this one.)

postindustrial (information) society a society based on information, services, and high technology, rather than on raw materials and manufacturing

I know that this sounds like science fiction, but we *already* have the goats that make spider silk and the part-human animals that produce medicine (Kristoff 2002; Osborne 2002). Some suggest that the changes in which we are immersed are revolutionary, that we are entering another new type of society (Holloway 2002; Oliver 2003). In this new **biotech society,** the economy will center on applying and altering genetic structures—both plant and animal—to produce food, medicine, and materials.

If there is a new society, then when did it begin? There are no firm edges to new societies, for each new one overlaps the one it is replacing. The biotech society could have begun in 1953, when Francis Crick and James Watson identified the double-helix structure of DNA. At this point, though, the best guess is that historians will trace the date to the decoding of the human genome in 2001.

Projecting a new type of society so soon after the arrival of the information society is risky. The wedding of genetics and economics could turn out to be simply another aspect of our information society—or we may have just stepped into a new type of society. In either case, we can anticipate revolutionary changes in health care (prevention, instead of treating disease) and, with cloning and bioengineering, perhaps even changes in the human species. The Sociology and the New Technology box on the next page examines implications of cloning.

Whether the changes that are swirling around us are part of a new type of society is not the main point. *The sociological significance of these changes is that just as the larger group called society always profoundly affects people's thinking and behavior, so, too, these recent developments will do the same for us.* As society is transformed, we will be swept along with it. The changes will be so extensive that they will transform even the ways we think about the self and life.

▰ ▰ ◣ ▰
IN SUM | Our society sets boundaries around our lives. It establishes the values and beliefs that prevail and also determines the type and extent of social inequality. These factors, in turn, set the stage for relationships between men and women, the young and the elderly, race–ethnic groups, the rich and the poor, and so on.

It is difficult to overstate the sociological principle that the type of society in which we live is the fundamental reason why we become who we are—why we feel about things the way we do, and even why we think our particular thoughts. On the obvious level, if you lived in a hunting and gathering society you would not be listening to your favorite music, watching TV programs, or playing video games. On a deeper level, you would not feel the same about life or hold your particular aspirations for the future.

Finally, we should note that not all the world's societies will go through the transformations shown in Figure 6.1 (page 149). Whether any hunting and gathering societies will survive, however, remains to be seen. Perhaps a few will, maybe kept on "small reserves" that will be off limits to developers—but open to guided ecotours at a hefty fee.

Now that we have reviewed the major historical shifts in societies, let's turn to groups within society. Just how do they affect our lives?

Groups Within Society

▰ ▰ ◤ ◢ ▰ Sociologist Emile Durkheim (1933) wondered what could be done to prevent *anomie* (AN-uh-mee), that bewildering sense of not fitting in, of not belonging. Durkheim found the answer in small groups. He said that small groups stand as a buffer between the individual and the larger society. If it weren't for these groups, we would feel oppressed by that huge, amorphous entity known as society. By providing intimate relationships, small groups give us a sense of meaning and purpose, helping to prevent anomie.

Before we examine groups in more detail, we should distinguish some terms. Two terms sometimes confused with "group" are *aggregate* and *category*. An **aggregate** consists of individuals who temporarily share the same physical space but who do not see themselves as belonging together. People waiting in a checkout line or drivers parked at a red light are an

biotech society a society whose economy increasingly centers around the application of genetics—human genetics for medicine, and plant and animal genetics for the production of food and materials

aggregate individuals who temporarily share the same physical space but who do not see themselves as belonging together

"So, You Want to Be Yourself?" Cloning in the Coming Biotech Society

NO TYPE OF SOCIETY ENDS ABRUPTLY. The edges are fuzzy, and one overlaps the other. As the information society matures, it looks as though it is being overtaken by a biotech society. Let's try to peer over the edge of our current society to glimpse the one that may be coming. What will life be like? There are many issues we could examine, but since space is limited, let's consider just one: cloning.

Consider this scenario:

Your four-year-old daughter has drowned, and you can't get over your sorrow. You go to the regional cloning clinic, where you have stored DNA from all members of your family. You pay the standard fee, and the director hires a surrogate mother to bring your daughter back as a newborn.

Will cloning humans become a reality? Since human embryos have already been cloned, it seems inevitable that some group somewhere will complete the process. If cloning humans becomes routine—well, consider these scenarios:

Suppose that a couple can't have children. Testing shows that the husband is sterile. The couple talk about their dilemma, and the wife agrees to have her husband's genetic material implanted into one of her eggs. Would this woman, in effect, be rearing her husband as a little boy?

Or suppose that you love your mother dearly, and she is dying. With her permission, you decide to clone her. Who is the clone? Would you be rearing your own mother?

What if a woman gave birth to her own clone? Would the clone be her daughter or her sister?

When genetic duplicates appear, the questions of what humans are, what their relationship is to their "parents," and indeed what "parents" and "children" are, will be brought up at every kitchen table.

for your Consideration

As these scenarios show, the issue of cloning brings up profound questions, perhaps the most weighty being about the future of society itself. Let's suppose that mass cloning becomes possible.

Many people object that cloning is immoral, but some will argue the opposite. They will ask why we should leave human reproduction to people who have inferior traits—genetic diseases, low IQs, perhaps even the propensity for crime and violence. They will suggest that we select people with the finer characteristics—high creative ability, high intelligence, compassion, and a propensity for peace.

Let's assume that scientists have traced these characteristics—as well as the ability and appreciation for poetry, music, mathematics, architecture, and love—to genetics. Do you think that it should be our moral obligation to populate society with people like this? To try to build a society that is better for all—one without terrorism, war, violence, and greed? Could this perhaps even be our evolutionary destiny?

Source: Based on Kaebnick 2000; McGee 2000; Bjerklie et al. 2001; Davis 2001; Weiss 2004; Regalado 2005.

---

aggregate. A **category** is a statistic. It consists of people who share similar characteristics, such as all college women who wear glasses or all men over 6 feet tall. Unlike groups, the individuals who make up a category neither interact with one another nor take one another into account. The members of a *group,* in contrast, think of themselves as belonging together, and they interact with one another. These concepts are illustrated in the photos on the facing page.

Primary Groups

Our first group, the family, gives us our basic orientations to life. Later, among friends, we find more intimacy and an additional sense of belonging. These groups are what sociologist Charles Cooley called **primary groups.** By providing intimate, face-to-face interaction, they give us an identity, a feeling of who we are. As Cooley (1909) put it,

By primary groups I mean those characterized by intimate face-to-face association and cooperation. They are primary in several senses, but chiefly in that they are fundamental in forming the social nature and ideals of the individual.

category people who have similar characteristics

primary group a group characterized by intimate, long-term, face-to-face association and cooperation

Categories, Aggregates, and Secondary Groups

Groups have a deep impact on our views, orientations, even what we feel and think about life. Yet, as illustrated by these photos, not everything that appears to be a group is actually a group in the sociological sense. You might also want to look at the photos of primary and reference groups on pages 156 and 158.

What outstanding trait do these people have in common? Their natural red hair does not make them a group, but a **category.**

Aggregates are simply people who happen to be in the same place at the same time.

Secondary groups are larger and more anonymous, formal, and impersonal than primary groups. Why is this photo of a political convention an example of a **secondary** group?

Primary groups such as the family play a key role in the development of the self. As a small group, the family also serves as a buffer from the often-threatening larger group known as society. The family has been of primary significance in forming the basic orientations of this Latino couple, as it will be for their daughter.

Producing a Mirror Within   Cooley called primary groups the "springs of life." By this, he means that primary groups are essential to our emotional well-being. You can see this in your own life with your family and friends. As humans, we have an intense need for face-to-face interaction that generates feelings of self-esteem. By offering a sense of belonging and a feeling of being appreciated—and sometimes even loved—primary groups are uniquely equipped to meet this basic human need. From our opening vignette, you can see that gangs are also primary groups.

Primary groups are also "springs of life" because their values and attitudes become fused into our identity. We internalize their views, which become the lenses through which we view life. Even as adults—no matter how far we move away from our childhood roots—early primary groups remain "inside" us. There they continue to form part of the perspective from which we look out onto the world. Ultimately, then, it is difficult, if not impossible, for us to separate the self from our primary groups, for the self and our groups merge into a "we."

Secondary Groups

Compared with primary groups, **secondary groups** are larger, more anonymous, more formal, and more impersonal. Secondary groups are based on some common interest or activity, and their members are likely to interact on the basis of specific statuses, such as president, manager, worker, or student. Examples are a college class, the American Sociological Association, and the Democratic Party.

In hunting and gathering and horticultural societies, the entire society forms a primary group. In industrial and postindustrial societies, secondary groups have become essential to our welfare. They are part of the way we get our education, make our living, and spend our money and leisure time.

As necessary as secondary groups are for contemporary life, they often fail to satisfy our deep needs for intimate association. Consequently, *secondary groups tend to break down into primary groups*. At school and work, we form friendship cliques. Our interaction with them is so important that we sometimes feel that if it weren't for our friends, school or work "would drive us crazy." The primary groups that we form within secondary groups, then, serve as a buffer between us and the demands that secondary groups place on us.

In-Groups and Out-Groups

Groups toward which we feel loyalty are called **in-groups**; those toward which we feel antagonism are called **out-groups**. For Monster Kody in our opening vignette, the Crips was an in-group, while the Bloods were an out-group. That the Crips—and we—make such a fundamental division of the world has far-reaching consequences for our lives.

Producing Loyalty, a Sense of Superiority, and Rivalries   Identification with a group can generate not only a sense of belonging, but also loyalty and feelings of superiority. These, in turn, often produce rivalries. Usually the rivalries are mild, such as sports rivalries between neighboring towns, in which the most extreme act is likely to be the furtive invasion of the out-group's territory to steal a mascot, paint a rock, or uproot a goal post. The consequences of in-group membership can also be discrimination, hatred, and, as we saw in our opening vignette, even participation in murder.

Implications for a Socially Diverse Society   The strong identifications with members of our in-groups are the basis of many gender and racial-ethnic divisions. As sociologist Robert Merton (1968) observed, our favoritism leads to biased perception. Following a fascinating double standard, we tend to view the traits of our in-group as virtues while

secondary group compared with a primary group, a larger, relatively temporary, more anonymous, formal, and impersonal group based on some interest or activity. Its members are likely to interact on the basis of specific statuses

in-groups groups toward which one feels loyalty

out-groups groups toward which one feels antagonism

we see those *same* traits in out-groups as vices. Men may perceive an aggressive man as assertive but an aggressive woman as pushy. They may think that a male employee who doesn't speak up "knows when to keep his mouth shut," while they consider a quiet woman as too timid to make it in the business world.

To divide the world into "we" and "they" poses a danger for a pluralistic society. As the Jews did for the Nazis, an out-group can come to symbolize evil. One consequence is that discrimination—even in extreme forms—seems to be justified. The Nazis weren't alone in their views; many ordinary, "good" Germans defended the Holocaust as "dirty work" that someone had to do (Hughes 1962/2005). This principle might seem to pertain only to the past, but it continues today—and likely always will. Consider what happened following the terrorist attacks of 9/11. Some Americans began to view Arabs as sinister, bloodthirsty villains. Some airline pilots refused to leave the ground until "Arab-looking" passengers had been forced to get off the plane. Even worse, U.S. politicians openly discussed the option of torturing Arab suspects who wouldn't talk. Mainstream journalists followed suit and wrote articles arguing that torture is moral—"the lesser of two evils."

Economic downturns pose an especially dangerous period. The Nazis took power during a debilitating depression. If a depression were to occur in the United States, immigrants could be transformed from "nice people who do jobs that Americans think are beneath them" to "people who steal jobs from friends and family." A national anti-immigration policy could follow, accompanied by a resurgence of hate groups such as the neo-Nazis or the Ku Klux Klan.

In short, to divide the world into in-groups and out-groups is a natural part of social life. But in addition to bringing functional consequences, it can bring dysfunctional ones.

"So long, Bill. This is my club. You can't come in."

How our participation in social groups shapes our self-concept is a focus of symbolic interactionists. In this process, knowing who we are *not* is as significant as knowing who we are.

Reference Groups

Suppose you have just been offered a good job. It pays double what you hope to make even after you graduate from college. You have only two days to make up your mind. If you accept it, you will have to drop out of college. As you consider the matter, thoughts like this may go through your mind: "My friends will say I'm a fool if I don't take the job . . . but Dad and Mom will practically go crazy. They've made sacrifices for me, and they'll be crushed if I don't finish college. They've always said I've got to get my education first, that good jobs will always be there. . . . But, then, I'd like to see the look on the faces of those neighbors who said I'd never amount to much!"

This is an example of how people use **reference groups,** the groups we use as standards to evaluate ourselves. Your reference groups may include your family, neighbors, teachers, classmates, co-workers, and the Scouts or the members of a church, synagogue, or mosque. If you were like Monster Kody in our opening vignette, the "set" would be your main reference group. Even a group you don't belong to can be a reference group. For example, if you are thinking about going to graduate school, graduate students or members of the profession you want to join may form a reference group. You would consider their standards as you evaluate your grades or writing skills.

Providing a Yardstick Reference groups exert tremendous influence over our lives. For example, if you want to become a corporate executive, you might start to dress more formally, try to improve your vocabulary, read the *Wall Street Journal,* and change your major to business or law. In contrast, if you want to become a rock musician, you might wear jewelry in several places where you have pierced your body, get outrageous tattoos,

reference group a group that we use as a standard to evaluate ourselves

All of us have *reference groups*—the groups we use as standards to evaluate ourselves. How do you think the reference groups of these members of the KKK who are demonstrating in Jaspar, Texas, differ from those of the police officer who is protecting their right of free speech? Although the KKK and this police officer use different groups to evaluate their attitudes and behaviors, the process is the same.

dress in ways your parents and many of your peers consider extreme, read *Rolling Stone,* drop out of college, and hang around clubs and rock groups.

Exposure to Contradictory Standards in a Socially Diverse Society   From these examples, you can see that the yardsticks provided by reference groups operate as a form of social control. When we see ourselves as measuring up to the yardstick, we feel no conflict. If our behavior, or even aspirations, do not match the group's standards, however, the mismatch can lead to inner turmoil. For example, to want to become a corporate executive would create no inner turmoil for most of us, but it would if we had grown up in an Amish home, for the Amish strongly disapprove of such aspirations for their children. They ban high school and college education, three-piece suits, and corporate employment. Similarly, if you wanted to become a soldier and your parents were dedicated pacifists, you likely would feel deep conflict, as your parents would hold quite different aspirations for you.

Given the social diversity of our society as well as our social mobility, many of us are exposed to contradictory ideas and standards from the many groups that become significant to us. The "internal recordings" that play contradictory messages from these reference groups, then, are one price we pay for our social mobility.

Social Networks

If you are a member of a large group, you probably associate regularly with a few people within that group. In a sociology class I was teaching at a commuter campus, six women who didn't know one another ended up working together on a project. They got along well, and they began to sit together. Eventually they planned a Christmas party at one of their homes. These clusters, or internal factions, are called **cliques** (cleeks).

The links between people—their cliques, as well as their family, friends, acquaintances, and even "friends of friends"—are called **social networks.** Think of a social network as lines that extend outward from yourself, gradually encompassing more and more people.

We all use *reference groups* to evaluate our accomplishments, failures, values, and attitudes. We compare what we see in ourselves with what we perceive as normative in our reference groups. As is evident in these two photos, the reference groups these youths are using are not likely to lead them to the same social destination.

Introductory Sociology 1
174

Facebooking: The Lazy (But Efficient) Way to Meet Friends

MAKING NEW FRIENDS AND MAINTAINING friendships can take effort. You have to clean up, put on clothes, leave your room, and engage in conversations. The talk can turn in directions that don't interest you, and people can drop into your group that you don't particularly care for. Situations can arise that make you feel awkward or embarrassed. Maybe you would like to disengage for a few minutes—to take a little power nap or to read a book. You can't do this without offending someone.

Not so with facebooking. You are in charge. Talk with people when you want. Stop when you want.

This is part of the allure of facebooking. The facebook is like an ever-changing, online yearbook. To find people with similar interests, just type in that interest. Your favorite book is Kerouac's *On The Road? The DaVinci Code?* Your favorite movie is *Fight Club? Barbarella?* You enjoy *J. Crew* or *Wheezer?* Your favorite activity is making out? Fiddling with guns? Looking at pink shoes? And you want to find people who share your interest? Just a mouse-click away.

You can even form your own group—and invite others to join it. The group can be as esoteric as you prefer. Some actual groups: "Ann Coulter Fan Club." "Republican Princesses." "Preppy Since Conception." "Cancer Corner" (for students who love to smoke). "I Want to Be a Trophy Wife and You Can't Stop Me." There is even an "anti-group" group.

You see a cute guy or girl, and you want to get to know them. Back in your room, with one click you learn not only their e-mail address, but also the classes they are taking and their interests. This will give you good pick-up info. That person won't even know you're stalking them.

One woman who contacted a man after reading his profile, said "We had all the same interests. Books. Movies. Everything. It was a little weird, though—like dating a website."

Facebooking is free. If you have a school e-mail address, just answer a few questions, post your picture—and start making friends. You can do a search of your own campus or even locate old friends who might be attending college somewhere else.

A photo blinks onto your computer screen, and someone asks to be listed as part of your social network. You consider it for a couple of seconds, faintly recalling the individual from high school, and you click yes. You have just "friended" him.

You have control. You can set the privacy settings to determine who can view which parts of your profile: the contact information, personal information, courses you are taking, and a list of your friends.

Many students find the allure of facebooking irresistible, a new form of creative procrastination. And in college, there is so much to procrastinate from.

Facebooking has a touch of whimsy. The poke option lets you "poke" anyone you want to. No one knows what the "poke" message really means, but it seems to be, "Hey. How ya doin'?" The poke can be a conversation starter, like "zup" (what's up?), a tap on the shoulder as it were.

Then there's The Wall, a virtual "wall" on which friends can scrawl messages. ("MEATHEAD WAS HERE.")

Change your mind about someone? It's so simple to drop them. Just click the "defriend" button. But risky. That's a slap in the face.

Not only do you see a list of your friends but also you can track your social network—-the friends of friends, the people you can reach in three or fewer steps. In just three steps, your network could balloon to several thousand.

The usual popularity contest has reared its head, of course. Who has the most friends listed? Some students even contact members they've never met just to ask to be "friended." Larger numbers give them bragging rights. Pathetic, but true.

There is something strange about groups that exist only in cyberspace, profiles that might be faked, and friends you may not even know. But life itself is strange.

On the serious side: Facebooking provides a sense of belonging on what can be large, impersonal campuses. It is reassuring to see that you are connected to others—even if most of the connections are in cyberspace.

Source: Based on Copeland 2004; Sales 2004; Schackner 2004.

As you may recall from Chapter 1 (page 21), analyzing social networks was the way that U.S. forces located Saddam Hussein.

Although we live in a huge society, we don't experience social life as a sea of nameless, strange faces. Instead, we interact within social networks. One of the more interesting ways that people are expanding their social networks is *facebooking*, the topic of the Down-to-Earth Sociology box above.

The Small World Phenomenon Social scientists have wondered just how extensive the connections are between social networks. If you list everyone you know, and each of

clique a cluster of people within a larger group who choose to interact with one another; an internal faction

social network the social ties radiating outward from the self that link people together

those individuals lists everyone he or she knows, and you keep doing this, would almost everyone in the United States eventually be included on those lists?

It would be too cumbersome to test this hypothesis by drawing up such lists, but psychologist Stanley Milgram (1933–1984) came up with an interesting idea. In a classic study known as "the small world phenomenon," Milgram (1967) addressed a letter to "targets," the wife of a divinity student in Cambridge and a stockbroker in Boston. He sent the letter to "starters," who did not know these people. He asked them to send the letter to someone they knew on a first-name basis, someone they thought might know the "target." The recipients, in turn, were asked to mail the letter to someone they knew who might know the "target," and so on. The question was, Would the letters ever reach the "target"? If so, how long would the chain be?

Think of yourself as part of this study. What would you do if you were a "starter," but the "target" lived in a state in which you know no one? You would send the letter to someone you know who might know someone in that state. This, Milgram reported, is just what happened. Although none of the senders knew the targets, the letters reached the designated individual in an average of just six jumps.

Milgram's study caught the public's fancy, leading to the phrase, "six degrees of separation." This expression means that, on average, everyone in the United States is separated by just six individuals. Milgram's conclusions have become so popular that a game, "Six Degrees of Kevin Bacon," was built around it.

Is the Small World Phenomenon an Academic Myth?   But things are not this simple. There is a problem with Milgram's research, as psychologist Judith Kleinfeld (2002a, 2002b) discovered when she decided to replicate Milgram's study. When she went to the archives at Yale University Library to get more details, she found that Milgram had stacked the deck in favor of finding a small world. The "starters" came from mailing lists of people who were likely to have higher incomes and therefore were not representative of average people. In addition, one of the "targets" was a stockbroker, and that person's "starters" were investors in blue-chip stocks. Kleinfeld also found another discrepancy: On average, only 30 percent of the letters reached their "target." In one of Milgram's studies, the success rate was just 5 percent.

Since most letters did *not* reach their targets, even with the deck stacked in favor of success, we can draw the *opposite* conclusion from the one that Milgram reported: People who don't know one another are dramatically separated by social barriers. How great the barriers are is illustrated by another attempt to replicate Milgram's study, this one using e-mail. Only 384 of 24,000 chains reached their targets (Dodds et al. 2003).

As Kleinfeld says, "Rather than living in a small world, we may live in a world that looks a lot like a bowl of lumpy oatmeal, with many small worlds loosely connected and perhaps some small worlds not connected at all." Somehow, I don't think that the phrase, "lumpy oatmeal phenomenon," will become standard, but the criticism of Milgram's research is valid.

Implications for a Socially Diverse Society   Besides geography, the barriers that separate us into many small worlds are primarily those of social class, gender, and race-ethnicity. Overcoming these social barriers is difficult because even our own social networks contribute to social inequality, a topic that we explore in the Cultural Diversity box on the next page.

Implications for Science   Kleinfeld's revelations of Milgram's research reinforce the need of replication, a topic discussed in the previous chapter. For our knowledge of social life, we cannot depend on single studies—there may be problems of generalizability on the one hand, or those of negligence or even fraud on the other. Replication by objective researchers is essential to build and advance solid social knowledge.

A New Group: Electronic Communities

electronic community individuals who regularly interact with one another on the Internet and who think of themselves as belonging together

In the 1990s, a new type of human group, the **electronic community**, made its appearance. People "meet" online in chat rooms and "news groups" to communicate about almost any conceivable topic, from donkey racing and bird-watching to sociology and quantum physics. Most news groups are simply an interesting way of communicating. Some, however, meet our definition of *group*, people who interact with one another and

Cultural Diversity *in the* United States

How Our Own Social Networks Perpetuate Social Inequality

CONSIDER SOME OF THE PRINCIPLES we have reviewed. People tend to form in-groups with which they identify; they use reference groups to evaluate their attitudes and behavior; and they interact in social networks. Our in-groups, reference groups, and social networks are likely to consist of people whose backgrounds are similar to our own. This means that, for most of us, just as social inequality is built into society, so it is built into our own relationships. One consequence is that we tend to perpetuate social inequality.

To see why, suppose that an outstanding job—great pay, interesting work, opportunity for advancement—has just opened up where you work. Who are you going to tell? Most likely it will be someone you know, a friend or at least someone to whom you owe a favor. And most likely your social network is made up of people who look much like yourself—especially their race-ethnicity, age, social class, and probably also, gender. This tends to keep good jobs moving in the direction of people whose characteristics are similar to those of the people already in an organization. So you can see how our social networks both reflect the inequality that characterizes our society and help to perpetuate it.

Consider a network of white men who are established in an organization. As they learn of opportunities (jobs, investments, real estate, and so on), they share this information with their networks. Opportunities and good jobs flow to people who have characteristics similar to their own. Those who benefit from this information, in turn, reciprocate with similar information when they learn of it. This bypasses people who have different characteristics, in this example women and minorities, while it perpetuates the "good old boy'" network. No intentional discrimination need be involved.

Social networks, *which open and close doors of opportunity, are important for careers. Despite the official program of sociology conventions, much of the "real" business centers around renewing and extending social networks.*

To overcome this barrier, women and minorities do **networking.** They try to meet people who can help advance their careers. Like the "good old boys," they go to parties and join clubs, churches, synagogues, mosques, and political parties. African American leaders cultivate a network of African American leaders. As a result, the network of African American leaders is so tight that one-fifth of the entire national African American leadership are personal acquaintances. Add some "friends of a friend," and *three-fourths* of the entire leadership belong to the same network (Taylor 1992).

Similarly, women cultivate a network of women. As a result, women who reach top positions end up in a circle so tight that the term "new girl" network is being used, especially in the field of law. Remembering those who helped them and sympathetic to those who are trying to get ahead, these women tend to steer business to other women. Like the "good old boys" who preceded them, the new insiders have a ready set of reasons to justify their exclusionary practice (Jacobs 1997).

for your Consideration

The perpetuation of social inequality does not require purposeful discrimination. Just as social inequality is built into society, so is it built into our personal relationships. How do you think your own social network helps to perpetuate social inequality? How do you think we can break this cycle? (The key must center on creating diversity in social networks.)

who think of themselves as belonging together. They pride themselves on the distinctive nature of their interest and knowledge—factors that give them a common identity and bind them together.

Group Dynamics

As you know from personal experience, the lively interaction *within* groups—who does what with whom—has profound consequences for how you adjust to

networking using one's social networks for some gain

Japanese who work for the same firm think of themselves more as a group or team, Americans perceive themselves more as individuals. Japanese corporations use many techniques to encourage group identity, such as making group exercise a part of the work day. Similarity of appearance and activity helps to fuse group identity and company loyalty.

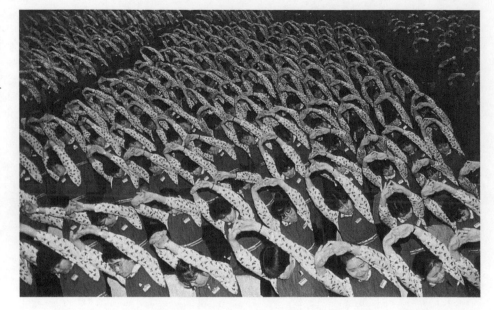

life. Sociologists use the term **group dynamics** to refer to how groups influence us and how we affect groups. Let's consider how the size of a group makes a difference, and then examine leadership, conformity, and decision making.

Before doing this, we should see how sociologists define the term *small group*. In a **small group,** there are few enough members that each one can interact directly with all the other members. Small groups can be either primary or secondary. A wife, husband, and children make up a primary small group, as do workers who take their breaks together, while bidders at an auction and guests at a cocktail party are secondary small groups.

Effects of Group Size on Stability and Intimacy

Writing in the early 1900s, sociologist Georg Simmel (1858–1918) noted the significance of group size. He used the term **dyad** for the smallest possible group, which consists of two people. Dyads, which include marriages, love affairs, and close friendships, show two distinct qualities. First, they are the most intense or intimate of human groups. Because only two people are involved, the interaction is focused on them. Second, because dyads require that both members participate and be committed, it takes just one member to lose interest for the dyad to collapse. In larger groups, by contrast, even if one member withdraws, the group can continue, for its existence does not depend on any single member (Simmel 1950).

A **triad** is a group of three people. As Simmel noted, the addition of a third person fundamentally changes the group. With three people, interaction between the first two decreases. This can create strain. For example, with the birth of a child, hardly any aspect of a couple's relationship goes untouched. Attention focuses on the baby, and interaction between the husband and wife diminishes. Despite the difficulty that this presents—including in many instances the husband's jealousy that he is getting less attention from his wife—the marriage usually becomes stronger. Although the intensity of interaction is less in triads, they are inherently stronger and give greater stability to a relationship.

Yet, as Simmel noted, triads, too, are inherently unstable. They tend to form **coalitions**—some group members aligning themselves against others. In a triad, it is not uncommon for two members to feel strong bonds and prefer one another. This leaves the third person feeling hurt and excluded. Another characteristic of triads is that they often produce an arbitrator or mediator, someone who tries to settle disagreements between the other two. In one-child families, you can often observe both of these characteristics of triads—coalitions and arbitration.

The general principle is this: *As a small group grows larger, it becomes more stable, but its intensity, or intimacy, decreases.* To see why, look at Figure 6.3. As each new person comes into a group, the connections among people multiply. In a dyad, there is only 1 relationship; in a triad, there are 3; in a group of four, 6; in a group of five, 10. If we expand the group to

group dynamics the ways in which individuals affect groups and the ways in which groups influence individuals

small group a group small enough for everyone to interact directly with all the other members

dyad the smallest possible group, consisting of two persons

triad a group of three people

coalition the alignment of some members of a group against others

162 CHAPTER 6 SOCIETIES TO SOCIAL NETWORKS

Group size has a significant influence on how people interact. When a group changes from a dyad (two people) to a triad (three people), the relationships among the participants undergo a shift. How do you think the birth of this boy affected the relationship between his mother and father?

Groups also mold our orientation to life. What assumptions of the world do you think this boy is growing up with?

six, we have 15 relationships, while a group of seven yields 21 relationships. If we continue adding members, we soon are unable to follow the connections: A group of eight has 28 possible relationships; a group of nine, 36 relationships; a group of ten, 45; and so on.

It is not only the number of relationships that makes larger groups more stable. As groups grow, they also tend to develop a more formal structure to accomplish their goals. For example, leaders emerge and more specialized roles come into play. This often results in such familiar offices as president, secretary, and treasurer. This structure provides a framework that helps the group survive over time.

Effects of Group Size on Attitudes and Behavior

Imagine that your social psychology professors have asked you to join a few students to discuss your adjustment to college life. When you arrive, they tell you that to make the discussion anonymous they want you to sit unseen in a booth. You will participate in the discussion over an intercom, talking when your microphone comes on. The professors say that they will not listen to the conversation, and they leave.

You find the format somewhat strange, to say the least, but you go along with it. You have not seen the other students in their booths, but when they talk about their experiences, you find yourself becoming wrapped up in the problems that they begin to share. One student even mentions how frightening he has found college because of his history of epileptic seizures. Later, you hear this individual breathe heavily into the microphone. Then he stammers and cries for help. A crashing noise follows, and you imagine him lying helpless on the floor.

Nothing but an eerie silence follows. What do you do?

Figure 6.3 The Effects of Group Size on Relationships

A Dyad	A Triad	A Group of Four
One relationship	Three relationships	Six relationships

A Group of Five	A Group of Six	A Group of Seven
Ten relationships	Fifteen relationships	Twenty-one relationships

Your professors, John Darley and Bibb Latané (1968), staged the whole thing, but you don't know this. No one had a seizure. In fact, no one was even in the other booths. Everything, except your comments, was on tape.

Some participants were told that they would be discussing the topic with just one other student, others with two, others with three, and so on. Darley and Latané found that all students who thought they were part of a dyad rushed out to help. If they thought they were part of a triad, only 80 percent went to help—and they were slower in leaving the booth. In six-person groups, only 60 percent went to see what was wrong—and they were even slower.

This experiment demonstrates how deeply group size influences our attitudes and behavior: It even affects our willingness to help one another. Students in the dyad knew that it was up to them to help the other student. The professor was gone, and if they didn't help there was no one else. In the larger groups, including the triad, students felt *a diffusion of responsibility:* Giving help was no more their responsibility than anyone else's.

You probably have observed the second consequence of group size firsthand. When a group is small, its members act informally, but as the group grows, the members lose their sense of intimacy and become more formal. No longer can the members assume that the others are "insiders" in sympathy with what they say. Now they must take a "larger audience" into consideration, and instead of merely "talking," they begin to "address" the group. Their speech becomes more formal, and their body language stiffens.

You probably have observed a third aspect of group dynamics, too. In the early stages of a party, when only a few people are present, almost everyone talks with everyone else. But as others arrive, the guests break into smaller groups. Some hosts, who want their guests to mix together, make a nuisance of themselves trying to achieve *their* idea of what a group should be like. The division into small groups is inevitable, however, for it follows the basic sociological principles that we have just reviewed. Because the addition of each person rapidly increases connections (in this case, "talk lines"), conversation becomes more difficult. The guests break into smaller groups in which they can see each other and comfortably interact directly with one another.

Leadership

All of us are influenced by leaders, so it is important to understand leadership. Let's look at how people become leaders, the types of leaders there are, and their different styles of leadership. Before we do this, though, it is important to clarify that leaders don't necessarily hold formal positions in a group. **Leaders** are simply people who influence the behaviors, opinions, or attitudes of others. Even a group of friends has leaders.

Who Becomes a Leader?

Are leaders born with characteristics that propel them to the forefront of a group? No sociologist would agree with such an idea. In general, people who become leaders are perceived by group members as strongly representing their values, or as able to lead a group out of a crisis (Trice and Beyer 1991). Leaders also tend to be more talkative and to express determination and self-confidence.

These findings may not be surprising, as such traits appear to be related to leadership. Researchers, however, have also discovered traits that seem to have no bearing on the ability to lead. For example, taller people and those who are judged better looking are more likely to become leaders (Stodgill 1974; Judge and Cable 2004). The taller and more attractive are also likely to earn more, but that is another story (Deck 1968; Feldman 1972; Katz 2005).

Many other factors underlie people's choice of leaders, most of which are quite subtle. A simple experiment performed by social psychologists Lloyd Howells and Selwyn Becker (1962) uncovered one of these factors. They formed groups of five people who did not know one another, seating them at a rectangular table, three on one side and two on the other. Each group discussed a topic for a set period of time, and then chose a leader. The findings are startling: Although only 40 percent of the people sat on the two-person side, 70 percent of the leaders emerged from that side. The explanation is that we tend to direct more interactions to people facing us than to people to the side of us.

leader someone who influences other people

Types of Leaders   Groups have two types of leaders (Bales 1950, 1953; Cartwright and Zander 1968). The first is easy to recognize. This person, called an **instrumental leader** (or *task-oriented leader*), tries to keep the group moving toward its goals. These leaders try to keep group members from getting sidetracked, reminding them of what they are trying to accomplish. The **expressive leader** (or *socioemotional leader*), in contrast, usually is not recognized as a leader, but he or she certainly is one. This person is likely to crack jokes, to offer sympathy, or to do other things that help to lift the group's morale. Both types of leadership are essential: the one to keep the group on track, the other to increase harmony and minimize conflicts.

It is difficult for the same person to be both an instrumental and an expressive leader, for these roles contradict one another. Because instrumental leaders are task oriented, they sometimes create friction as they prod the group to get on with the job. Their actions often cost them popularity. Expressive leaders, in contrast, who stimulate personal bonds and reduce friction, are usually more popular (Olmsted and Hare 1978).

Leadership Styles   Let's suppose that the president of your college has asked you to head a task force to determine how the college can improve race relations on campus. Although this position requires you to be an instrumental leader, you can adopt a number of **leadership styles,** or ways of expressing yourself as a leader. The three basic styles are those of **authoritarian leader,** one who gives orders; **democratic leader,** one who tries to gain a consensus; and **laissez-faire leader,** one who is highly permissive. Which style should you choose?

Social psychologists Ronald Lippitt and Ralph White (1958) carried out a classic study of these leadership styles. Boys who were matched for IQ, popularity, physical energy, and leadership were assigned to "craft clubs" made up of five boys each. The experimenters trained adult men in the three leadership styles. As the researchers peered through peepholes, taking notes and making movies, each adult rotated among the clubs, playing all three styles to control possible effects of their individual personalities.

The *authoritarian* leaders assigned tasks to the boys and told them exactly what to do. They also praised or condemned the boys' work arbitrarily, giving no explanation for why they judged it good or bad. The *democratic* leaders held discussions with the boys, outlining the steps that would help them reach their goals. They also suggested alternative approaches and let the boys work at their own pace. When they evaluated the projects, they gave "facts" as the bases for their decisions. The *laissez-faire* leaders were passive. They gave the boys almost total freedom to do as they wished. They offered help when asked, but made few suggestions. They did not evaluate the boys' projects, either positively or negatively.

The results? The boys who had authoritarian leaders grew dependent on their leader and showed a high degree of internal solidarity. They also became either aggressive or apathetic, with the aggressive boys growing hostile toward their leader. In contrast, the boys who had democratic leaders were friendlier, and looked to one another for mutual approval. They did less scapegoating, and when the leader left the room they continued to work at a steadier pace. The boys with laissez-faire leaders asked more questions, but they made fewer decisions. They were notable for their lack of achievement. The researchers concluded that the democratic style of leadership works best. Their conclusion, however, may have been biased, as the researchers favored a democratic style of leadership in the first place (Olmsted and Hare 1978). Apparently, this same bias in studies of leadership continues (Cassel 1999).

You may have noted that only boys and men were involved in this experiment. It is interesting to speculate how the results might differ if we were to repeat the experiment with all-girl groups and with mixed groups of girls and boys—and if we used both men and women as leaders. Perhaps you will become the sociologist to study such variations of this classic experiment.

Leadership Styles in Changing Situations   Different situations require different styles of leadership. Suppose, for example, that you are leading a dozen backpackers in the Sierra Madre mountains north of Los Angeles, and it is time to make dinner. A

Adolf Hitler was one of the most influential—and evil—persons of the twentieth century. Why did so many people follow Hitler? This question stimulated the research by Stanley Milgram.

instrumental leader an individual who tries to keep the group moving toward its goals; also known as a *task-oriented leader*

expressive leader an individual who increases harmony and minimizes conflict in a group; also known as a *socioemotional leader*

leadership styles ways in which people express their leadership

authoritarian leader an individual who leads by giving orders

democratic leader an individual who leads by trying to reach a consensus

laissez-faire leader an individual who leads by being highly permissive

laissez-faire style would be appropriate if the backpackers had brought their own food, or perhaps a democratic style if everyone were supposed to pitch in. Authoritarian leadership—you telling the hikers how to prepare their meals—would create resentment. This, in turn, would likely interfere with meeting the primary goal of the group, which in this case is to have a good time while enjoying nature.

Now assume the same group but a different situation: One of your party is lost, and a blizzard is on its way. This situation calls for you to take charge and be authoritarian. To simply shrug your shoulders and say, "You figure it out," would invite disaster—and probably a lawsuit.

The Power of Peer Pressure: The Asch Experiment

How influential are groups in our lives? To answer this, let's look first at *conformity* in the sense of going along with our peers. Our peers have no authority over us, only the influence that we allow.

Imagine that you are taking a course in social psychology with Dr. Solomon Asch and you have agreed to participate in an experiment. As you enter his laboratory, you see seven chairs, five of them already filled by other students. You are given the sixth. Soon the seventh person arrives. Dr. Asch stands at the front of the room next to a covered easel. He explains that he will first show a large card with a vertical line on it, then another card with three vertical lines. Each of you is to tell him which of the three lines matches the line on the first card (see Figure 6.4).

Dr. Asch then uncovers the first card with the single line and the comparison card with the three lines. The correct answer is easy, for two of the lines are obviously wrong, and one is exactly right. Each person, in order, states his or her answer aloud. You all answer correctly. The second trial is just as easy, and you begin to wonder why you are there.

Then on the third trial, something unexpected happens. Just as before, it is easy to tell which lines match. The first student, however, gives a wrong answer. The second gives the same incorrect answer. So do the third and the fourth. By now, you are wondering what is wrong. How will the person next to you answer? You can hardly believe it when he, too, gives the same wrong answer. Then it is your turn, and you give what you know is the right answer. The seventh person also gives the same wrong answer.

On the next trial, the same thing happens. You know that the choice of the other six is wrong. They are giving what to you are obviously wrong answers. You don't know what to think. Why aren't they seeing things the same way you are? Sometimes they do, but in twelve trials they don't. Something is seriously wrong, and you are no longer sure what to do.

When the eighteenth trial is finished, you heave a sigh of relief. The experiment is finally over, and you are ready to bolt for the door. Dr. Asch walks over to you with a big smile on his face, and thanks you for participating in the experiment. He explains that you were the only real subject in the experiment! "The other six were stooges. I paid them to give those answers," he says. Now you feel real relief. Your eyes weren't playing tricks on you after all.

What were the results? Asch (1952) tested fifty people. One-third (33 percent) gave in to the group half the time, giving what they knew to be wrong answers. Another two out of five (40 percent) gave wrong answers, but not as often. One out of four (25 percent) stuck to their guns and always gave the right answer. I don't know how I would do on this test (if I knew nothing about it in advance), but I like to think that I would be part of the 25 percent. You probably feel the same way about yourself. But why should we feel that we wouldn't be like *most* people?

The results are disturbing, and more researchers have replicated Asch's experiment than any other study (Levine 1999). In our "land of individualism," the group is so powerful

Figure 6.4 **Asch's Cards**

Card 1

Card 2

The cards used by Solomon Asch in his classic experiment on group conformity

Source: Asch 1952:452–453.

that most people are willing to say things that they know are not true. And this was a group of strangers! How much more conformity can we expect when our group consists of friends, people we value highly and depend on for getting along in life? Again, maybe you will become the sociologist to run that variation of Asch's experiment, perhaps using female subjects.

The Power of Authority: The Milgram Experiment

Even more disturbing are the results of the experiment described in the following Thinking Critically section.

Thinking Critically

If Hitler Asked You to Execute a Stranger, Would You?
The Milgram Experiment

Imagine that you are taking a course with Dr. Stanley Milgram (1963, 1965), a former student of Dr. Asch. Assume that you do not know about the Asch experiment and have no reason to be wary. You arrive at the laboratory to participate in a study on punishment and learning. You and a second student draw lots for the roles of "teacher" and "learner." You are to be the teacher. When you see that the learner's chair has protruding electrodes, you are glad that you are the teacher. Dr. Milgram shows you the machine you will run. You see that one side of the control panel is marked "Mild Shock, 15 volts," while the center says "Intense Shock, 350 Volts," and the far right side reads "DANGER: SEVERE SHOCK."

"As the teacher, you will read aloud a pair of words," explains Dr. Milgram. "Then you will repeat the first word, and the learner will reply with the second word. If the learner can't remember the word, you press this lever on the shock generator. The shock will serve as punishment, and we can then determine if punishment improves memory." You nod, now very relieved that you haven't been designated the learner.

"Every time the learner makes an error, increase the punishment by 15 volts," instructs Dr. Milgram. Then, seeing the look on your face, he adds, "The shocks can be extremely painful, but

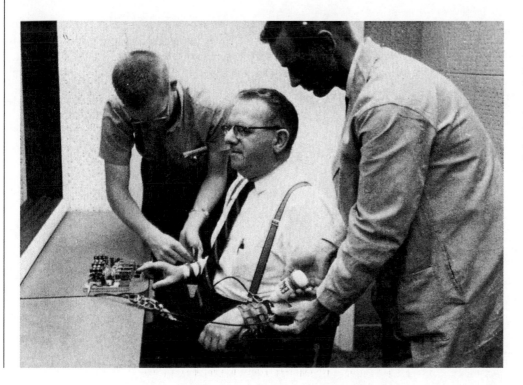

In the 1960s, U.S. social psychologists ran a series of creative but controversial experiments. Among these were Stanley Milgram's experiments. From this photo of the "learner" being prepared for the experiment, you can get an idea of how convincing the situation would be for the "teacher."

they won't cause any permanent tissue damage." He pauses, and then says, "I want you to see." You then follow him to the "electric chair," and Dr. Milgram gives you a shock of 45 volts. "There. That wasn't too bad, was it?" "No," you mumble.

The experiment begins. You hope for the learner's sake that he is bright, but unfortunately he turns out to be rather dull. He gets some answers right, but you have to keep turning up the dial. Each turn makes you more and more uncomfortable. You find yourself hoping that the learner won't miss another answer. But he does. When he received the first shocks, he let out some moans and groans, but now he is screaming in agony. He even protests that he suffers from a heart condition.

How far do you turn that dial?

By now, you probably have guessed that there was no electricity attached to the electrodes and that the "learner" was a stooge who only pretended to feel pain. The purpose of the experiment was to find out at what point people refuse to participate. Does anyone actually turn the lever all the way to "DANGER: SEVERE SHOCK"?

Milgram wanted the answer because millions of ordinary people did nothing to stop the Nazi slaughter of Jews, gypsies, Slavs, homosexuals, people with disabilities, and others whom the Nazis designated as "inferior." That seeming compliance in the face of all of these deaths seemed bizarre, and Milgram wanted to see how ordinary, intelligent Americans might react in an analogous situation.

Milgram was upset by what he found. Many "teachers" broke into a sweat and protested to the experimenter that this was inhuman and should be stopped. But when the experimenter calmly replied that the experiment must go on, this assurance from an "authority" ("scientist, white coat, university laboratory") was enough for most "teachers" to continue, even though the "learner" screamed in agony. Even "teachers" who were "reduced to twitching, stuttering wrecks" continued to follow orders.

Milgram varied the experiments (Brannigan 2004). He used both men and women. In some experiments, he put the "teachers" and "learners" in the same room, so the "teacher" could clearly see the suffering. In others, he put the "learners" in a separate room, and had them pound and kick the wall during the first shocks and then go silent. The results varied. When there was no verbal feedback from the "learner," 65 percent of the "teachers" pushed the lever all the way to 450 volts. Of those who could see the "learner," 40 percent turned the lever all the way. When Milgram added a second "teacher," a stooge who refused to go along with the experiment, only 5 percent of the "teachers" turned the lever all the way, a result that bears out some of Asch's findings.

A stormy discussion about research ethics erupted. Not only were researchers surprised and disturbed by what Milgram found but also they were alarmed at his methods. Universities began to require that subjects be informed of the nature and purpose of social research. Researchers agreed that to reduce subjects to "twitching, stuttering wrecks" was unethical, and almost all deception was banned.

for your Consideration

What is the connection between Milgram's experiment and the actions of Monster Kody in our opening vignette? Taking into account how significant these findings are, do you think that the scientific community overreacted to Milgram's experiments? Should we allow such research? Consider both the Asch and Milgram experiments, and use symbolic interactionism, functionalism, and conflict theory to explain why groups have such influence over us.

Global Consequences of Group Dynamics: Groupthink

Suppose you are a member of the President's inner circle. It is midnight, and the President has just called an emergency meeting to deal with a terrorist attack. At first, several options are presented. Eventually, these are narrowed to only a couple of choices, and at some point, everyone seems to agree on what now appears to be "the only possible course of action." To express doubts at that juncture will bring you into conflict with all the other important people in the room. To criticize will mark you as not being a "team player." So you keep your mouth shut, with the result that each step commits you—and them—more and more to the "only" course of action

From the Milgram and Asch experiments, we can see the power of authority and the influence of peers. Under some circumstances, as in this example, this can lead to **groupthink**. Sociologist Irving Janis (1972, 1982) coined this term to refer to the collective tunnel vision that group members sometimes develop. As they begin to think alike, they become convinced that there is only one "right" viewpoint and a single course of action to follow. They take any suggestion of alternatives as a sign of disloyalty. With their perspective narrowed and fully convinced that they are right, they may even put aside moral judgments and disregard risk (Hart 1991; Flippen 1999).

Groupthink can bring serious consequences. Consider the *Columbia* space shuttle disaster of 2003.

Foam broke loose during launch, and engineers were concerned that it might have damaged tiles on the nose cone. Because this would make reentry dangerous, they sent e-mails to NASA officials, warning them about the risk. One engineer even suggested that the crew do a "space walk" to examine the tiles (Vartabedian and Gold 2003). The team in charge of the Columbia shuttle, however, disregarded the warnings. Convinced that a piece of foam weighing less than two pounds could not seriously harm the shuttle, they refused to even consider the possibility (Wald and Schwartz 2003). The fiery results of their mental closure were transmitted around the globe.

The consequences of groupthink can be even greater than this. In 1941, President Franklin D. Roosevelt and his chiefs of staff had evidence that the Japanese were preparing to attack Pearl Harbor. They simply refused to believe it and decided to continue naval operations as usual. The destruction of the U.S. naval fleet ushered the United States into World War II. In the war with Vietnam, U.S. officials had evidence of the strength and determination of the North Vietnamese military. They arrogantly threw such evidence aside, refusing to believe that "little, uneducated, barefoot people in pajamas" could defeat the U.S. military.

In each of these cases, options closed as officials committed themselves to a single course of action. Questioning the decisions would have indicated disloyalty and disregard for "team playing." Those in power plunged ahead, unable to see alternative perspectives. No longer did they try to objectively weigh evidence as it came in; instead, they interpreted everything as supporting their one "correct" decision.

Preventing Groupthink Groupthink is a danger that faces government leaders, who tend to surround themselves with an inner circle that closely reflects their own views. In "briefings," written summaries, and "talking points," this inner circle spoon feeds the leaders carefully selected information. The result is that top leaders, such as the president, become cut off from information that does not support their own opinions.

Perhaps the key to preventing the mental captivity and intellectual paralysis known as groupthink is the widest possible circulation—especially among a nation's top government officials—of research that has been conducted by social scientists independent of the government and information that has been freely gathered by media reporters. If this conclusion comes across as an unabashed plug for sociological research and the free exchange of ideas, it is. Giving free rein to diverse opinions can curb groupthink, which—if not prevented—can lead to the destruction of a society and, in today's world of nuclear, chemical, and biological weapons, the obliteration of Earth's inhabitants.

groupthink a narrowing of thought by a group of people, leading to the perception that there is only one correct answer, in which to even suggest alternatives becomes a sign of disloyalty

Summary *and* Review

Social Groups and Societies

What is a group?

Sociologists use many definitions of groups, but, in general, **groups** consist of people who interact with one another and think of themselves as belonging together. **Societies** are the largest and most complex group that sociologists study. P. 148.

The Transformation of Societies

How is technology linked to the change from one type of society to another?

On their way to postindustrial society, humans passed through four types of societies. Each emerged from a social revolution that was linked to new technology. The **domestication revolution**, which brought the pasturing of animals and the cultivation of plants, transformed **hunting and gathering societies** into **pastoral** and **horticultural societies**. Then the invention of the plow ushered in the **agricultural society**, while the **Industrial Revolution**, brought about by machines that were powered by fuels, led to the **industrial society**. The computer chip ushered in a new type of society called **postindustrial** (or **information**) **society**. Another new type of society, the **bioetech society**, may be emerging. Pp. 148–153.

How is social inequality linked to the transformation of societies?

Social equality was greatest in hunting and gathering societies, but over time social inequality grew. The root of the transition to social inequality was the accumulation of a food surplus, made possible through the domestication revolution. This surplus stimulated the division of labor, trade, accumulation of material goods, the subordination of females by males, the emergence of leaders, and the development of the state. Pp. 150–153.

Groups Within Society

How do sociologists classify groups?

Sociologists divide groups into primary groups, secondary groups, in-groups, out-groups, reference groups, and networks. The cooperative, intimate, long-term, face-to-face relationships provided by **primary groups** are fundamental to our sense of self. **Secondary groups** are larger, relatively temporary, and more anonymous, formal, and impersonal than primary groups. **In-groups**

provide members with a strong sense of identity and belonging. **Out-groups** also foster identity by showing in-group members what they are *not*. **Reference groups** are groups whose standards we refer to as we evaluate ourselves. **Social networks** consist of social ties that link people together. The new technology has given birth to a new type of group, the **electronic community**. Pp. 153–161.

Group Dynamics

How does a group's size affect its dynamics?

The term **group dynamics** refers to how individuals affect groups and how groups influence individuals. In a **small group**, everyone can interact directly with everyone else. As a group grows larger, its intensity decreases but its stability increases. A **dyad**, consisting of two people, is the most unstable of human groups, but it provides the most intense or intimate relationships. The addition of a third person, forming a **triad**, fundamentally alters relationships. Triads are unstable, as **coalitions** (the alignment of some members of a group against others) tend to form. Pp. 161–164.

What characterizes a leader?

A **leader** is someone who influences others. **Instrumental leaders** try to keep a group moving toward its goals, even though this causes friction and they lose popularity. **Expressive leaders** focus on creating harmony and raising group morale. Both types are essential to the functioning of groups. Pp. 164–165.

What are the three main leadership styles?

Authoritarian leaders give orders, **democratic leaders** try to lead by consensus, and **laissez-faire leaders** are highly permissive. An authoritarian style appears to be more effective in emergency situations, a democratic style works best for most situations, and a laissez-faire style is usually ineffective. Pp. 165–166.

How do groups encourage conformity?

The Asch experiment was cited to illustrate the power of peer pressure, the Milgram experiment to illustrate the influence of authority. Both experiments demonstrate how easily we can succumb to **groupthink**, a kind of collective tunnel vision. Preventing groupthink requires the free circulation of contrasting ideas. Pp. 166–169.

Thinking Critically

about **Chapter 6**

1. How would your orientations to life (your ideas, attitudes, values, goals) be different if you had been reared in an agricultural society?
2. Identify your in-groups and your out-groups. How have your in-groups influenced the way you see the world?
3. Asch's experiment illustrates the power of peer pressure. How has peer pressure operated in your life? Think about something that you did not want to do but did anyway because of peer pressure.

Additional Resources

Companion Website www.ablongman.com/henslin8e

- *Content Select* Research Database for Sociology, with suggested key terms and annotated references
- Link to 2000 Census, with activities
- Flashcards of key terms and concepts
- Practice Tests
- Weblinks
- Interactive Maps

Where Can I Read More on This Topic?

Suggested readings for this chapter are listed at the back of this book.

Suggested Readings
to Selected Chapters

SUGGESTED READINGS

CHAPTER 2 Culture

Berger, Peter L., and Samuel P. Huntington, eds. *Many Globalizations: Cultural Diversity in the Contemporary World.* New York: Oxford University Press, 2002. One of the recurring themes of this book is how globalization is changing cultures.

Borofsky, Robert, and Bruce Albert. *Yanomani: The Fierce Controversy and What We Can Learn from It.* Berkeley: University of California Press, 2006. The authors criticize the research on the Yanomani, including that by Chagnon in the next book, with an emphasis on anthropologists' inconsideration of human rights.

Chagnon, Napoleon A. *Yanomamö: The Fierce People,* 5th ed. New York: Harcourt, Brace, Jovanovich, 1997. This account of a tribal people whose customs are extraordinarily different from ours will help you to see how arbitrary the choices are that underlie human culture.

Edgerton, Robert B. *Sick Societies: Challenging the Myth of Primitive Harmony.* New York: Free Press, 1993. The author's thesis is that cultural relativism is misinformed, that we have the obligation to judge cultures that harm its members as inferior to those that do not.

Hull, John R., Mary Jo Neitz, and Marshall Battani. *Sociology on Culture.* New York: Routledge, 2003. The authors present an overview of sociological approaches to culture.

Jacobs, Mark D., and Nancy Weiss Hanrahan, eds. *The Blackwell Companion to the Sociology of Culture.* Malden, MA.: Blackwell Publishing, 2005. The authors of this article explore cultural systems, everyday life, identity, collective memory, and citizenship in a global economy.

Smith, Shawn Michelle. *American Archives: Gender, Race, and Class in Visual Culture.* Princeton, N.J.: Princeton University Press, 2000. The photos in this book show how gender, race, and class have been portrayed in U.S. history and how these portrayals have helped to maintain white dominance.

Stinson, Kandi M. *Women and Dieting Culture: Inside a Commercial Weight Loss Group.* New Brunswick: Rutgers University Press, 2001. Through participant observation, the author provides an insider's perspective on women and dieting.

Sullivan, Nikki. *Tattooed Bodies: Subjectivity, Textuality, Ethics, and Pleasure.* Westport, Conn.: Praeger, 2001. A sociological analysis of this very old and very new custom.

Wolf, Mark J. P., and Bernard Perron, eds. *The Video Game: Theory Reader.* New York: Routledge, 2003. The authors of these articles on gamers and games examine sociological and economic issues that surround gaming.

Zellner, William W. *Countercultures: A Sociological Analysis.* New York: St. Martin's Press, 1995. The author's analysis of skinheads, the Ku Klux Klan, survivalists, satanists, the Church of Scientology, and the Unification Church (Moonies) helps us understand why people join countercultures.

CHAPTER 3 Socialization

Ariès, Philippe. *Centuries of Childhood: A Social History of Family Life.* New York: Vintage Books, 1972. The author analyzes how childhood in Europe during the Middle Ages differs from childhood today.

Blumer, Herbert. *George Herbert Mead and Human Conduct.* Lanham, Md.: AltaMira Press, 2004. An overview of symbolic interactionism by a sociologist who studied and taught Mead's thought all of his life.

Heywood, Colin. *A History of Childhood: Children and Childhood in the West from Medieval to Modern Times.* Cambridge, UK: Polity Press, 2001. Critical of the Ariès book listed above, the author explores the changing experiences and perceptions of childhood from the early Middle Ages to the beginning of the twentieth century.

Hunt, Stephen J. *The Life Course: A Sociological Introduction.* New York: Palgrave McMillan, 2006. Gives an overview of the life course while considering what is distinct about a sociological approach to this topic.

Lareau, Annette. *Unequal Childhoods: Class, Race, and Family Life.* Berkeley: University of California Press, 2003. The author documents differences in child rearing in poor, working-class, and middle-class U.S. families.

Rymer, Russ. *Genie: A Scientific Tragedy.* New York: Harper Perennial Library, 1994. This account of Genie includes the battles to oversee Genie among linguists, psychologists, and social workers, all of whom claimed to have Genie's best interests at heart.

Segal, Nancy L. *Entwined Lives: Twins and What They Tell Us About Human Behavior.* New York: Plume, 2001. This summary of research on twins and human behavior is thorough, but, unfortunately, provides little basis to draw firm conclusions.

Settersten, Richard A., Jr., and Timothy J. Owens, eds. *New Frontiers in Socialization.* Greenwich, Conn.: JAI Press, 2003. The authors of these articles focus on the adult years in the life course, examining the influence of families, neighbourhoods, communities, friendship, education, work, volunteer associations, medical institutions, and the media.

Sociological Studies of Child Development: A Research Annual. Greenwich, Conn.: JAI Press, published annually. Along with theoretical articles, this publication reports on sociological research on the socialization of children.

Walters, Glenn D. *Criminal Belief Systems: An Integrated-Interactive Theory of Lifestyles.* Westport, Conn.: Greenwood Publishing Group, 2003. The author analyzes how five belief systems (selfview, world-view, past-view, present-view, future-view) explain crime initiation and maintenance.

CHAPTER 4 Social Structure and Social Interaction

Goffman, Erving. *The Presentation of Self in Everyday Life.* New York: Peter Smith, Publisher, 1999. First published in 1959. This classic statement of dramaturgical analysis provides a different way of looking at everyday life. As a student, this was one of the best books I read.

Johnson, Kim K. P., and Sharron J. Lennon, eds. *Appearance and Power.* Oxford, England: Berg Publishers, 2000. The authors of these articles analyze how significant appearance, especially clothing, is for what happens to us in social life.

LeBesco, Kathleen. *Revolting Bodies: The Struggle to Redefine Fat Identity.* Amherst, MA.: University of Massachusetts Press, 2004. This analysis of the political struggle over the cultural meaning of fatness examines oppression and negative stereotypes.

Schauer, Frederick. *Profiles, Probabilities, and Stereotypes.* Cambridge, MA: Belknap Press, 2004. The focus of this book is the question of whether we can generalize about members of a group on the basis of the statistical tendencies of that group.

Schmidt, Kimberly D., Diane Zimmerman Umble, and Steven D. Reschly, eds. *Strangers at Home: Amish and Mennonite Women in History.* Baltimore: Johns Hopkins University Press, 2002. These accounts of the experiences of Amish and Mennonite women provide a window onto history, as well as insight into how social structure influences social interaction.

Seidman, Steven. *The Social Construction of Sexuality.* New York: W.W. Norton, 2004. The author explores how society influences our sexual choices, our beliefs about sexuality, and our sexual standards.

Tönnies, Ferdinand. *Community and Society (Gemeinschaft und Gesellschaft).* New York: Dover Publications, 2003. Originally published in 1887, this classic work, focusing on social change, provides insight into how society influences personality. Rather challenging reading.

Whyte, William Foote. *Street Corner Society: The Social Structure of an Italian Slum,* 4th ed. Chicago: University of Chicago Press, 1993. Originally published in 1943. The author's analysis of interaction in a U.S. Italian slum demonstrates how social structure affects personal relationships.

Journals

Qualitative Sociology, Symbolic Interaction, and *Urban Life* feature articles on symbolic interactionism and analyses of everyday life.

CHAPTER 6 Societies to Social Networks

Brown, Rupert. *Group Processes: Dynamics Within and Between Groups.* Boston: Blackwell, 2000. Among the group dynamics analyzed here is how groups are a primary source of our identity.

Cross, Robert, and Andrew Parker. *The Hidden Power of Social Networks: Understanding How Work* Really *Gets Done in Organizations* Cambridge, Mass: Harvard Business School Press, 2004. Based on their research and experience in organizations, the authors explain how understanding networks can improve communication and productivity.

Homans, George C. *The Human Group.* New Brunswick, N.J.: Transaction Publishers, 2001. First published in 1950. In this classic work, the author develops the idea that all human groups share common activities, interactions, and sentiments.

Hughes, Richard L., Robert C. Ginnett, and Gordon J. Curphy. *Leadership: Enhancing the Lessons of Experience,* 5th ed. New York: McGraw-Hill, 2005. Supplementing empirical studies with illustrative anecdotes, the authors focus on what makes effective leaders.

Janis, Irving L. *Groupthink: Psychological Studies of Policy Decisions and Fiascoes,* 2nd ed. New York: Houghton Mifflin, 1982. Janis analyzes how groups can become cut off from alternatives, interpret evidence in light of their preconceptions, and embark on courses of action that they should have seen as obviously incorrect.

Putnam, Robert D., and Lewis M. Feldstein. *Better Together.* New York: Simon and Schuster, 2003. The authors' premise is that Americans' sense of community has deteriorated over the past two generations; provides case studies on what some communities have done to develop networks of mutual support.

Stewart, Greg L., Charles C. Manz, and Henry P. Sims. *Team Work and Group Dynamics.* New York: John Wiley, 2000. Based on theoretical research and case studies, the authors try to pinpoint how to work effectively in groups.

Wilson, Gerald L. *Groups in Context: Leadership and Participation in Small Groups,* 6th ed. New York: McGraw-Hill, 2001. An overview of principles and processes of interaction in small groups, with an emphasis on how to exercise leadership.